HACKS

family handyman

HACKS

family handyman

Family Handyman Hacks

Project Editor Mary Flanagan
Cover Photography Tom Fenenga
Cover Art Direction Vern Johnson
Page Layout David Farr

Text, photography and illustrations for
Family Handyman Hacks are based on articles
previously published in *Family Handyman* magazine
(2915 Commers Dr., Suite 700, Eagan, MN 55121,
familyhandyman.com). For information on advertising
in *Family Handyman* magazine, call (646) 518-4215.

Paperback book: Colorful paint cans with paintbrush
©Sebastian Duda/Shutterstock

Hardcover: 978-1-62145-536-3
Paperback: 978-1-62145-537-0

A NOTE TO OUR READERS: All do-it-yourself activities
involve a degree of risk. Skills, materials, tools and site
conditions vary widely. Although the editors have made
every effort to ensure accuracy, the reader remains
responsible for the selection and use of tools, materials
and methods. Always obey local codes and laws, follow
manufacturer instructions and observe safety
precautions.

Family Handyman

Chief Content Officer Nick Grzechowiak
Editor-in-Chief Gary Wentz
Associate Editors Bill Bergmann, Mike Berner, Jay Cork,
   Brad Holden
Creative Director Vern Johnson
Design and Production Mariah Cates, Jenny Mahoney,
   Andrea Sorensen
Illustrations Steve Björkman, Ron Chamberlain,
   Ken Clubb, Jeff Gorton, John Hartman,
   Trevor Johnston, Don Mannes, Christopher Mills,
   Frank Rohrbach
Photography Tom Fenenga
Managing Editor Donna Bierbach
Set Builder Josh Risberg
Editorial Services Associate Peggy McDermott
Production Manager Aracely Lopez

Trusted Media Brands, Inc.

President & Chief Executive Officer Bonnie Kintzer

PRINTED IN THE UNITED STATES OF AMERICA
13 5 7 9 10 8 6 4 2

SAFETY FIRST–ALWAYS!

Tackling home improvement projects and repairs can be endlessly rewarding. But as most of us know, with the rewards come risks. DIYers use chain saws, climb ladders and tear into walls that can contain big and hazardous surprises.

The good news is, armed with the right knowledge, tools and procedures, homeowners can minimize risk. As you go about your projects and repairs, stay alert for these hazards:

Aluminum wiring

Aluminum wiring, installed in about 7 million homes between 1965 and 1973, requires special techniques and materials to make safe connections. This wiring is dull gray, not the dull orange characteristic of copper. Hire a licensed electrician certified to work with it. For more information go to cpsc.gov and search for "aluminum wiring."

Spontaneous combustion

Rags saturated with oil finishes like Danish oil and linseed oil, and oil-based paints and stains can spontaneously combust if left bunched up. Always dry them outdoors, spread out loosely. When the oil has thoroughly dried, you can safely throw them in the trash.

Vision and hearing protection

Safety glasses or goggles should be worn whenever you're working on DIY projects that involve chemicals, dust and anything that could shatter or chip off and hit your eye. Sounds louder than 80 decibels (dB) are considered potentially dangerous. Sound levels from a lawn mower can be 90 dB, and shop tools and chain saws can be 90 to 100 dB.

Lead paint

If your home was built before 1979, it may contain lead paint, which is a serious health hazard, especially for children six and under. Take precautions when you scrape or remove it. Contact your public health department for detailed safety information or call (800) 424-LEAD (5323) to receive an information pamphlet. Or visit epa.gov/lead.

Buried utilities

A few days before you dig in your yard, have your underground water, gas and electrical lines marked. Just call 811 or go to call811.com.

Smoke and carbon monoxide (CO) alarms

The risk of dying in reported home structure fires is cut in half in homes with working smoke alarms. Test your smoke alarms every month, replace batteries as necessary and replace units that are more than 10 years old. As you make your home more energy-efficient and airtight, existing ducts and chimneys can't always successfully vent combustion gases, including potentially deadly carbon monoxide (CO). Install a UL-listed CO detector, and test your CO and smoke alarms at the same time.

Five-gallon buckets and window covering cords

Anywhere from 10 to 40 children a year drown in 5-gallon buckets, according to the U.S. Consumer Products Safety Commission. Always store them upside down and store ones containing liquid with the covers securely snapped.

According to Parents for Window Blind Safety, hundreds of children in the United States are injured every year after becoming entangled in looped window treatment cords. For more information, visit pfwbs.org.

Working up high

If you have to get up on your roof to do a repair or installation, always install roof brackets and wear a roof harness.

Asbestos

Texture sprayed on ceilings before 1978, adhesives and tiles for vinyl and asphalt floors before 1980, and vermiculite insulation (with gray granules) all may contain asbestos. Other building materials, made between 1940 and 1980, could also contain asbestos. If you suspect that materials you're removing or working around contain asbestos, contact your health department or visit epa.gov/asbestos for information.

For additional information about home safety, visit homesafetycouncil.org. This site offers helpful information about dozens of home safety issues.

Contents

CHAPTER 1
Cleaning Hacks 11

CHAPTER 2
Gardening &
Lawn Care Hacks 51

Contents *(continued)*

CHAPTER 5
Storage & Organizing Hacks 169

CHAPTER 6
Safety & Security Hacks 235

CHAPTER 7
Pets 259

SPECIAL SECTION: IKEA HACKS 278

KEEP THOSE HACKS COMING! 284

Cleaning Hacks

Clean grime with a toothpaste

Everybody saves old toothbrushes for cleaning jobs, but an electric toothbrush is even better, and you can get one for less than 10 bucks at a discount store.

Scuff mark eraser

Clean off shoe scuff marks from vinyl flooring with a clean, dry tennis ball. A light rub and heel marks are "erased."

Clean range hood filters

If you've had disappointing results after cleaning your vent hood grease filters in the dishwasher or with grease-cutting household cleaners, try a water-based degreaser from the auto parts store. Fill the sink with hot water and degreaser, drop in the filter and let the degreaser do the work. The filter will be sparkling clean in just a few minutes. Then, rinse it off and reinstall.

Remove stains from plastic laminate countertops

Stubborn stains on countertops can be frustrating, but they don't have to be permanent. Standard household spray cleaners will remove most of them. Check the label and make sure any product you use is recommended for laminate countertops. The secret to success with these products is patience; let the cleaner work for five minutes or so before you wipe off the countertop. A plastic brush is helpful on stubborn spots. If a standard cleaner won't do the job, read on for more options.

Soak stains with baking soda

Paste made from baking soda and a little water often removes stains left by fruit juices and other liquids **(Photo 1)**. Baking soda is slightly abrasive and can leave fine scratches, so don't scrub. Just let the paste work for one to two hours and then wipe it off gently.

Use solvents sparingly

Gentle solvents like paint thinner, or harsher solvents like denatured alcohol, acetone and nail polish removers, often work on the toughest stains, including Ink **(Photo 2)**. These solvents are flammable and give off nasty fumes, so the best way to use them is to apply a small amount to a soft rag or cotton ball. Most solvents won't harm or discolor plastic laminate, but play it safe and test them on an inconspicuous spot first.

What about bleach?

There's no doubt that bleach is a great stain remover. Some laminate manufacturers suggest using it undiluted on stains, while others warn against using any product that contains bleach. Since you may not know what brand of laminate you have, test bleach before using it. Wipe a little on an inconspicuous spot and let it dry. Check the spot for discoloration before you use bleach on a stain.

Stain prevention

The best way to prevent stains is to wipe up messes immediately; the longer something sits, the more likely it is to leave a stain. A coating of countertop polish can also help **(Photo 3)**. Coating products usually aren't necessary on

1 Mix baking soda with just enough water to form a thick paste. Apply the paste to the stain and lay a wet paper towel over the paste to keep it moist.

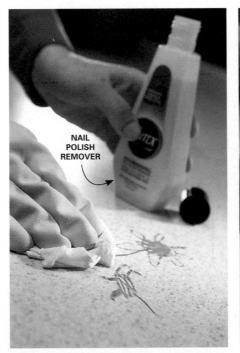

2 Wet a rag with a solvent such as nail polish remover and rub away stains. Use white rags to avoid staining the countertop with fabric dye.

3 Apply a protective coating to prevent stains. Spray or wipe on a product meant for countertops and wipe off the excess.

newer laminate. But years of wear leave the surface more porous and stain-prone; that's when these protective coatings can make a big difference. One such product,

Countertop Magic, is available at Ace Hardware, Lowe's and The Home Depot. Any coating product will wear off and should be reapplied every few weeks.

Replace disposer splash guard

Got a garbage disposer that spits, um, garbage at you? Forget about replacing the entire unit. You could try to clean the splash guard with a toothbrush, but that's messy and you can install a new splash guard (purchase at a home center) in about 20 minutes. You don't need any special tools.

If your garbage disposer is hard-wired, start by flipping off the circuit breaker. If it plugs in, unplug it. Stack up books or lumber to support the disposer. Then remove the drainpipe and disconnect the quick-connect fitting **(Photo 1)**. Replace the old splash guard with a new one **(Photo 2)**.

The hardest part of reinstallation is hoisting the disposer up and into place with one hand while you try to engage the locking ring with the other. Forget about that. Use our tip in **Photo 3**.

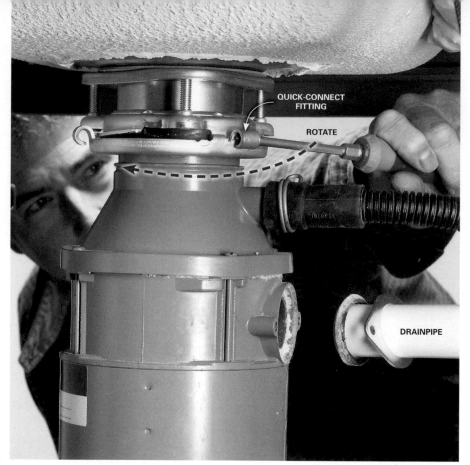

QUICK-CONNECT FITTING

ROTATE

DRAINPIPE

1 Disconnect the disposer Jam a screwdriver into the locking ring and rotate it away from you. The disposer will drop onto the books. Support it with one hand so it doesn't tip over.

NEW SPLASH GUARD

2 Replace the splash guard Grab the lower edge of the old rubber guard and peel it up and off. Then slip the new one on and push it down until it seats.

HOLD-DOWN PLATE

SHIMS

UNDERSTANDING PHYSICS ISAAC ASIMOV

GROB BASIC ELECTRONICS

3 Reconnect the disposer Shove several shims between the books and the bottom of the disposer until the locking ring just touches the sink flange. Then just rotate the ring to lock it in place. Reinstall the drain line, do a leak test and grind away.

Clean a clogged aerator

If you get weak water flow when you turn on the faucet, don't assume your water pressure has suddenly gone bad. You could simply have a filter screen, or aerator, that's clogged. Remove the aerator as shown in the photo, rinse it out and reinstall it. If it's corroded or worn, take it to a home center and pick up a new one ($3 to $5). Most stores have a slick gauge you can screw your old aerator onto to determine which replacement to buy. If you can't find a replacement for your aerator, soak the parts in vinegar overnight, scrub them with an old toothbrush and reinsert into the faucet (make sure to reassemble the parts in the same order you removed them).

TURN DIRECTION

ELECTRICAL TAPE

Wrap the jaws of pliers with tape to keep them from scratching the aerator. Unscrew the aerator body from the faucet and remove all the internal components. Clean and reassemble.

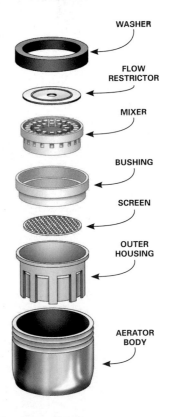

WASHER

FLOW RESTRICTOR

MIXER

BUSHING

SCREEN

OUTER HOUSING

AERATOR BODY

Aerator Parts

Dirt usually collects on the mixer and screen.

How to clean oven door glass

It's a mystery how baking slop gets deposited between oven door glass panels. But it's clear that you can't remove it without disassembling the door. The job's not that hard and takes less than an hour.

Remove the oven door (consult the manual for how to unlock the hinges and lift the door off). Then remove the exterior trim panel **(Photo 1)** and the glass hold-downs **(Photo 2)**. Lift out the glass and handle it carefully (it's expensive and breaks easily!).

Clean off the crud with a nylon scrub pad, hot water and degreaser. Rinse and dry, then clean with glass cleaner. Wear gloves to prevent fingerprints as you place the glass back onto the oven door. Be sure the glass sits inside the locating tabs before you reassemble the hold-downs. Then install the hold-down channels and screws and the trim panel. Put the door on the oven.

1 Remove the panel Remove the screws that secure the front panel to the oven door frame. Note their location and store them in a cup. Then carefully lift off the panel and set it aside.

GLASS HOLD-DOWN

2 Remove the glass Remove the screws from the glass hold-downs and set them aside. Note the location of the retaining tabs above and below the glass. Then lift off the glass and clean it.

Microwave cleaner

It's easy to clean baked-on food and spills from your microwave! Partially fill a measuring or coffee cup with water and add a slice of lemon. Boil the water for a minute, and then leave the door closed and let the steam loosen the mess. After 10 minutes, open the door and wipe away the grime.

Freshen with citrus and ice cubes

If your disposer has developed an odor, it may contain bits of rotted food. Here's how to clean them out:

1. With the water running at about half throttle, drop in orange or lemon peels. Run the disposer for five seconds. Citric acid from the peels softens crusty waste and attacks smelly bacteria. Give the acid about 15 minutes to do its work.

2. Turn on the water and the disposer and drop in a few ice cubes. Flying shards of ice work like a sandblaster inside the disposer.

3. Run the water until the sink is about half full. Then pull the stopper and turn on the disposer to flush it out.

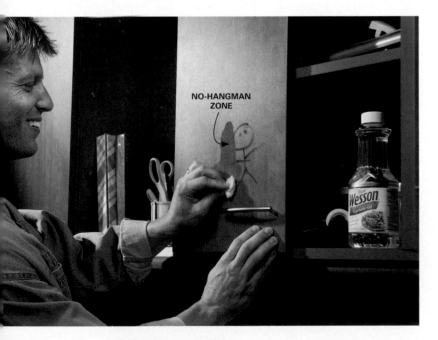

Marker cleanup

When the permanent marker has ended up in the wrong hands, vegetable oil can clean it off lots of surfaces—even skin! Then just wipe up with a damp cloth and you're done.

Restore a shower head

If the flow from your shower head is growing weaker, the cause is probably mineral buildup. Many manufacturers recommend that you remove the shower head and soak it in a half-and-half mixture of warm water and vinegar (any type). But there's really no need to remove the head. Just pour the mix into a heavy-duty plastic bag and attach it to the shower arm with a rubber band. The acid in the vinegar dissolves minerals, but prolonged contact can harm some plastics and metal finishes, so remove the bag every 15 minutes and check the shower flow.

WATER/VINEGAR MIX

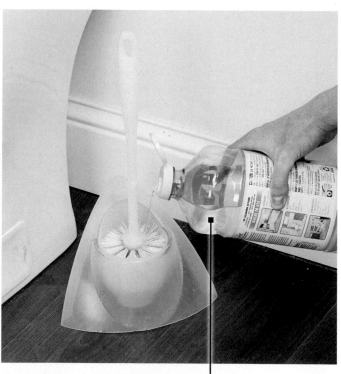

Toilet brush freshener

To keep your toilet brush as fresh as possible, put a splash of pine-scented cleaner in the bottom of the brush holder. This will disinfect the brush and keep your bathroom smelling clean.

Vacuum first, then scrub

Do you ever find yourself chasing strands of wet hair or running into dust balls in the corners with your sponge or cleaning rag? You can eliminate this nuisance by vacuuming the bathroom before you get out your cleaning solutions.

For a really thorough cleaning, start at the top, vacuuming the dust from light fixtures and the top of window casings. Then work your way down. And finally, vacuum the floor methodically so you cover every inch. You don't want to leave any stray hair or dust bunnies to muck up your cleaning water. A soft-bristle upholstery brush works best for this type of vacuuming.

Synthetic soap simplifies bathroom cleaning

In terms of chemistry, some soaps aren't really true soap. Any soap in a liquid or gel form and some bar soaps, such as Zest and Ivory, are synthetic soap. These non-soap soaps are much less likely to form that dreaded layer of tough scum on your sink or tub.

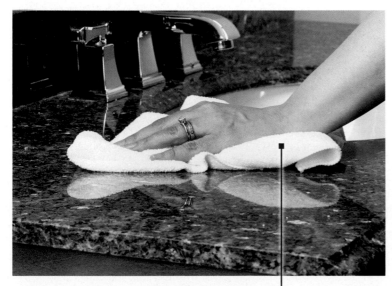

Polish with a microfiber cloth

Microfiber cloths excel at putting the finishing touches on mirrors, countertops, and even tile and fixtures. After cleaning surfaces with your favorite cleaning solution and drying them off with a terry cloth rag or a separate microfiber cloth, polish them to a mirror finish with a dry microfiber cloth.

Microfiber cloths are perfect for this because they pick up dust, wipe off smudges and don't shed any fibers. You'll find microfiber cloths wherever cleaning supplies are sold. You can even buy them in bulk at wholesale clubs and use them throughout your house for all kinds of other cleaning chores.

FOAM BRUSH WITH ACID MAGIC

Remove tough water stains

If you have a lot of iron in your water and struggle with rust stains in your toilet or bathtub, here's a perfect solution. Acid Magic dissolves rust like, um, magic. It's as powerful as muriatic acid but much safer and more pleasant to use. You should still take all the precautions you would with any strong cleaning solution, like wearing gloves and safety glasses when you're using it. But it's better than regular acid because there are no noxious fumes, and it won't burn your skin.

To clean rust from toilets and other porcelain surfaces, add one part Acid Magic to three parts water. Apply the mixture to the rust stains with a sprayer, brush or foam pad and watch the stain dissolve. Rinse with clear water. You can also use it full strength for stubborn stains. Avoid getting the acid on metal parts because they can discolor. Acid Magic is available online and at Ace and True Value stores.

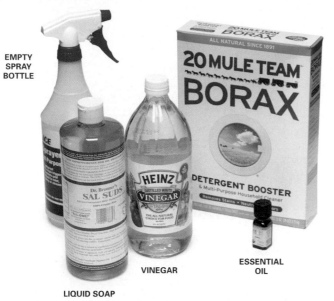

EMPTY SPRAY BOTTLE

LIQUID SOAP

VINEGAR

ESSENTIAL OIL

Make your own greener cleaning solution

Professional housecleaner Maggie Orth likes to make her own cleaning products. Here's her recipe for an all-purpose cleaning solution, modified from a recipe she found in the book *Clean House, Clean Planet* by Karen Logan.

In a 5-quart bucket, mix: 1 cup of distilled vinegar, 3 tablespoons of borax, 1 gallon of hot water and 1/2 cup of soap (Maggie uses Dr. Bronner's Sal Suds). Maggie likes to add 10 or 15 drops of tea tree, lavender or lemon oil for a nice fragrance. Mix the ingredients and then pour some of the mixture into a spray bottle. Save the rest in a gallon jug. You'll have enough to last for years!

Use this mixture to clean tile, countertops and painted woodwork. It's a good all-purpose cleaner, but it's not the best for cleaning glass. Maggie uses club soda to clean glass.

A scrub and a wax

Every three months, use CLR Calcium, Lime and Rust Remover and an old toothbrush to clean faucets. Then apply an automotive car wax like Turtle Wax and buff after the wax hazes. Your fixtures will look like new.

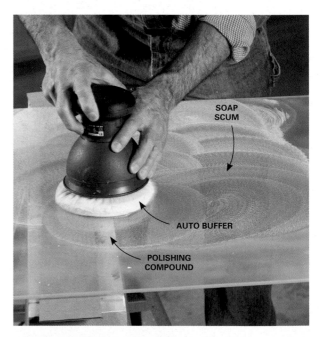

SOAP SCUM

AUTO BUFFER

POLISHING COMPOUND

Buff off heavy grime

If you have glass shower doors in your bathroom and don't keep on top of the cleaning, you can end up with soap scum so tough that it's nearly impossible to remove. That's when you bring out the heavy equipment.

Pick up some polishing compound at a home center or an auto parts store and use an auto buffer to polish off the offending scum. If you don't own a buffer, you can buy one for as little as $20 or borrow one from a gearhead friend. If possible, remove the doors and take them out to the garage to avoid messing up the bathroom.

Clean grout with a bleach pen

Use a bleach pen to transform your grout from grungy to great. This method is tedious, but the payoff is crisp, clean grout lines. Use the pen to "draw" bleach across the grout lines. The pen allows you to target the grout without getting bleach all over the tile. Wait 10 minutes and then rinse.

For really mildewed grout, you may need a second application, and it can help to gently scrub the bleach into the grout with a toothbrush before allowing it to work for 10 minutes. Make sure to run the fan in the bathroom and to avoid skin contact. This method is best for light or white grout. If you have colored grout, test a small area first. It might fade.

Install a detachable toilet seat

It seems like no matter how hard you try, you can never get the hinges on the toilet seat clean. There's always a bit of cleaning solution that seeps underneath and creeps out later. Installing a detachable toilet seat solves the problem. This Bemis brand seat is easy to remove by just twisting two hinge caps about a quarter of a turn. Then you have easy access to clean under the hinges. Installation is straightforward and requires only a wrench.

Remove tough grime with less scrubbing

Whether it's built-up soap scum on the shower walls, ground-in dirt on the floor tile, or dried toothpaste on the vanity top, a Magic Eraser sponge will make short work of it. Just dampen it and rub it on the offending mess. In most cases, the mess will come right off. These sponges are especially useful for removing ground-in dirt from porous floor tile and getting those pesky nonslip strips in the bottom of your tub clean.

Magic Eraser sponges are available at grocery stores, hardware stores and wherever cleaning supplies are sold. Unlike regular sponges, they wear out pretty fast, so stock up.

Wash your shower curtain

Toss your grimy shower curtain or liner in the washing machine instead of the garbage and save a trip to the store and a few bucks. Add about a quarter cup of vinegar to a warm-water wash cycle and your shower curtain will come out fresh and clean. The vinegar also helps to kill mold and mildew.

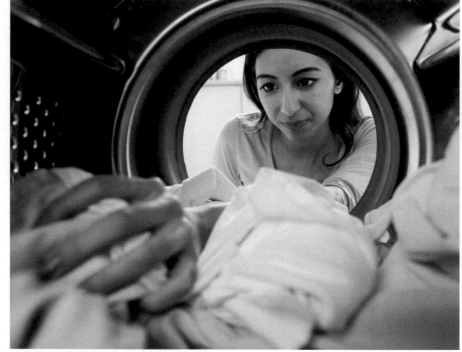

Scum-proof your shower doors

Keeping shower doors clean and streak free is a challenge—unless you know the pros' secrets. Start by cleaning any mold, mildew or streaks off the glass with a glass cleaner. Use a Mr. Clean Magic Eraser to get into the cracks in textured glass. Scrape off tough buildup with a razor blade. Dry the doors with a cloth.

Treat the doors with a product like Aquapel ($8; autobodydepot.com) or Rain-X ($5 at auto parts stores and home centers). These glass treatments form an invisible film on the glass to increase water repellency, causing water and soap to bead up and run off the glass. (Squeegee off the water after bathing or showering to keep soap scum from building up again.) Spray or wipe on the glass treatment, then wipe it off with a microfiber cloth. Overspray won't harm surrounding surfaces. The products repel water for six months.

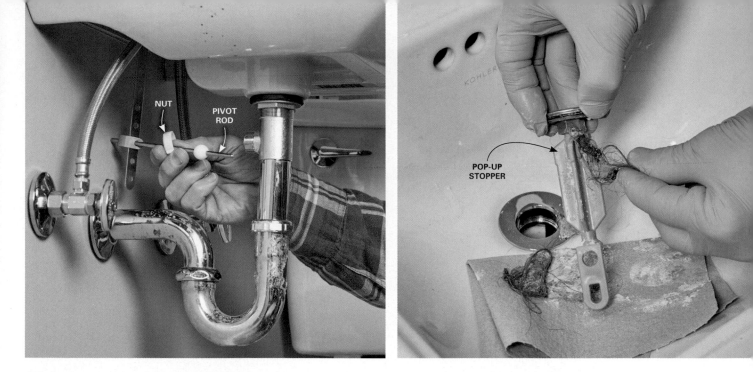

Clean your pop-up stopper

The pop-up stopper on your bathroom sink is a magnet for hair, dental floss and other yucky stuff. And it's probably a good thing because it keeps all of that out of your drains. But allowing this waste to build up for too long can cause the sink to drain slower and slower and eventually not empty at all. And because the water flow down the drain is also slowed, clogs in the drain lines can form more easily.

When you notice that your bathroom sink is draining slowly, remove the stopper and clean it. Most pop-ups can be installed two ways. They can either be hooked into the pivot rod that lifts them, or simply rest on it. If your pop-up stopper is hooked in, you'll have to unscrew the nut on the back of the tailpiece (under the sink) and pull out the pivot rod to release the pop-up (left photo). When you reassemble it, try reinstalling the rod without running it through the hole in the pop-up stopper. Then drop the stopper into the drain hole. In most cases, it will work fine this way, and you'll be able to remove the pop-up stopper for cleaning without removing the rod.

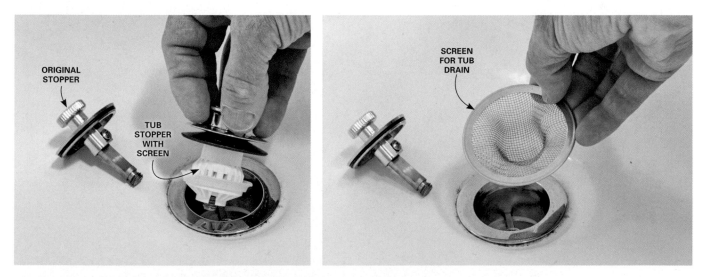

Catch hair before it reaches the drain

Hair and soap combine in your tub or shower drain to create clogs that could end up requiring a drain snake to remove. But you can avoid that task by catching the hair before it reaches the drain.

Various sizes of mesh screens are available for this purpose. One good source for these stainless steel strainers is plumbingsupply.com.

Another option is to replace the stopper assembly with one that includes a built-in screen. One choice is the DrainEASY Bathtub Stopper shown here ($14 at home centers or online). It's designed to replace stopper assemblies that screw into the drain.

Remove tough water stains on your toilet

2. FLUSH

1. TURN OFF WATER

3. PLUNGE OUT WATER

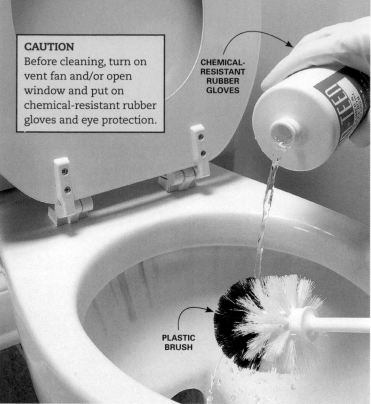

CAUTION
Before cleaning, turn on vent fan and/or open window and put on chemical-resistant rubber gloves and eye protection.

CHEMICAL-RESISTANT RUBBER GLOVES

PLASTIC BRUSH

1 Close the water shutoff valve by turning it clockwise until it stops. Flush the toilet and plunge out as much water as possible.

2 Pour an aggressive cleaner (such as Acid Magic; see p. 19) on a plastic toilet brush and spread it over the entire bowl surface.

3 Force the brush tip back and forth, especially along the toilet jets (holes under rim), around the water line and on visible stains. Scrub until stains are gone, reapplying cleaner as necessary, then flush twice.

GET JETS CLEAN

Remove tough water stains on your faucet

READ AND FOLLOW THE LABEL
Make sure the cleaner is safe to use on both the faucet surface and the tub, tile or sink surfaces. Do not use abrasive cleaners. Do not use all-purpose cleaners on marble or other natural stone surfaces. Buy a special stone cleaner.

1 Soak the entire faucet surface from base to tip with an all-purpose bathroom cleaner, or use a lime-removing product if the buildup is extremely thick and crusty.

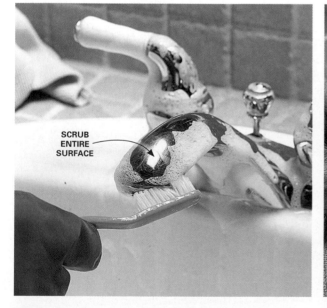

SCRUB ENTIRE SURFACE

SOFT COTTON CLOTH

2 Scrub the surface with an old toothbrush, pushing bristles into crevices on the end of the spout (aerator and screen) and on the handles, as well as at the base of the faucet.

3 Once all deposits have been removed, rinse the cleaner off immediately by wiping the entire surface down with a dripping wet sponge. Dry and polish with a soft cloth.

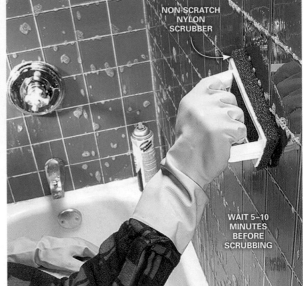

1 Coat the entire tiled surface (grout, caulk and all) with an all-purpose cleaner that attacks soap scum. Wait 5 to 10 minutes to allow the product to work, which saves your scrubbing elbow.

2 Remove remaining visible scum and deposits by applying light pressure with a non-scratch nylon scrubber. Reapply product to difficult areas and scrub until clean.

3 Remove stains and deposits on grout or caulk by lightly scrubbing back and forth with a grout brush or old toothbrush. Reapply product as needed.

4 Rinse the entire tiled surface thoroughly with a dripping wet sponge. Push it back and forth across the top of the wall so rinse water streams to the bottom of the wall. Repeat until all cleaner is removed. Then, start at the top of the tile with a bathroom squeegee and move downward to remove as much water as possible.

Grille duster

If the grille on your bathroom exhaust fan is clogged with dust, try a trick that's faster and more effective than vacuuming: Turn on the fan and blast out the dust with "canned air." The fan will blow the dust outside. This works on the return air grilles of your central heating/cooling system too. Run the system so that the return airflow will carry the dust to the filter. You'll find canned air at home centers and hardware stores, usually in the electrical supplies aisle. **Caution:** The cans contain chemical propellants, not just air. Don't let children play with them.

Water-saving toilet upgrade

When your toilet flapper fails, water leaks into the bowl and then triggers the fill valve to refill the tank. It's annoying and it wastes water. Instead of just putting up with the rhythmic sound of running water, fix it with Fluidmaster's Toilet Fill Valve and Flapper Repair Kit ($14). It's a great kit for repairing common problems that can be solved with a new flapper, and while you're at it, upgrading to a quicker, quieter fill valve.

   If you want to take it one step further, Fluidmaster also sells an easy retrofit flush valve kit called the DuoFlush System Toilet Converter ($25). It will turn your toilet into a dual flusher, letting you flush only half a tank, lowering your water bill and reducing water waste. You can find both products at home centers and online.

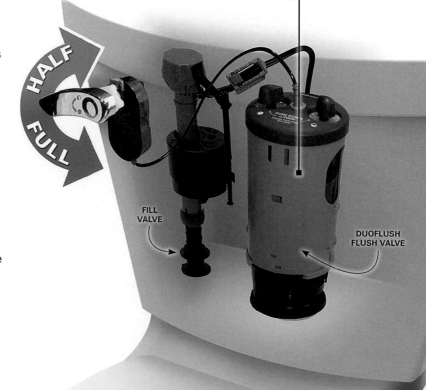

HALF

FULL

FILL VALVE

DUOFLUSH FLUSH VALVE

Clean up pet messes

Many pet owners do exactly what they shouldn't do when they clean up pet messes. But if you learn how to clean up the right way, with the right products, you can prevent a permanent stain. Here are three tips that work with all pet messes and discuss a few cleaning products. You'll get the best results if you have the products and a carpet extractor in hand when you discover the accident.

Wet messes

Using paper towels to blot up urine and vomit soaks up the surface liquid but still leaves a lot in the carpet. And stomping on those paper towels only makes it worse. That forces the liquid deeper into the padding and then into the subflooring. Instead, invest in a handheld carpet extractor. Don't use a shop vacuum—the smell will linger in the filter and it's much harder to clean than a small extractor. Hit the carpet as soon as possible and vacuum like there's no tomorrow.

Solid messes

Scooping up the solids with paper towels or rags can actually force them into the carpet. Instead, use a putty knife and dustpan to scrape them up as shown.

Treating the carpet

To treat a urine stain, fresh or dried, use a urine-specific bio-enzymatic cleaner (one choice is Nature's Miracle Urine Destroyer). It neutralizes the urea and uric acid and eliminates proteins and starches. Ordinary carpet cleaners can't do that. In fact, using a carpet cleaner before a bio-enzymatic cleaner can set the stain permanently.

Liquid messes spread as they're absorbed into the carpet, so always treat a larger area than the original stain. For all solid messes, saturate the stain with an oxygenated bio-enzymatic cleaner. Let it sit for 45 minutes to separate additional solids from the carpet fibers. Then clean up those solids.

Bio-enzymatic cleaners take a long time to work. Just let the treated area air-dry. Then vacuum to raise the nap.

The best tool for the job Buy a handheld extractor to suck liquids from the carpet. It works much better than trying to absorb a mess with paper towels or rags. An extractor is made for this task and, unlike a shop vacuum, is easy to clean.

Use a putty knife for solids Sink the edge of the putty knife into the carpet at the edge of the mess. Then push it forward to scrape the solid waste up and into the dustpan.

Cleaning solutions

Home remedies that use vinegar and baking soda simply mask the odor for a short time and don't eliminate the cause. Instead, buy a product made for your particular type of pet mess.

Commercial pet cleaning products range in price from a few dollars to more than $20 per quart. The least expensive products usually contain a carpet detergent for the stain and an odor-masking chemical. Since they don't actually neutralize the substance, the smell usually returns on humid days.

Spend more to get a product with enzymes. These products are good for small surface stains. But if you're dealing with a large stain, one that has soaked deep into the carpet, or one that has already dried, spend more yet and use a product with bacteria, enzymes and an oxygen booster.

Clean up stains right away

Act quickly

If you get to a stain immediately, there's a 99 percent chance you can remove it. The longer a stain reacts chemically with the carpeting, the harder it is to remove.

Try water first

Eighty percent of stains can be removed using plain tap water. To remove a stain, press a clean, dry, white cloth over the stain to absorb the spill. Repeat until the spill is absorbed. Then gently work water into the stain with a damp white towel and blot until the stain is gone. Change cloths when necessary. For a particularly stubborn spot, go to the online "spot solver" resource at carpet-rug.org to find your stain and a suggested solution. Use a fan to dry the area if it's very wet.

Blot—don't rub or scrub

Scrubbing a stain will damage the fibers and create a fuzzy area. Always blot from the outer edge toward the center of the stain to avoid spreading the spot and creating a larger problem.

Be patient

Work water gently into the spill and then blot with a dry cloth. Repeat until the stain is gone and all the water has been absorbed. If you're patient, you'll almost always be able to remove the stain.

On tough spots, try vinegar or club soda

If water alone doesn't remove a stain, try a white vinegar and water solution (equal amounts) or club soda before trying stronger commercial cleaning products.

Test commercial products first

Some products can cause carpet to get dirty faster or damage the carpet's color and texture. For a list of carpet manufacturer-approved spot and stain cleaners, go to carpet-rug.org and under the residential customer tab you'll see a "Find a Seal of Approval Certified Product" search box. Test carpet-cleaning products on an inconspicuous area before using.

For more cleaning tips, search "carpet cleaning" at familyhandyman.com

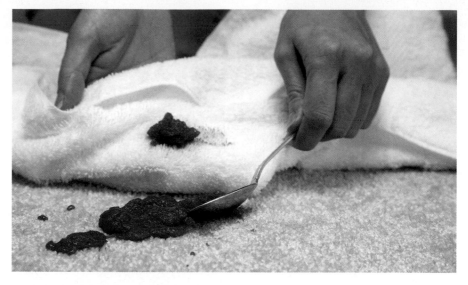

Don't dig or scoop food spills Digging or scooping can work the stain into the carpet. If there are solids on top of the stain, use a spoon or dull knife to carefully scrape the food toward the middle of the spill and into a white towel and then treat the stain.

Use a shop vacuum on wet spills Keep vacuuming until no more liquid can be removed. If the spill was a colored liquid, treat it as you would a stain, after vacuuming.

Spot removal and more

The Carpet and Rug Institute, a nonprofit trade association of carpet manufacturers, has a great Web site (carpet-rug.org) for consumers. It's filled with information about carpet care, including a list of CRI-approved, off-the-shelf cleaning products, a state-by-state list of member service providers and lots of stain removal advice in its "spot solver" database on the residential customer tab. You can type in your specific stain for advice about how to remove it.

After a carpet spill, doing the right thing—right now—can make the difference between a complete recovery and permanent damage. You can treat most food or drink spills with the steps shown here, whether it's wine, coffee or spaghetti sauce.

Clean up food and drink spills

Use the wet/dry vacuum first

Getting as much of the liquid and solids out of the carpet as quickly as possible is the single most important part of removing a carpet stain. But blotting and scooping can actually drive the stain deep into the carpet backing and pad. Instead, reach for your wet/dry vacuum and vacuum up the spill. Convert your wet/dry vac to wet mode by removing the paper filter and installing a foam cover (if equipped) before sucking anything up **(Photo 1)**.

Apply a cleaning solution

After sucking up as much of the spill as possible, resist the temptation to hit the stain with strong cleaners like vinegar and hydrogen peroxide right out of the gate. Those products can set the stain and even discolor your carpet. They can be used in some cases to remove a stubborn stain, but only as a last resort after you've used a milder cleaning solution.

If you keep a store-bought carpet stain removal product on hand, great. Use it. If not, you can make your own by mixing 1/4 teaspoon dish soap (clear is best) to 1 cup of water. Pour the homemade solution into a spray bottle and apply a generous amount to the soiled area, but don't saturate it. Let the cleaning solution soak into the fibers for a few minutes before moving on to the next step.

Blot from the outside in

Blot the stain with a clean white cloth (dyed fabric can transfer color to the carpet), working from the outside in **(Photo 2)**. Your goal is to move the carpet fibers, spread the cleaner slightly, and soak up the stain. Avoid aggressive blotting, scrubbing and stomping on the blotter. That just drives the stain deeper into the pile, backing and padding, making stain removal even more difficult. After blotting, use your wet/dry vac again to remove as much cleaning solution as possible.

Rinse, rinse, rinse

Leaving cleaning solution in the carpet is a big mistake. The leftover cleaning chemicals attract dirt, causing the spot to get soiled faster than the rest of the carpet. Even if you remove the stain, you'll eventually have a dirty area at the exact spot of the stain. Plus, the rinsing step helps remove any leftover stain liquid. So rinse the stained area multiple times with clear water **(Photo 3)**. Vacuum the rinse water between applications and continue vacuuming until you remove as much final rinse water as possible.

WET VAC NOZZLE

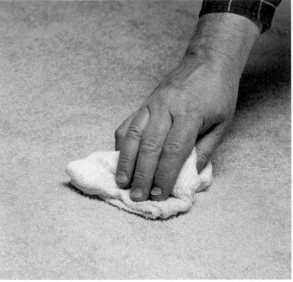

1 Suck up the mess. Push the hose directly onto the carpet fibers and leave it in place for several seconds. Don't rub or drag the hose over the carpet. Move to an adjoining spot and repeat as many times as required to remove as much of the spill as possible.

2 Blot gently. Fold a clean white cloth into a small square and dab the carpet, starting at the outside edge. Roll the cloth toward the center and refold the cloth to a clean section as you soak up more stain.

3 Rinse the stained area. Dab or spray clean water onto the stained area. Never pour water directly onto the carpet—it'll push the cleaning solution and stain into the backing and padding and can cause mold.

4 Clean your shop vacuum the easy way. Dump some disinfecting cleaner into a bucket of warm water and drop your hose into it. Empty the tank and rinse both the hose and tank with water.

Leaving food or organic matter in your shop vacuum will turn it into a stinky science experiment in no time. So clean it right away **(Photo 4)**.

What to do next

These techniques won't set the stain or damage your carpet, so if your stain is particularly stubborn, you can proceed to the next level and follow specific spot removal advice. Pet vomit, and fecal and urine stains, require additional neutralization and disinfection steps. Find advice for treating those stains by searching for "carpet pet" at familyhandyman.com.

Clean the outside of your car

Tired of your bumper stickers?

Soak the sticker in warm soapy water for at least 10 minutes, then take a plastic putty knife and get under a corner and start working it loose. Never use a metal scraper or razor blade because they can scratch the finish. If the sticker still won't budge, wipe off the soap solution and give the sticker a spray of WD-40, let it absorb and start scraping again. The WD-40 will loosen the adhesive and act as a lubricant for the putty knife without harming your car's finish. Keep spraying as needed if you run into stubborn spots. Once the sticker is removed, you may have adhesive still stuck to the bumper. Dab rubbing alcohol onto a clean rag and scrub until it's gone. Wash and dry the area, then put on a coat of wax.

Wash the entire car one section at a time

Soak the entire car with your hose to get rid of loose dirt and dust, and use a heavy jet spray under the wheel wells where road dirt accumulates. Then fill a bucket with warm water and add car-washing soap. Dish soap is generally too harsh. Avoiding the direct sun, wash a section at a time and then rinse it immediately. Start from the top down: first the roof, then the hood, the trunk and finally the sides. Use a special wash mitt or a heavy terry cloth towel. Work the soapy water in a circular motion and get into corners and detail lines. Use a soft-bristled washing brush to get at areas where a rag or mitt can get caught (racks and license plate brackets, door handles, trim, etc.). Open the hood and trunk and wash the crevices where dirt gets trapped. When you've finished washing the last section, rinse the whole car again and then dry it with a chamois, starting from the top down. Wring out the chamois often to keep it absorbent. The idea is to avoid water spots and streaks.

Use a spray-on solution to clean doorjambs and weather-stripping

You can use a hose and bucket, but it's often tough to keep water from spraying into the interior. A spray-on wash such as Bucket-Free Car Wash is great for this because you'll have a lot more control and won't be flooding delicate door mechanisms with water. Get into all the nooks and crannies around the weatherstrip and hinges to make your car look showroom perfect.

Scrub the wheels and tires with a brush

Ordinary soap and water often aren't enough to get rid of caked-on brake dust and road grime, so buy a specialty cleaner for your type of wheels (painted, chrome, alloy or clear coat). Spray the wheel and let the solution work for about 30 seconds, then scrub with a soft-bristled brush to work the cleaner into all the small recesses. Flush with water and repeat the process if necessary. After you've dressed the tires to make them look showroom new (see next step), put a coat of wax on the wheels. Spray-on wax works best.

Wash the tires with soap and water, then rinse and dry

Next spray on a tire dressing like Tire Foam & Shine and let it dry. The tires will look new and be protected for up to 30 washings.

Revive a dull paint finish

Contamination from brake dust and air pollution dulls painted finishes and eventually leads to surface rust. The best way to revive the finish is with a clay bar that actually absorbs these contaminants as you rub it back and forth across the paint. Professional detailers have been using this product for years. Now you can find it at auto supply stores or amazon.com. Spray the surface with either the lubricant that comes with your clay bar or liquid wax. Never use plain water. Rub the clay back and forth on the freshly lubricated section, overlapping each stroke and using light pressure. It will sound harsh at first, but as the clay bar absorbs contaminants, it will get quieter and smoother. Rework as needed until the finish feels as smooth as glass. Remove any residue by spraying on more lubricant and then buff with a clean terry cloth towel.

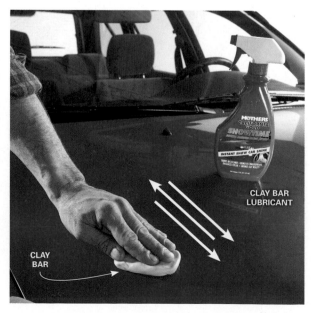

CLAY BAR LUBRICANT

CLAY BAR

Wax your car at least twice a year.

Very lightly mist a 2 x 2-ft. section with clean water then apply a good-quality wax. Do a panel at a time, such as the hood or the roof, just as you do when you wash. We used a new product called Nano Wax, which has super-fine particulates that hide surface scratches much better than ordinary car waxes, resulting in a deep shine. Apply the wax with the applicator, rubbing in a circular motion. Let the wax dry to a haze and remove it with a lint-free, soft terry towel. Open the doors, the hood and the trunk to remove haze from the edges. Never wax in direct sun.

Give your weatherstripping renewed life.

Dress door, trunk and hood weatherstripping with a silicone spray like Armor All. Wash the weatherstrip first, then apply Armor All to a rag (prepackaged wipes are available) and work it into the weatherstrip until it shines. You'll restore its suppleness, protect it from aging and keep it from freezing to the door in icy winter weather.

Clean the inside of your car

Slide the seat all the way forward and clean out all the junk underneath

You'll be surprised by what you find. We found a lost cell phone, enough pens and pencils to equip a small office, and enough change for several vending machine lunches. Vacuum the seats, remove the mats and vacuum the carpet. Use a brush attachment for the dash and door panels. Don't forget to clean out and vacuum those handy door pockets (another source of buried treasure).

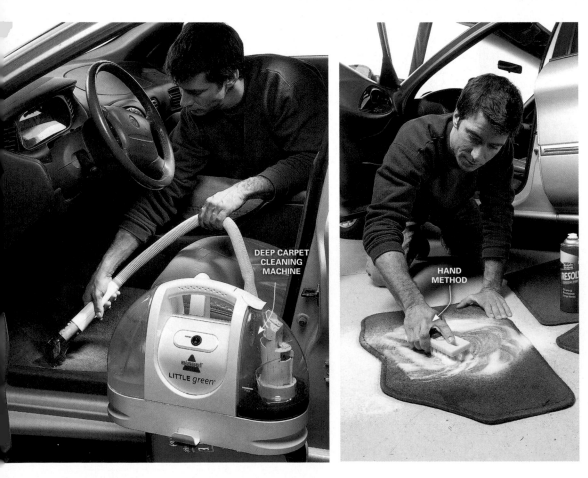

DEEP CARPET CLEANING MACHINE

HAND METHOD

Deep-clean carpeting and upholstery

Use a carpet cleaning machine to get the deep dirt that settles into the fibers of the carpet. (Clean cloth seats this way as well.) It sprays the carpet with a solution of water and cleaner and then sucks the dirt and grime into a reservoir. A machine like this pays for itself after just a few uses. You can also rent one from a rental center or use a spray-on cleaner and a scrub brush instead.

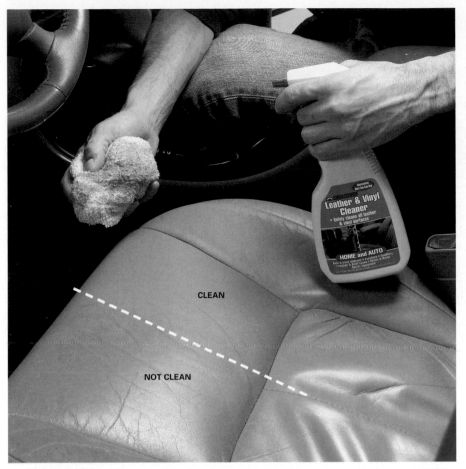

CLEAN

NOT CLEAN

Clean and condition the leather or vinyl

After a couple of years, you'll notice that the color of the leather seats no longer matches the rest of the interior. It's not enough just to condition the leather. First spray on leather cleaner and rub vigorously with a clean terry cloth towel. To avoid rubbing the grime back into the seats, keep flipping the cloth to expose a fresh surface. Let the seats dry for an hour and then rub in a leather conditioner like Lexol to keep the leather supple. It's available at discount stores and auto stores.

Remember to get into the nooks and crannies

Detailing means just that— finding and dealing with all the trim lines and recesses that a quick once-over cleaning job misses. Wrap a cloth around an old, worn screwdriver (without sharp edges) and spray Simple Green or other all-purpose cleaner on the cloth. Move it gently along the trim lines to pick up the gunk. Keep refreshing the surface of the cloth. Go around all the buttons and controls as well. Follow up with a rejuvenator like Armor All.

Brush out the air vents

These louvers are a real magnet for dust, and a vacuum with a brush attachment just won't get it all. Take an inexpensive paint brush and give it a light shot of Endust or Pledge furniture polish. Work the brush into the crevices to collect the dust. Wipe the brush off with a rag and move on to the next one.

LONG-BRISTLED ARTIST'S BRUSH

Wash the windows, including the top edges

Ever notice that line of grime on the tops of windows when they're partially rolled down? Most people overlook this detail when giving their vehicle a quick wash. A few minutes with Windex and a clean rag is all it takes.

GRIME AT TOP OF WINDOW

Scrape off those annoying stickers

While all of your national and state park stickers may call to mind great memories, they can be a visual hazard as they accumulate. The high-quality stickers will pull off if you can get under a corner and carefully pull them free at a 90-degree angle. Others will leave a gummy residue and require a bit more attention. Cover your dash with an old towel and dab on Goo Gone. Then scrape and wipe it off.

PLASTIC PUTTY KNIFE

Kill bad odors

Whether your vehicle smells like a Big Mac or cigarettes, one pump of the Odor Gun will solve the problem.

ODOR ELIMINATOR

Mini blind cleaning tongs

Dusting mini blinds is a pain. It's difficult to thoroughly wipe both sides of the slats without bending them in the process. A pair of kitchen tongs makes it a lot easier.

First, cut a rag into two small pieces. Then use twist ties or rubber bands to secure the rags around the tongs. You can close the tongs around each slat and wipe away the dust.

Power scrubber

You can buy scrub brushes for your drill, or you can make your own rather than spend $15. Once you gather the materials-which you may already have-it takes about five minutes. You'll need a 4-in. carriage bolt, a washer, a nut and a scrub brush.

Start by cutting the handle off your brush. Drill a hole through the brush and slide the carriage bolt through. Slip on the washer, thread on the nut and you're set. Chuck the carriage bolt into your drill and clean with power!

Coat hanger drain snake

A wire coat hanger makes an excellent drain snake for pulling out hair clogs. First, untwist the wire under the hook. This leaves the hook at one end and a miniature "auger" at the other end. Push the auger end down the drain to the clog. Bend the free end 90 degrees, forming a handle. Crank the handle so the auger bores into the clog, allowing you to pull it out.

MINI AUGER

Handy broom cleaner

Every time you sweep, clumps of dust and hair collect at the ends of the broom bristles. To get rid of them neatly, hot-glue a wide-tooth comb to the top of the dustpan. Just run the bristles through it to remove the debris.

CARPET SCRAP

Grout haze cleaner

When you tile a backsplash or floor, use a scrap of carpet to clean off the grout haze and buff the tiles to a shine in one easy step. The carpet fibers are slightly more abrasive than a sponge or cotton rag but not abrasive enough to scratch the tiles. They just remove the grout haze quickly with minimal elbow grease. If you don't have a clean carpet scrap handy, check at a home center-most have small samples available for free.

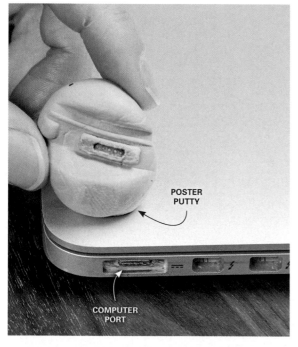

POSTER PUTTY

COMPUTER PORT

Poster-putty port cleaner

If you use your If you use your computer in your shop, the magnetic charging port can collect dust and metal filings. Blowing out the filings with compressed air doesn't work; the magnet wouldn't let go of them. What does the trick is a ball of poster putty. It removes debris without leaving any residue.

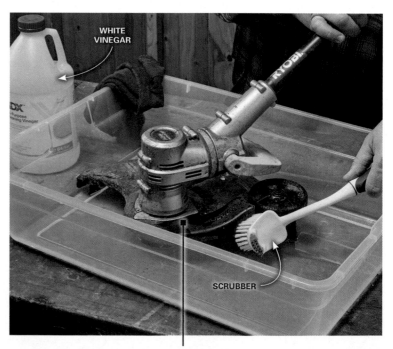

WHITE VINEGAR

SCRUBBER

Lawn equipment cleaner

To keep your lawn equipment really clean, scrub off all the muck with an old dish brush and white vinegar. It takes about 15 minutes for a string trimmer to go from drab to fab!

12 ways to clean with vinegar

Clean window blinds

Give your mini-blinds or venetians "the white glove treatment." Put on a white cotton glove and moisten the fingers in a solution of equal parts white vinegar and hot tap water. Slide your fingers across both sides of each slat to quickly clean them. Periodically rinse the glove in a container of clean water.

Get rid of smoke odor

Remove the lingering odor of burned food or cigarettes by setting out shallow bowls about three-quarters full of white or cider vinegar. The odor should be gone in less than a day. To quickly banish the smell of fresh cigarette smoke, moisten a cloth with vinegar and wave it around a bit.

Erase ballpoint-pen marks

Dab some full-strength white vinegar onto the marks, using a sponge. Repeat until the marks are gone.

Restore rugs

Bring a rug or carpet back to life by brushing it with a clean push broom dipped in a solution of 1 cup white vinegar in 1 gallon water. The faded threads will perk up, and you don't even need to rinse off the solution.

Keep rugs from mildewing

To prevent mildew from forming on the bottoms of carpets and rugs, mist the backs with full-strength white vinegar from a spray bottle.

Revitalize wood paneling

To liven up dull wood paneling, mix 2 cups warm water, 4 tablespoons white or cider vinegar, and 2 tablespoons olive oil in a container, give it a couple of shakes, and apply with a clean cloth. Let it soak in for several minutes, then polish with a dry cloth.

Brighten up brickwork

To clean brick floors without breaking out the polish, just go over them with a damp mop dipped in 1 cup white vinegar mixed with 1 gallon warm water. Brighten fireplace bricks the same way.

Wipe away mildew

To remove mildew stains, reach for white vinegar. It can be safely used without additional ventilation and can be applied to almost any surface—bathroom fixtures and tile, clothing, furniture, painted surfaces, plastic curtains and more. For heavy mildew accumulations, use it full strength. For light stains, dilute it with an equal amount of water.

Unglue stickers, decals and price tags

To remove a sticker or decal on painted furniture or a painted wall, saturate the corners and sides of the sticker with full-strength white vinegar and carefully scrape it off, using an expired credit card. Remove any residue by pouring on a bit more vinegar. Let it sit for a minute or two, then wipe with a clean cloth. This is equally effective for removing price tags and other stickers from glass, plastic and other glossy surfaces.

Clean piano keys

To get grimy fingerprints and stains off piano keys, dip a soft cloth into a solution of 1/2 cup white vinegar mixed with 2 cups water, squeeze it out thoroughly, then gently wipe each key. Use a second cloth to dry each key as you move along. Let the keyboard dry uncovered for 24 hours.

Freshen a musty closet

Got a closet that doesn't smell fresh? Empty it, then wash the walls, ceiling, and floor with a cloth dampened in a solution of 1 cup vinegar, 1 cup ammonia, and 1/4 cup baking soda in 1 gallon water. Let the interior dry with the door open before refilling it.

Remove carpet stains

You can lift out many stains from your carpet with vinegar.

- Rub light carpet stains with a mixture of 2 tablespoons salt dissolved in 1/2 cup white vinegar. Let dry, then vacuum.
- For larger or darker stains, add 2 tablespoons borax to the mixture and use in the same way.
- For tough, ground-in dirt and other stains, make a paste of 1 tablespoon vinegar with 1 tablespoon cornstarch, and rub on with a dry cloth. Let it sit for two days, then vacuum.

Easier bottle cleaning

Clean those narrow-necked jars and vases with small gravel (aquarium gravel works the best). Fill one-third of the jar with water. Add a handful of gravel, and then stir and shake the jar. The gravel will scour the inside of the jar clean. Dump the gravel into a strainer, give it a quick rinse (so it doesn't stink!) and save it for next time.

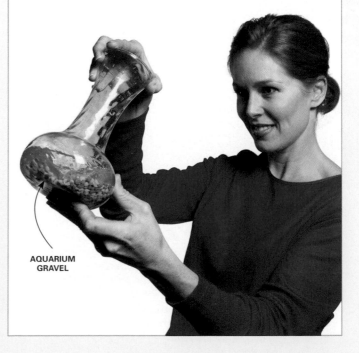

AQUARIUM GRAVEL

How to clean and restore your deck

1 Pressure-wash the railings with stripper. Keep the tip 6 to 10 in. from the wood and work from the top down. Spray balusters at the corners to scour two sides at once.

2 Spray one deck board at a time, using a gentle sweeping motion. Avoid sudden stops. Work from the end of the deck toward the exit. Then rinse the entire deck with a garden hose.

1,200 PSI PRESSURE WASHER

6" TO 10"

3 Dig out trapped debris from between deck boards with a putty knife. Spray the deck lightly with a mixture of oxalic acid and water to brighten the wood.

4 Rinse the siding and windows with clean water at low pressure to remove chemical residue.

CORROSION-RESISTANT DECK SCREWS

5 Sink any raised nails and screws. Replace loose and missing fasteners with screws at least 1/2 in. longer than the original.

6 Remove mold, mildew or algae using non-chlorine bleach. Scrub the area with a nylon brush, then rinse with water. For tougher stains, repeat the process with a TSP substitute.

RUST STAINS FROM NAILS

7 Drive the heads of stain-causing fasteners below the wood surface. Then sand out the stains using 80-grit sandpaper. Also sand rough or splintered areas.

APPLY FROM TOP DOWN

8 Apply stain to the top rail, then the balusters and the posts. Work from the top down. Stain one section at a time, using a foam applicator pad. Brush out drips as you work.

9 Stain the deck boards using a foam applicator pad with an extension handle. Stain the full length of two or three boards at a time, working with the grain.

Pressure washer safety

To use the pressure washer:

- Wear appropriate safety gear and clothes. Rubber boots and gloves will protect your hands and feet. Safety goggles will keep the chemicals from splashing into your eyes, and a disposable respirator or dust mask will filter fumes.

- Keep the exhaust from the pressure washer at least 3 ft. away from any objects, including your house.

- Practice spraying the water until you find an appropriate power setting.

- Never point the wand at anything you don't want to spray.

- Cover electrical outlets.

10 Spray on the finish in hard-to-reach areas or surfaces that are difficult to cover with a paintbrush. Use a wide spray to avoid streaks. Work stain into crevices and narrow areas between balusters and posts with a paintbrush.

How to remove roof stains

To see an immediate improvement, you'll need to climb onto your roof, spray it with a cleaning solution and rinse with water. A cleaning solution and water will remove most algae stains right away, but some can be especially difficult. If you have a steep roof, it's best to call a pro.

1 Mix a homemade solution To save money, you can make your own solution. Commercial roof cleaners are available at most home centers, but they're expensive and won't work any better than a homemade solution. Plus, it's easy to make your own. Mix 15 oz. of an oxygen bleach powder (we used OxiClean Stain Remover, available at home centers for about $12) with 2 gallons of warm tap water in a garden sprayer. Don't use chlorinated bleach; it'll kill the lawn and plants on the ground below.

2 Spray the shingles Once you're on the roof, start at the edge and spray the shingles with your homemade solution, working your way up to the ridge. A wet roof is a slippery roof, so leave a dry path back to your ladder. Allow the solution to sit for 20 minutes before rinsing. Tough stains may require an additional application and a mild scrubbing with a stiff-bristle brush.

3 Rinse with a garden hose After you've waited for the solution to do its work, douse the roof with a garden hose, clearing suds and algae off the shingles. You'll see a big improvement unless your stains are especially stubborn. Never use a pressure washer to clean the algae; the roof will be clean, but its life will be shortened by the loss of granules.

Be safe!
Climbing a roof is dangerous. Use a safety harness, wear boots or shoes with good traction and consider installing a slide guard. For more information, search "roof safety" at familyhandyman.com.

Reduce home allergens

When pollen and mold levels are high, allergy symptoms might force you indoors. But indoor allergens are troublesome too. They can cause sneezing, a stuffy or runny nose, and itchy, watery eyes. Your best bet for beating indoor allergies is to banish the things that trigger them. For starters, vacuum regularly, preferably with a HEPA-rated vacuum cleaner so you're not blasting allergens back into the air. When you dust, use a damp cloth to help trap the allergens. Below are a few specific allergy triggers and ways to combat them.

Pet allergens

The cause:

Dead skin flakes and saliva in dogs and cats, and urine in rabbits, guinea pigs, hamsters and mice. Although some animals trigger more allergic reactions than others, there is no such thing as a hypo-allergenic pet.

The fix:

■ Keep pets out of your bedroom.

■ Regularly wash or replace your pet's bedding and toys.

■ In extreme cases, consider replacing carpets with hard-surface floors.

Mold & mildew

The cause:

Dampness.

The fix:

■ Repair roof and plumbing leaks.

■ Keep damp spaces—such as kitchens, bathrooms and basements—clean and well-ventilated.

■ Replace vent switches with timers to fully vent moisture during and after showers.

■ Don't install carpeting on concrete or damp floors.

■ Don't store items like towels, bedding or clothes in damp areas.

Cockroaches

The cause:

Saliva, feces and body parts of cockroaches, which are often found in urban areas and in the southern United States.

The fix:

■ Block any cracks or gaps in walls and windows where cockroaches can enter.

■ Repair roof and plumbing leaks to eliminate the water sources needed by cockroaches.

■ Apply bug barrier products around your home's exterior perimeter.

Pollen

The cause:

Spores that make their way inside your home.

The fix:

■ Keep doors and windows closed to prevent pollen from drifting in.

■ Weatherproof around your doors and windows to seal any gaps.

■ Change your air conditioner filter regularly.

Dust mites

The cause:

Warm, humid areas such as bedding and carpeting.

The fix:

■ Allergen-proof covers on bedding.

■ Wash bedding weekly in hot water and dry with high heat.

■ Consider replacing carpeting with hard-surface flooring like tile, hardwood or vinyl. If you don't want bare floors, use washable area rugs.

CHAPTER 2

Gardening & Lawn Care Hacks

Low-maintenance perennial garden

Looking for a way to reduce the weed-pulling chore around your plants that come back every year? When you start a new perennial border, spread a nonwoven polypropylene black landscape fabric over the soil. The fabric keeps weeds under control, holds heat in cool spring weather (giving your plants a faster start), and lets water soak through to the roots. At a local garden center, buy a nonbiodegradable fabric that weighs about 3.4 ozs. per square yard. U-shaped metal stakes **(Photo 2)**, which are ideal to hold down the fabric, come in packs of 10.

While this system works best for plants already started, you can also start your perennials from seed. Simply prep the soil and plant the seed.

Space plants according to the recommendations on the labels when you buy them. The hardy, drought-resistant plants shown here will fill in and cover the mulch completely in two years. Then they will need annual pruning or even dividing.

1 Dig and break up compacted soil with a sharp spade or U-bar and remove the weeds. Mix peat moss and/or composted manure into the soil if necessary.

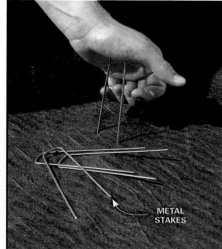

2 Lay down landscape fabric, securing it at the corners with metal stakes.

METAL STAKES

3 Draw the garden pattern, including paths, onto the fabric with a light-colored crayon or chalk. Cut the plant holes with a utility knife and set the plants.

UTILITY KNIFE

CHALK MARK

LANDSCAPE FABRIC

POULTRY NETTING

TENT STAKES

Munch-proof your flower bulbs

Keep hungry critters from snacking on your freshly planted flower bulbs by staking poultry netting over the bed. You can either remove the cloth in the early spring or let plants grow through the holes and leave it throughout the growing season.

No-stick shovel

Whether you're dealing with wet snow or mucky soil, a dose of spray lubricant on your shovel will make the sticky stuff slip right off. Use a lubricant that contains silicone or Teflon and recoat the shovel occasionally.

Rein in an invasive plant

Plants like gooseneck loosestrife have underground rhizomes (roots) that can spread to all corners of your garden before you know it. To contain them, slice out the bottom of a plastic container with a utility knife (**Photo 1**) and push this "collar" into the soil (or drive it down with a mallet) to encircle the plant and its invasive root system (**Photo 2**). If the soil has become compacted, cut around the plant with a spade first. Note: This technique won't contain plants that spread above ground like strawberries and mint.

10 tips for a no-fuss garden

1 Forget the stereotypes

Not all pretty gardens are neat rows of shrubs and sprawling beds of cascading flowers. To cut down on garden upkeep, why not include a paved patio or gravel path? After all, when's the last time your driveway needed to be watered?

2 Use common sense

Remember those words of wisdom from your mother? They apply to planning a garden, too. Plant flowers near a faucet, keep your compost pile near your planting beds—anything to minimize trips across the yard. They may seem short, but they add up and take time.

3 Bigger is not always better

This one's a no-brainer: The smaller your garden, the fewer plants to care for. Don't go too tiny, but make it manageable. You can always expand later.

4 Space it out

If planting directions recommend leaving 6 inches between flowers, don't leave less. Your garden may seem bare at first, but it will fill in. Plant too closely now, and you'll be thinning, pruning or even removing plants later.

5 Think outside the (flower) box

Container gardening is easy and fun, but it can be time-consuming. Some potted plants need to be watered daily. Cut back on the number of containers in your garden, and you'll cut back on watering chores—guaranteed.

6 Mulch is a must

Mulching is a great way to control weeds, keep soil moist and improve the overall health of your plants. That means you spend less time weeding, watering and tending to wilted blooms.

7 It's easy being evergreen

When planting trees and shrubs, choose evergreens over deciduous plants, which shed seasonally and need more pruning. That's more work in the leaf-sweeping department.

8 Pick perennials

Perennials are perfect for an easy-care garden. They die back in winter and re-emerge in spring—no replanting necessary. Annuals, on the other hand, must be planted each year.

9 Know your nursery

Every region is different, so the best recommendations for easy-care plants often come from staff at a nearby garden center. Live in a dry area? Ask for a list of drought-resistant plants. You get the idea.

10 Stick to your plan

When buying plants, you'll almost always see a colorful bloom that looks too good to pass up. But remember, you preplanned your shopping list for a reason. The blooms on that list are the ones that are best for your garden and lifestyle. So buy them and get planting. Then kick back and enjoy your low-maintenance backyard!

Laundry jug watering can

Instead of throwing away empty laundry detergent containers, rinse them out thoroughly and then recycle them for watering plants. Drill 1/8-in. holes in the top of the cap, and a 1/2-in. hole just above the handle to relieve pressure so the water flows freely.

1/2" HOLE DRILLED FOR AIR

1/8" HOLES DRILLED FOR WATER

1" PVC

Sprinkler socket system

If you use spike-type sprinklers, try setting them in permanent sockets made from 1-in. PVC pipe. These sockets will make it a snap to move the sprinklers, and they'll keep them upright and shooting water where you want it.

STEEL PIPE

Space-saving hose storage

If you have a small yard, don't waste any precious real estate on a bulky hose reel. Pound a 4-ft. length of galvanized steel pipe into the ground, coil up to 50 ft. of hose around it and top the end with a nozzle that hooks into the pipe's end. This hose holder's narrow profile is both space saving and attractive.

Leaf hamper

Leaf bags have an irritating tendency to close and collapse, making them difficult to fill. Cut out the bottom of a laundry hamper and insert the hamper into the leaf bag. Fill the bag with leaves or grass clippings and pull out the hamper when it's full.

CARDBOARD TUBE

Weedy tip

When you sow seeds, it can be hard to tell little weeds from the young sprouts. Cut cardboard tubes from toilet paper into one-third sections to encircle the seed and keep you from plucking out your young plants.

LAUNDRY HAMPER

Help for root-bound plants

If you buy potted plants or shrubs, they may well be root-bound. With nowhere else to grow, roots form tight circles inside the pot. As the plant grows, the tightly wound roots prevent water and nutrients from reaching the leaves. Before planting, gently coax these roots outward with your fingers. If the roots are very stubborn, make three or four vertical cuts in the root-ball with a sharp knife. Once planted, water often to help the plant get established.

10 tips for planting flowers in the sun

- Choose the right site. Even sun lovers need a little relief, especially at midday. So avoid growing them in full sun, especially on south-facing exposures. Part-day shade minimizes stress and also preserves flower color longer.

- While you can't turn down the heat, you can change the soil. Dig in plenty of organic matter prior to planting. This improves the soil's texture, fertility and ability to retain moisture. Plus, the soil stays cooler. This should be an annual task.

- An inch or two of mulch can make a world of difference. Organic mulch will hold moisture in the soil, keep plant roots cool and even improve the soil as it breaks down.

- Group plants with similar moisture needs in the same area. This cuts down on the special trips you'll need to make to water just one or two plants.

- One of the best ways to prevent drought stress is proper watering. Instead of giving your plants frequent, shallow waterings, water less often and more deeply. Let a soaker hose give plants a good drink for several hours, or use a sprinkler at a low setting. Always water plants at ground level so that the moisture goes directly to the roots.

- Try desert and dry-meadow natives and plants that survive at high altitudes. These plants survive nicely in the wild, without human help, so they're sure to survive in your backyard.

- Young plants purchased from native nurseries may start out as ugly ducklings but, once established, provide beauty with little care.

  Hot, dry weather is the worst possible time to fertilize your flower garden. This is because plant roots respond to the difficult condition by slowing or shutting down. The nitrates in plant foods will only injure them in this dormant state.

- Experiment with plant placement if you live in the South. You may find that the light is intense enough for you to grow even sun-loving plants in the shade.

- Try spring bulbs! Many spring-flowering bulbs will survive in hot, dry locations, since the most extreme weather hits after they've already flowered and are resting. Mulch or cover them with other plants to keep them safe and cool.

- Many ornamental grasses are prairie natives, so they're well suited to hot, dry conditions. Look for ones native to your area.

Seedlings on the half shell

You don't have to buy seedling pots in the spring. Instead, make your own from eggshells, using the egg carton as a tray. Next time you use eggs, carefully crack them in half, rinse out the egg residue, then poke a drainage hole in the bottom of each half shell with sharp scissors or an ice pick. Fill the shells with a lightweight, sterile potting mix formulated for seed starting, and sow the seeds. When the seedlings are ready for transplanting, gently crush the eggshell with your fingers and plant them, eggshell and all. The shell will improve your soil as it decomposes.

HOOK-AND-LOOP STRIP

Potted plant transport

The spaces between the rungs of a stepladder are great spots to transport tender plants. No more messy spills during turns!

DOOMED

Drive-by weeding

Attach a bottle of herbicide to your lawn tractor with a hook-and-loop strip (like Velcro) in a spot where you can easily grab it. When you're mowing your lawn, pause the tractor and spray weeds right when you see them for weed control on the fly.

HOOK-AND-LOOP STRIP

Easy-read rain gauge

Drip food coloring into the bottom of your rain gauge the next time you empty it out. When it showers, the coloring will reconstitute and tint the water to make the gauge easier to read.

10 tips for planting flowers in the shade

- Different areas of shade allow freedom of plant selection. A spot that gets morning sun will dry dew and allow plants that prosper in drier conditions to grow. A bit of afternoon sun lures reluctant blooms into developing buds.

- Lousy soil is the leading cause of poor growth—not lack of sun. Add organic matter in late spring or early fall when the ground is neither soggy nor frozen.

- Intermix shade plants as artistically as you would in a sunny spot. Position taller growers like astilbe in back, shorter ones like foam flower and hosta in front, and low-growing ground covers to fill in your display.

- Shade doesn't mean your color choices are limited. Experiment with different plants and color schemes. A few to try are the white wands of astilbe flowers along brunnera's sprays of little blue flowers, or bugleweed's sapphire-blue spikes next to a light-hued rhododendron.

- Another great way to liven up a shady spot is to pick plants with varying textures. Combine the fine leaves of ferns with bold hostas. Or mix leafy bergenia with spiky ornamental grasses such as hakone grass. Even in complete shade, you'll still have visual appeal.

- For a low-maintenance, attractive shady spot, try ground covers. Plant seedlings in staggered rows rather than straight lines. They'll expand, fill the area and form a nice carpet.

- Want flower color in late summer or early fall? Several plants are adapted to this. Rhododendrons bloom from early spring to midsummer with an array of color. Toad lily produces adorable violet-dabbed flowers.

- Don't overpamper your shade garden in fall. Allow the leaves to break down and they'll contribute valuable humus to the soil. Remove them only if they're smothering your plants.

- Consider how changing seasons affect sun and shade conditions in your yard. Even a yard filled with shade trees can support bright, spring-flowering bulbs, as long as they emerge before the trees leaf out fully.

  Pick up hints from previous seasons. If sun lovers like marigolds died where astilbe thrived, you've likely found a hot spot for a shade garden.

- Resist the temptation to give shade plants a nudge by overwatering or overfertilizing them. Shade slows plant growth, so your plants in low light need less water and energy, not more. Mulching will also keep your workload light. It helps retain soil moisture and minimizes weeds.

Bulb storage solution

Tender bulbs that must be overwintered indoors are hard to keep organized. These include canna lilies, freesias, caladiums, gladioluses, dahlias and tuberous begonias. Keep track of the bulbs by storing them in egg cartons, with each bulb identified on the top of the carton. The cartons even have ventilation holes that help prevent rot and mildew.

OLD HOSE

12d NAIL

STICK

Homemade soaker hose

A sprinkler isn't always the most efficient way to water your plants, especially if you live in a hot, dry climate. Soaker hoses ensure that the plants get most of the water, and you don't need to spend money at a garden center to get one. Give your worn-out hoses a second career by converting them. Just plug the end of the hose with a round stick and perforate the hose with a sharp nail. You'll get a free soaker hose and conserve water at the same time.

No-trim wall border

If you're building a fence, a retaining wall or a planter, set a course of protruding stones in the soil beneath it. That way, your mower can cut all the grass—no trimming by hand needed. The stones should protrude about 4 in. from the wall and stand at least an inch above the soil so grass doesn't creep over them. You will still have to pull out grass from between the stones occasionally.

Portable potting

Cut a piece of plywood roughly to the shape of your wheelbarrow's back end and screw a few wood cleats along the sides to keep it from slipping off while you wheel. Now you'll have both soil and a potting surface right at hand when you take the wheelbarrow to the garden.

STAY-PUT CLEAT

Ice cube trick

Tired of water draining too quickly through hanging baskets? Try ice cubes. They'll melt slowly enough so plants can absorb as much water as they need.

Flag your lawn problems

If you have a really big lawn, you probably mow it with a riding mower. If you keep a supply of marking flags—sometimes called "stake" or "irrigation" flags—on hand, then when you stumble on a problem like weeds or an anthill that you can't deal with right away, you can mark it! The flags cost about $2 for a 10-pack at home centers. After you're done mowing, you can easily find the spots that need attention.

Easy apple cleanup

Bending over to pick up fallen fruit from apple trees is hard on your back, but here's a solution that works really well. Buy a three-tine frog spear ($4 at Cabela's) and fasten it to the end of a broom handle. Now just spear the apples. If you're careful, you can spear more than one at a time. Mashing small apples with my your foot makes them easier to spear.

5 tips for pet-friendly gardens

- Include sweeps of lawn where dogs can wander aimlessly, roll about or frolic freely.
- Guide pets through your gardens by laying clearly defined pathways that are easy on their feet.
- Keep dogs safely contained, and keep unwanted visitors out, by fencing in your yard.
- Run lattice around the bases of porches and decks to prevent pets from burrowing into these spaces and getting stuck beneath the floorboards.
- When buying products to treat lawns or gardens, read the labels to ensure the products are pet-safe.

Watering jug

When your trusty old metal watering can rusts through, reuse and recycle instead of buying a new one. Rinse out a milk jug and drill a few holes in the cap. It's a good size, lighter weight and easy to carry.

Hold your hostas!

If your hostas are always spreading and taking over entire flower beds, divide them with a spade and remove the excess plants, roots and all. Then stick 12-in. lengths of 8-in.-diameter duct around each plant. Works like a charm!

Garden straightedge

If you need to pull up sod for a new garden or flower bed, one good way to cut straight lines is to use an edger and a 2x6.

5 downspout upgrades

Water puddling around a foundation from an ineffective downspout can create major problems, ranging from damp basements to structural damage. It's worth finding a system that works for you. Here are the pros and cons of a variety of options.

RETRACTED

1 Vinyl recoiling sleeves These install with a simple strap and automatically unfurl as they fill with water.

Pros: They move water away from the foundation by dispersing it sprinkler-style, then recoil when it stops raining. They work well when you need to move water only 3 or 4 ft. away from the house to a slope where it will then run off naturally.

Cons: You need to remove the end clip to flush out built-up debris, and you should remove the entire sleeve in freezing temperatures to prevent damage.

2 Flip-up/swiveling/telescoping spouts Some simply flip up and out of the way, while others telescope for extra length and swivel 180 degrees to direct water away from the building at any angle.

Pros: The open-top design makes them easy to maintain. Fully extended, some carry water up to 6 ft. away from the foundation.

Cons: The most expensive option, one vulnerable to damage in areas where there's lots of foot traffic.

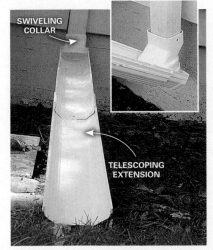
SWIVELING COLLAR

TELESCOPING EXTENSION

3 Flexible accordion spouts Attaches to your downspout with two screws.

Pros: Can be easily twisted to go around corners, shrubs or other obstacles and are easily moved when mowing. Two or more segments can be snapped together, making them ideal for situations where you need to move water over longer distances.

Cons: They look a little industrial—but none of these products is going to win any beauty contests.

OUTLET

4 A below-grade extension You'll need a downspout adapter and end cap, some 4-in. PVC pipe and adapters.

Pros: This is especially effective when the extension needs to cross a walkway or is in a "knock-off-prone" area.

Cons: Connecting and burying everything takes more time than other methods, but it's the most permanent solution. For this system to work, your lawn needs a little slope; make certain the pipe slants away from the house at least 1/4 in. per ft. If it clogs, clean it out with a plumbing snake.

5 Do-it-yourself flip-up spout Create your own by removing a 2-in. section from the top of a standard extension, then use two screws to create a "hinge" when securing it to the downspout elbow.

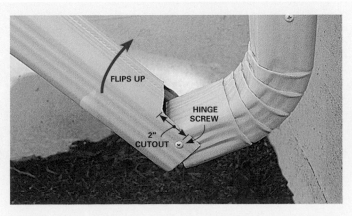
FLIPS UP
HINGE SCREW
2" CUTOUT

Pros: When it's time to mow, simply flip the extension up. It's inexpensive.

Cons: They are subject to "operator malfunction"—if they're left in the "up" position, you'll get water around your foundation during a storm.

Bamboo teepee

Climbing plants add an attractive third dimension to gardens. And the good news is that they don't care if their support is a pricey architectural statement or a couple of sticks.

A "teepee" made of bamboo stakes fits right in with a country flower or vegetable garden. It's cheap and simple to build and store. All you need are twine and some 3/4-in.-dia. bamboo stakes. Plunge the stakes (three or more, depending on how big you want it) into the soil so they form a teepee when the tops are bound together with twine as shown. Annual vines from beans and peas to morning glories will scramble up just about any support and quickly cover it up, so if this bamboo doesn't look attractive to begin with, just wait a few weeks.

Seed library

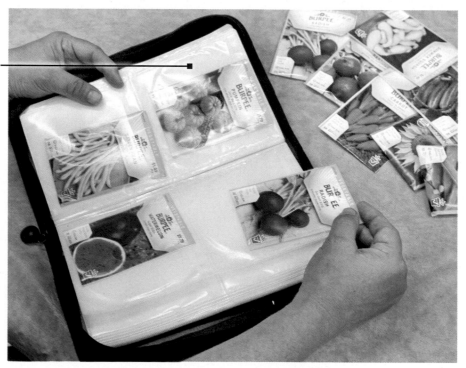

Now that CDs have been replaced with smartphones and other devices, you can use your old CD case to organize and store your seed packets. It works great to store them by seed type or even alphabetically. It's a convenient reference to have for the following year. Write notes on the packets to remember which seed variety worked and which didn't.

Weatherproof plant labels

Labeling rows of plants in a garden can be difficult. Even permanent markers can't stand up to constant sun and moisture. Here's one solution: a label maker and recycled vinyl window blinds. Cut the slats into 9-in. lengths and stick on the labels. They stand up to any kind of weather without smearing, dissolving or rotting away.

Reader photo

Easier vegetable planting

If you have a big vegetable garden and you have a lot of plants to get in the ground, put away your trowel and grab a posthole digger. Just one or two plunges into the soil for each plant and you've got perfectly sized holes for all of your crops.

Here's another easy way to keep a paper seed packet from getting destroyed by wind and rain out in your garden: Slip a small zipper-type plastic bag over the packet, with the bag upside down so the rain doesn't get in.

Save your lawn products

Leave a bag of fertilizer or weed killer open for long and it'll soak up moisture from the air and won't go through a spreader. Even grass seed could use an extra layer of protection from a moisture-wicking concrete floor. Place opened bags of lawn products in large resealable plastic bags. The products will be free of clumps or pests when you need them.

GIANT RESEALABLE PLASTIC BAG

Twig pickup on the go

Before you mow, you probably go around and pick up fallen twigs and other debris. Inevitably, you miss some and have to stop and pick them up while you're mowing. To solve the problem, attach a wastebasket to your mower. Now when wrappers, cans and sticks suddenly appear, you can stuff them into the basket and keep moving.

Better lawn mower traction

The drive wheels on self-propelled lawn mowers sometimes spin on hills, especially when the grass is damp. To improve the traction, drive a few self-tapping sheet metal screws with hex-shaped heads into the wheels. Now the tires will perform like those knobby tires on off-road vehicles

HEX-HEAD SCREWS

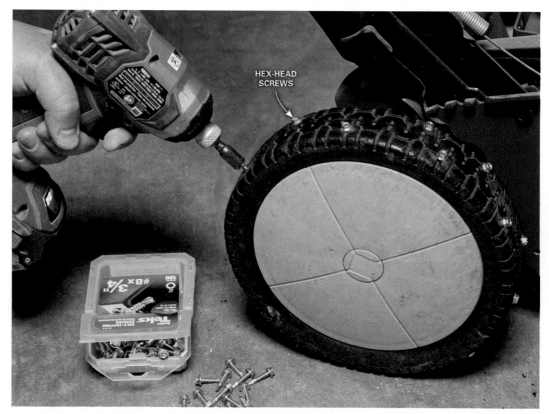

Mowing in comfort

Tape pipe insulation to the handle of your lawn mower and it will be a pleasure to use—no more numb hands or blisters. Make sure the insulation doesn't interfere with your auto-shutoff bar, if you have one.

Pinecone scooper

If your pine trees drop cones all summer long, you probably get pretty tired of bending over and picking them up. So, even if you don't have a dog, a pooper scooper could become your best friend! Gently squeezing the handle opens its jaws, allowing you to pick up pinecones with no back pain.

Better tree watering

If you've ever gotten tired of hauling buckets of water to distant trees, dumping the water at the base of the trees, and watching it quickly run off, take some old 5-gallon buckets and drill a 1/4-in. hole near the bottom of each one. After plugging the holes with dowels, fill the buckets and haul them in your wheelbarrow to the trees. Once you unplug the holes, it takes several minutes for the buckets to drain, allowing the soil to soak up every drop.

Fertilizing dense plants

To get fertilizer to the base of bushes and other dense plants, use a length of 2-in. PVC. Slide one end down to the plant base and pour the fertilizer into the pipe. Cut the top of the pipe at 45 degrees to give yourself a larger opening for pouring in the fertilizer.

Citrus-rind seed starters

Grapefruit, orange and other citrus rinds are just the right size for starting new seedlings. Make a hole in the bottom of each one for drainage and add some damp seed-starting mix and seeds. Then, when it's time to move them outside, plant the whole works in the ground—peels and all. The citrus rinds make the soil more acidic, however, so only do this with acid-loving plants like radishes, peppers and the like.

Flower-pot filler

Water settling at the bottom of pots can lead to root rot from poor aeration. To combat this, toss a few old sponges in the bottom of the pot. The sponges retain moisture and create necessary air space. They also help prevent water from running out the bottom.

PUNCH HOLES IN LID

Salad bar greenhouse

The next time you hit the salad bar for lunch, save the plastic container to make a mini greenhouse for starting seeds. Wash the container and then punch some air holes in the top. Fill the bottom with potting soil, plant your seeds, add a little water and close the lid. Set the container in a sunny spot and watch your seeds sprout! Once the seeds sprout, take off the lid.

Seed starter tubes

Empty tubes of toilet paper and paper towels make perfect seed starters. Set the tubes in a tray, fill them with potting soil and plant your seeds. The tubes decompose when you plant the seedlings in the garden. Keep the tubes below the soil surface so they don't wick moisture away from the roots.

No more rusty garden tools

When you change the oil in your lawn mower, here's a great way to reuse some of it. Pour a quart or so into a bucket filled with sand, and store your garden tools in it. This keeps them rust free and ready for use.

Tree protector

If you have a lot of deer where you live, they can do a lot of damage by stripping the bark off newly planted trees. And in the fall, the bucks rub their antlers on the bark to scrub off the velvet.

To prevent such damage, cut lengths of 4-in. flexible drainage pipe, slit them and wrap them around the base of the trees. Use the kind with holes in it so air can circulate and keep the trunk from rotting. The pipe also protects the base of the tree whenever you run your string trimmer and it prevents winter burn from the sun reflecting off the snow.

SPRING CLAMPS

Trash-can helpers

You can line a trash barrel with a plastic bag when doing yard cleanup, but when you push yard waste down into the barrel, the bag is going to slide toward the bottom. To remedy this, use a few spring clamps to hold the bag in place.

Need a hole in hard soil? Use a drill!

Have you ever waited too long to install your reflective driveway markers and discovered the ground was frozen? Or tried to install a yard sale sign in dry soil that's as hard as concrete? Well, why not treat it as if it really were concrete and drill holes into it with a masonry bit? This 3/8-in. x 12-in. bit costs less than $15 at home centers.

MASONRY BIT

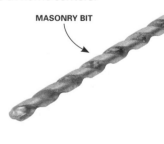

Berry box seed spreader

If you have just a few small bare spots in the lawn, use a berry container to spread the seed. They have small holes just right for shaking out grass seed. Just clean and dry the container, fill it with grass seed and you're ready to go.

Double potting

Ever wish you could reorganize your garden in the middle of the growing season? Here's a clever way to do it. You'll need a bunch of pots of similar sizes. Put your plants in doubled pots, and then bury them up to their rims. Whenever you want a change, lift out the top pot and put in a different one. This method is also really slick for bringing plants indoors over the winter.

ROPE
ATTACHMENT
POINT

CHUTE

ROPE

Cut trimming time

To cut your string trimmer work in half,
run a rope through your mower's grass
chute and tie a knot. Tie the other end of
the rope to the tractor so it can't get
caught in the blades. Now you can pull
up the grass chute and get closer to
trees and other obstacles from the
comfort of your tractor seat.

Sharpen your lawn mower blade

1 Pull the wire from the spark plug. Remove the gas cap, put a piece of plastic over the opening and replace the cap. This will help prevent gas spills when you flip the mower to access the blade.

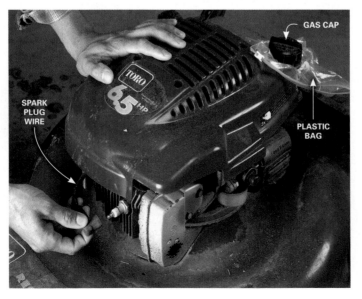

GAS CAP

SPARK PLUG WIRE

PLASTIC BAG

You wouldn't take care of grass that's too long by tearing off the end of each blade, would you? But that's exactly what a dull lawn mower does, leaving the torn grass vulnerable to sun damage and disease. You could sharpen your mower blade with a file (it takes forever!), a rotary tool or a bench grinder, but we'll show you how to do the job with an angle grinder. It's fast and easy. If you don't own a grinder, you can buy one for about $60 and use it for all kinds of other tasks too.

To sharpen your lawn mower blade, you'll need a socket or wrench to fit the blade nut. Tough nuts may call for a breaker bar and/or a penetrating lubricant. You'll also need two clamps, a block of wood and, of course, an angle grinder with a metal grinding blade.

Start by disconnecting the spark plug wire **(Photo 1)**. Next, place a piece of plastic (a sandwich bag works well) under the gas cap to prevent gas from leaking out of the vent hole when you tip the mower. Tip the mower so the side with the carburetor faces up.

Clamp a 2x4 block to the side of the mower to keep the blade from turning while you loosen it. Mark the "grass side" of the blade so you don't reinstall it upside down. Use a socket wrench or a breaker bar to turn the nut counterclockwise to loosen it **(Photo 2)**. If it's stubborn, soak it with penetrating oil for a half hour and try again.

Clamp the blade securely in a vise or to the edge of your workbench. Prepare for grinding by putting on your gloves, face shield, hearing protection and a long-sleeve shirt. Before you start grinding, hold the grinder against the blade and tip it up or down until the grinding disc is aligned with the angle on the blade. Try to maintain this angle as you grind. Keep the grinder moving and apply only light pressure so you don't overheat the blade or grind away too much **(Photo 3)**. If you overheat the metal, it'll turn dark blue or black and become brittle. Then it won't hold an edge. Your goal is to remove the nicks and dents and create an edge that's about as sharp as a butter knife. A razor-sharp edge will dull quickly and chip more easily.

Make several passes across the blade with the grinder, checking your progress frequently. You don't want to grind off more than necessary. If your blade has a lot of nicks and gouges, try this. Start by holding the grinder at a right angle to the blade and grinding the edge of the blade flat to remove the nicks. Be careful to use light pressure and move quickly. It's easy to burn the thin edge. After you've removed the nicks, go back to grinding at the correct blade angle.

If your blade has deep nicks or is cracked, bent or worn thin, don't sharpen it; buy a new one. You'll find the best selection at stores that sell and service lawn equipment. Take the old blade with you to get an exact match.

If you don't grind away the same amount of metal from both sides, the blade can become unbalanced. You can buy a special blade-balancing cone or simply hang the blade on a nail **(Photo 4)**. Correct an unbalanced blade by grinding a little metal from the blunt end of the heavy side of the blade until it balances on the nail. Make sure the marked side is toward you when you reinstall it and that you tighten the nut securely.

2 Clamp a block to the lawn mower skirt to stop the blade from spinning while you unscrew the nut. Use the longest wrench you can find to loosen the nut. It's likely to be very tight.

MARK GRASS SIDE OF BLADE

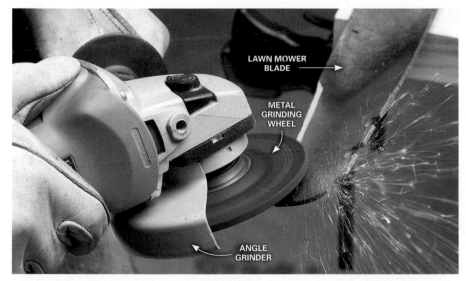

3 Grind the blade carefully with an angle grinder to remove nicks and dents and restore the edge. Make several light passes to avoid overheating the blade.

LAWN MOWER BLADE

METAL GRINDING WHEEL

ANGLE GRINDER

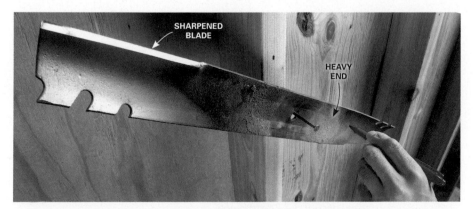

4 Balance the blade on a nail after you've sharpened both edges. If one side is heavy, it'll drop. Mark the heavy side so you'll know which end to grind. Grind a little off the heavy side and hang the blade on the nail again to recheck it. Repeat this process until the blade hangs level.

SHARPENED BLADE

HEAVY END

Digging holes

Digging is bonehead simple. But as with any other job, a little know-how lets you do it smarter and faster and with less strain.

By Gary Wentz

ELECTRICAL LINE

MARK EXCAVATION SITE WITH WHITE PAINT

1 Call before you dig Cutting into a buried utility line can kill or cost you—yes, you're responsible for damage to underground lines on your property. To avoid that risk, call 811 or visit call811.com three or four days before you dig. It's a good idea, though usually not mandatory, to mark the area you plan to excavate with white spray paint before utility lines get marked.

Color Code for Buried Utilities

	Proposed excavation
	Electric power lines, cables, conduit, lighting cables
	Electric power lines, cables, conduit, lighting cables
	Telecom, alarm or signal lines, cables or conduit
	Drinking water

CHOPPING BLADE

TAPE

3 **Trench with a mattock** A mattock is designed for digging narrow trenches—just right for running cable or pipe. Swing it like an ax to cut into hard soil, and then lift out the dirt with the wide blade. The chopping blade slices through roots. Wrap tape around the shaft to gauge the depth of your trench.

2 **Sharpen your shovel** A sharp edge makes all the difference when you're slicing through hard soil or roots. A file will do the job, but a grinder equipped with a metal-grinding disc is the fastest way to sharpen. A knife-sharp angle will dull instantly, so grind a blunter edge, about 45 degrees or so.

4 **Fold back the sod** When you're digging a trench, slice the sod along one side of the trench's path and fold it over. Then, after refilling the trench, you can just flip it back into place.

SOD FOLDED BACK

KNOCK
BLOCK

POWER
SOD
CUTTER

5 Knock off sticky soil Soil clinging to your posthole digger makes progress almost impossible. To knock off the sticky stuff, keep a "knock block" within reach and slam your digger against it. It can be a stone, a brick or a face-down shovel.

6 Save the sod Digging a hole is an opportunity to harvest some sod and patch up bad areas of your lawn. With a square spade, you can neatly slice up small pieces of sod, but it's slow going. For larger areas, rent a manual kick-type sod cutter. For major sod harvesting, rent a power sod cutter.

8 Get a tile shovel The long, narrow blade is great for trenching. It also works well for breaking up tough soil and enlarging postholes.

7 Rent a posthole auger—or not Gas-powered augers can make deck footings or fence-post holes fast and easy, but only in some types of soil. In hard clay, an auger is slower than a spade. In rocky soil, you'll have to stop occasionally to pull out rocks with a clamshell digger. Because of these frustrations, some deck and fence contractors don't bother with power augers and simply hand-dig every hole.

9 Get tough on tough soil A long, heavy digging bar is the ultimate tool for loosening rock-hard soil and dislodging rocks.It may seem crazy to buy a special tool for these tasks, but you won't regret it when you're in tough digging conditions.

10 **Cover your grass** To avoid raking soil out of the grass later, pile soil on cardboard or plywood. They work well because you can scoop dirt off them when refilling the hole. Tarps are fine too, but they're easily punctured by a shovel.

11 **Dig postholes with a clamshell digger** A clamshell digger is best for most jobs. Just plunge it into the ground, spread the handles and pull out the dirt. As your hole gets deeper, you have to enlarge the top of the hole so you can spread the handles.

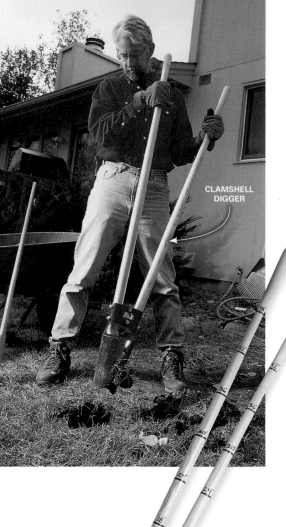

CLAMSHELL DIGGER

12 **Mark the depth** A tape measure isn't the tool for checking depth—it will get filled with dirt and wrecked. Instead, mark depths on your shovel or posthole digger. That way, you can measure as you dig.

13 **Improvised shovel**
A tile shovel is the best tool for flaring out the base of footing holes. But if you don't have one handy, remove the bolt from your clamshell-style posthole digger and use half of the digger as a tile shovel.

14 **Mark with a hose and paint** Lay out the footprint of your hole or trench with a garden hose. When you've got the layout right, mark it with spray paint.

15 **Beware of auger-type diggers** Just twist the handle and an auger-style digger drills a perfect posthole. Unlike a clamshell digger, it doesn't require you to enlarge the hole. But there's a catch: Augers work well only in soil that's soft, rock-free and not too sticky. In most soils, a clamshell digger is a better choice.

Spike's wonder cart

Better than a wheelbarrow and easy to build

By Spike Carlsen

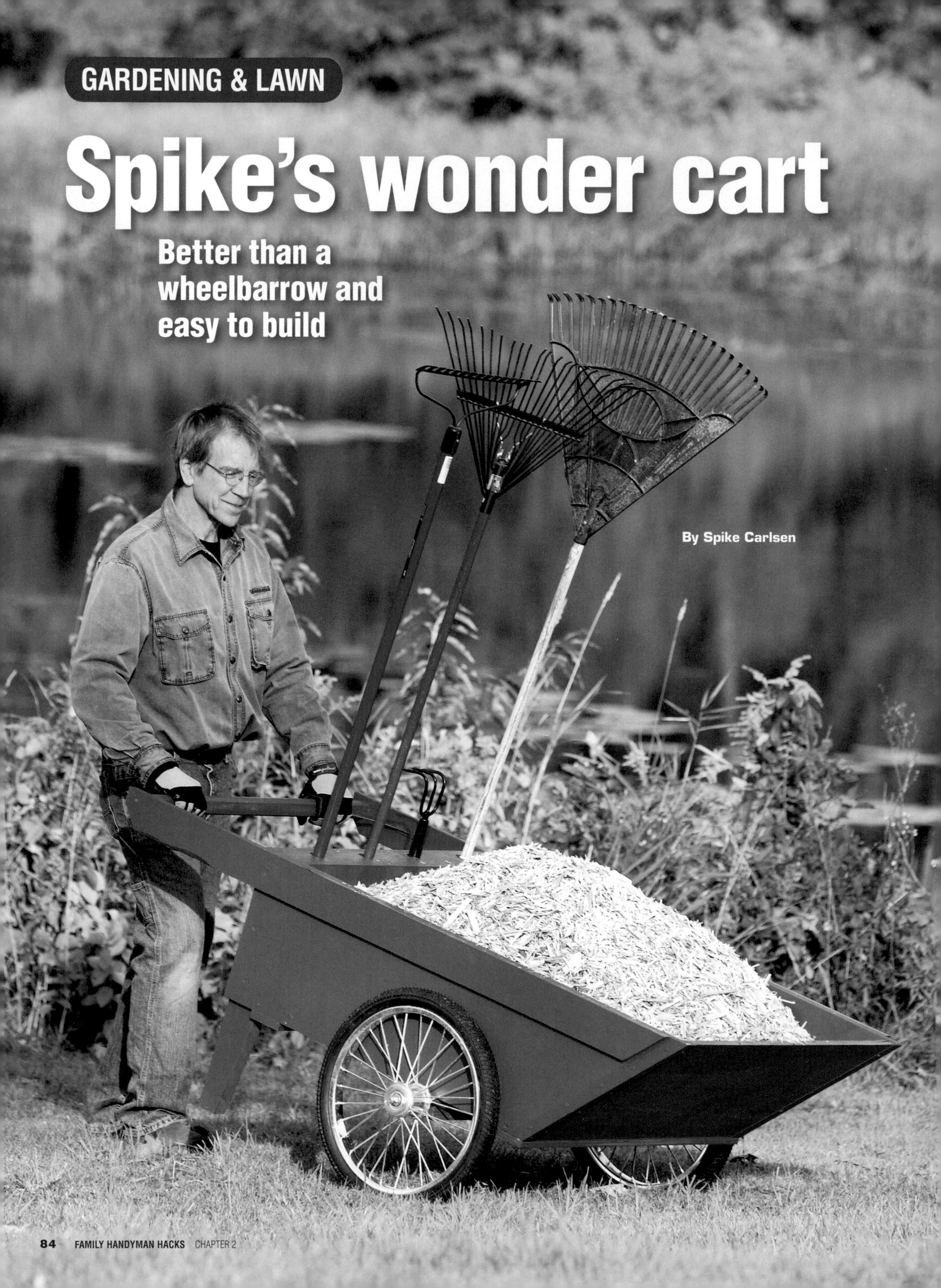

Wheelbarrows are great for hauling stuff around the yard—unless you're working on a hill ... or trying to negotiate steps and rough terrain ... or moving a lot of bulky material like leaves and branch trimmings ... or trying to load something big into them.

Since I added this garden cart to my outdoor arsenal of tools, life has gotten way easier. Two wheels means it doesn't tip; large pneumatic tires means it's easy to push; a big box lets me haul 10 bags of mulch in one load; and because the front tilts down for loading, my aching back doesn't ache as much. I'll still use my trusty wheelbarrow for mixing concrete and hauling the super-heavy stuff, but these days I "cart" nearly everything else.

I designed this cart to be as rugged and durable as any cart you can buy at any price. Yet it's one of the most useful projects I've ever built.

Meet the builder

A former editor at *Family Handyman*, Spike Carlsen now spends his days dreaming up ingenious DIY projects.

Easy to load

Onboard tool storage

Huge load? No problem

STRAIGHT-CUTTING JIG

1 **Cut the plywood parts** A homemade straight-cutting jig turns your circular saw into a precision plywood slicer. To see a video on how to make one, go to familyhandyman.com and search for "straight cuts."

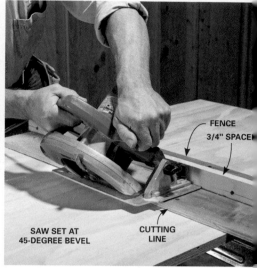

FENCE 3/4" SPACE

SAW SET AT 45-DEGREE BEVEL

CUTTING LINE

2 **Cut the beveled edges** Screw a spacer to the fence of your jig and line up the edge with your cutting line just like you would for a standard cut. Then make the long 45-degree cuts.

FRONT

SIDE

BOTTOM

CONSTRUCTION ADHESIVE

BACK

3 **Build the box** Secure the panels to one another using construction adhesive and 2-in. screws. Drill pilot holes to avoid splintering the edges of the plywood. Flip the cart upside down and install the three bottom braces (E).

Round up materials

You'll need a straight-cutting jig to cut the plywood. To learn how to make one, go to familyhandyman.com. Search for "straight cuts" to see a video, or "cutting guides" for written instructions. I used exterior plywood and standard pine boards for the structure. You can use treated plywood and lumber, but it may be hard to find treated material that's dry and flat.

I bought wheels at northerntool.com (item No. 145120). The threaded rod, washers and nuts are available at home centers and hardware stores.

Assemble the box

Lay out the plywood as shown in **Figure B**. Start by cutting the sheet lengthwise into 14-in., 30-in. and 3-1/2-in. strips **(Photo 1)**. After positioning the jig for each cut, clamp or screw it into place. Cut the angled sides (A) from the 14-in. strip and the bottom braces (E) from the 3-1/2-in. strip. Cut the front (C), bottom (D) and back (B) from the 30-in. strip.

If you use your straight-cutting jig, as is, for cutting the 45-degree bevels,

Figure A Garden cart

Overall Dimensions:
66" long x 24-1/2" tall x 41" wide
(including wheels)

J

A

P

3/4"
SCREW

J

T

A

C

L

B

K

D

N

M

H

20-3/4"

R

E

F

G

Q

S

10"

2"

CUTTING LIST

PART	QTY.	SIZE
A - Sides	2	3/4" x 14" x 50" *
B - Back	1	3/4" x 14" x 30"
C - Front	1	3/4" x 19-3/4" x 30" ‡
D - Bottom	1	3/4" x 31-5/8" x 30" §
E - Bottom braces	3	3/4" x 3-1/2" x 31-1/2"
F - Axle braces	2	1/2" x 1-1/2" x 31-1/2"
G - Axle cover	1	3/4" x 3-1/2" x 31-1/2" pine
H - Legs	2	1-1/2" x 3-1/2" x 23-3/4" pine
J - Handles	2	3/4" x 3-1/2" x 64-1/2" pine #
K - Corner braces	2	Cut to fit #
L - Long tool rack slat	1	3/4" x 3-1/2" x 30"
M - Short tool rack slats	2	3/4" x 3-1/2" x 27"
N - Tool rack blocks	2	3/4" x 3-1/2" x 3"
P - Handle bar	1	1-1/4" handrail
Q - Washers	4	1/2" fender washer
R - Wheels	2	20" w/pneumatic tire
S - Locknut	2	1/2" locknut
T - L-brackets	2	6" shelf brackets (or similar)

NOTES:
*Angled cut
‡ 45-degree bevel cut, both ends
§ 45-degree bevel cut, one end
# 45-degree cuts, both ends

MATERIALS LIST

ITEM	QTY.
4' x 8' x 3/4" exterior plywood	1
2x4 x 48" pine	1
1x4 x 96" pine	3
1-1/4" x 30" handrail	1
1/2" x 3" x 31-1/2" plywood or solid wood	1
20"-diameter wheels	2
1/2" x 48" threaded rod	1
1/2" washers	4
1/2" locknuts	2
6" L-shaped shelf brackets	2
1" x 1" x 2' aluminum angle	2
3/4" exterior screws	20
1-1/4" exterior screws	1 lb.
2" exterior screws	2 lbs.
Heavy-duty construction adhesive (pint tubes)	2

Figure B
Plywood diagram

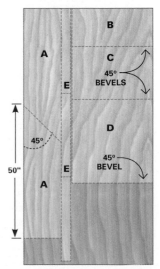

B

A

C

45°
BEVELS

E

D

45°

50"

E

45°
BEVEL

A

4 Install the wheel assembly Install a washer, a wheel, another washer and a locknut on one end of the threaded rod. Measure the overhang required by the wheel assembly, add that length to the other end, then cut the rod to length. Install the axle braces and cover.

5 Install the legs Apply two beads of construction adhesive, clamp the legs into place and secure them with screws. The spacer block positions the leg, leaving room for the tool rack.

6 Strengthen the corners Cut aluminum angle stock to length, then drill holes and countersink "dimples" for the screw heads. Install the corner braces using construction adhesive and screws.

HANDLE BAR (P)

L-BRACKET (T)

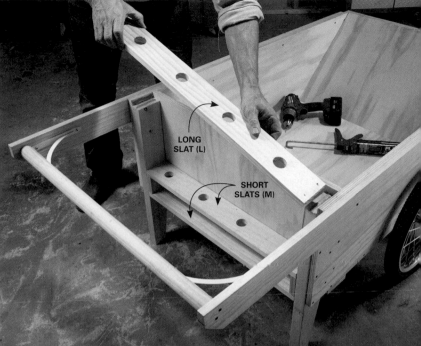

LONG SLAT (L)

SHORT SLATS (M)

7 **Install the handle bar** Secure the handle bar by driving screws through each handle into the end of the rail. Add the L-brackets to beef up the connection.

8 **Add a tool rack** Cut three tool rack slats and drill holes for tool handles. Adjust the size and spacing of the holes to suit your tools. Use adhesive and screws to install the slats.

you'll cut a bevel on the jig itself, making it unusable for future square cuts. Temporarily modify your jig by screwing a 3/4-in. strip of wood to the jig's fence **(Photo 2)**, positioning the edge of the guide on the cutting line (like you would for a square cut), then make your 45-degree cut.

Drill 1/8-in. holes about 3/8 in. away from the edges of the sides (A), spaced about 4 in. apart. Then secure the front with 2-in. exterior screws through the predrilled holes in the sides. **Note:** To ensure maximum sturdiness, use construction adhesive for all the connections—even for the metal corners.

Install the bottom **(Photo 3)** flush with the edges of the sides (A). Make sure the front beveled edge of the bottom makes solid contact with the bottom edge of the front (C). To complete the box, add the back (B). If you've cut and assembled everything correctly, there will be a 3-1/2-in. cavity at the back of the box to accommodate the tool rack. If it's a little larger or smaller, no big deal.

Install the wheels

Turn the cart box upside down. Secure the bottom braces (E). Secure the middle bottom brace so the center of it is exactly 20-3/4 in. away from the back of the back bottom brace (E). If you don't get this positioned right, it will affect the balance of the cart.

Position this assembly **(Photo 4)** snugly against one side of the cart and measure the amount of space it takes up. Transfer that measurement to the other end of the rod and mark the rod. Cut the rod and install the other wheel assembly. **Tip:** Before cutting the rod to length, twist a regular nut onto it beyond the cut mark. After making the cut, twist the nut off; it will "recut" any damaged threads so the locknut will go on easier.

Apply glue to the axle braces (F), snug them tightly against the axle, then secure them to the middle bottom brace (E) with 2-in. screws. Finally, install the axle cover (G). **Note:** If you want to strengthen the wheel assembly for hauling heavier loads, use oak for the middle bottom brace, two axle braces and cover.

Install the legs, handles and tool rack

Cut the legs and screw them to the protruding sides **(Photo 5)**. Use the spacer block as shown so the legs can accommodate the upper tool rack slat. Cut and install the handles (J), leaving space at the front for the aluminum angle.

Cut two lengths of aluminum angle. Don't try to measure them; just hold them in place and mark them for cutting. Drill holes and drill countersink "dimples" for the heads of the screws to nest into. Install the aluminum using adhesive and 3/4-in. screws **(Photo 6)**.

Position the handle bar (P) and add the L-brackets **(Photo 7)** to reinforce the handle. Finally, install the three tool rack slats **(Photo 8)**.

Remove the wheels and apply a coat of high-quality exterior primer, followed by two coats of exterior paint. To keep your cart in good condition, store it inside; if it will be outside, flip it upside down on a couple of scrap 4x4s.

CHAPTER 3

Painting Hacks

Roller spinner

To spin-dry a mini roller, chuck a 1/4-in. bit into your drill. Slip the roller onto the bit and pull the trigger. Centrifugal force whips the water right out. Do this in a bucket, utility sink or outdoors.

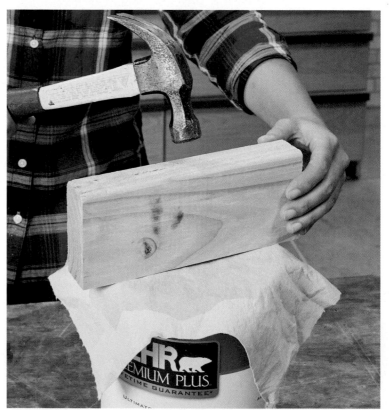

Handy paint-can opener

Every time you buy paint, you get a free paint-can opener, but you'll still never find one when you need it. So, grab a pair of pliers and open the loop on the handle just enough to slip it around the bail. No more hunting for openers—all of your paint cans have one attached.

Tidy paint-can closing

After you pour paint from a can, some paint always ends up in the can's rim. When you tap the lid back on, paint splatters everywhere. To avoid this, throw a rag over the lid before tapping it shut. Also, use a block of wood that spans the lid so you don't deform the can or lid with the hammer. Just tap the block a couple of times, give it a quarter turn and tap again.

C-clamp handles

Quart-size paint cans don't have handles, but they'd be so much easier to use if they did. Here's a solution: Attach a C-clamp to the can. It actually works better than a bail because it's out of the way for dipping the brush, and it keeps the can from swinging. Your clamp will get paint on it, but cleaning it up is easy.

C-CLAMP

24 in/po
60,9 cm

Paintbrush protectors

After thoroughly washing and air-drying brushes, wrap them with the same painter's plastic that you use to mask off trim and protect the floors. The tape on the edge sticks to the metal ferrule, and the plastic is the perfect length to cover the bristles and help maintain their shape.

Make exterior paint last

1 Clean siding and trim Dirty surfaces won't hold paint. Remove dirt, mildew, cobwebs and anything else that isn't meant to be there. Do the cleaning in stages. Start by applying a solution of bleach, water and a cleaner such as JOMAX (a bleach activator), using a garden sprayer. Next, remove weathered paint and dirt using a pressure washer. Be careful, as you can easily damage siding and trim with a pressure washer. If you don't feel confident using a pressure washer, a siding cleaner and scrub brush will do the job. Thoroughly rinse to remove any cleaner residue and let the surfaces dry.

2 Scrape After the surfaces have dried completely, scrape off any remaining loose or flaking paint. Applying new paint over flaking paint will cause it to peel far sooner than it should. Before scraping, pound in any nail heads that could nick your scraper blade. You can buy a hardened steel scraper, or for about twice the price, you can buy a carbide scraper. Carbide holds an edge far longer than hardened steel. With either option, buy a couple replacement blades so you don't have to sharpen as often. You can sharpen a carbide blade using a diamond stone.

FOUR-SIDED HARDENED
STEEL SCRAPER BLADE

TWO-SIDED CARBIDE
SCRAPER BLADE

3 Remove old caulk While you're scraping, check the caulking around windows, doors and trim. If the caulk is in good shape and still adhering, leave it in place. If not, dig it out with a 5-in-1 tool (shown), utility knife or putty knife.

4 Sand off ridges After scraping, sand any sharp paint edges, blending them with the surrounding surface. If you don't blend them in, the sharp edges will create thin, weak areas in the new paint. Brush away any dust created by sanding, and then rinse the siding and trim thoroughly.

Make exterior paint last *continued*

EXTERIOR PUTTY

5 **Repair damaged surfaces** Don't paint over rotten or insect-damaged wood. Even if it covers, the paint won't last. Replace or repair any damaged wood. Fill nail holes and other small imperfections with exterior wood putty. Sand off excess putty after it's dry.

1/4" SPACER

3/4" SPACER

6 **Create a gap between trim and concrete** Boards that come in contact with concrete won't hold paint for long. Water on the concrete wicks up into the wood, loosening the bond between the wood and the paint. To remedy this, trim any wood so that it's about 1/4 in. above concrete.

7 **Keep space between trim and shingles** If trim or siding contacts the shingles, water will wick into the wood and the paint won't last. Lay a 3/4-in.-thick spacer on the shingles and cut any trim or siding to create a gap between the wood and the shingles.

8 **Spot-prime** Prime nail heads, putty and knots before priming the whole surface. These areas are more difficult to cover, so they need a little extra attention.

9 **Prime all bare wood** You can get good results with oil or latex primer. For bare woods with a high tannin (a dark, natural pigment) content, such as cedar and redwood, use a stain-blocking exterior primer. Stain-blocking primers prevent "bleed-through" of tannin as well as stains from old, rusty nails.

10 **Caulk all cracks & gaps** Caulk around windows, doors, trim and anywhere else water could get behind a painted surface. Use interior/exterior paintable latex caulk. Be sure to prime first; primer adheres to bare or slightly dirty surfaces much better than caulk.

Make exterior paint last *continued*

11 **Don't forget the threshold**
The bottom of a wood doorjamb will rot prematurely if you don't caulk the line where the threshold meets the jamb.

12 **Seal end grain**
When you install or expose new wood, seal any end grain with a paintable water repellent, such as Woodlife Classic clear wood preservative. Allow the repellent to dry according to the directions, then prime and paint.

13 Wait for good painting weather
Avoid painting on hot days, in direct sun and in windy weather. Ideal temperatures for painting are between 50 and 90 degrees F. Temperatures below 50 degrees can prevent the paint from adhering to the surface properly. Hot weather, wind and direct sun all cause paint to dry too quickly, preventing adequate penetration of the primer and/or paint. It can also cause oil paint to blister. When possible, work in the shade, following the path of the sun throughout the day. Never paint when rain is imminent or right after it rains. Painting a damp surface can cause paint to bubble.

More exterior paint hacks

Keep vegetation trimmed
Plants that come into contact with your exterior walls hold moisture against the paint, which can lead to compromised paint and rotting wood. That means more repair work, more money and more frequent painting.

Keep an eye on your paint job
Whenever you're out doing yard work, check in on your paint. Look closely for areas of cracked or peeling paint, or wood that might be rotting. With a little spot maintenance, you can extend the life of your paint job by a few years.

Ease sharp edges
Sharp edges won't hold paint; there just isn't enough surface area. If you install any new wood, be sure to give any sharp edges a slight round-over. It doesn't take much; a single pass with a sanding block is usually sufficient.

Don't stall on painting
Primer loses its bonding properties with prolonged exposure to UV light. After priming, you have a window of time to apply paint. Check the label on your can, as the amount of time can vary among manufacturers. We checked with two major companies. One said that paint must be applied within one week; the other said anywhere from four to six weeks.

Kitchen-whisk paint stirrer

Paint mixers that you can chuck in a drill are nothing new, but if you don't have one on hand, find a whisk in one of your kitchen drawers, cut off the loop on the end of the handle, and chuck it in your cordless drill. It will do a great job of mixing old paint.

Prepainting nail heads

When you're installing prepainted wood or engineered-wood siding, paint the tops of galvanized nail coils the color of the house before loading them into the gun. It's much faster than going back and painting them one at a time later. Use a foam brush and apply the paint sparingly so it doesn't drip over the edges of the nail heads. Let the paint dry completely before loading the coils into the nail gun.

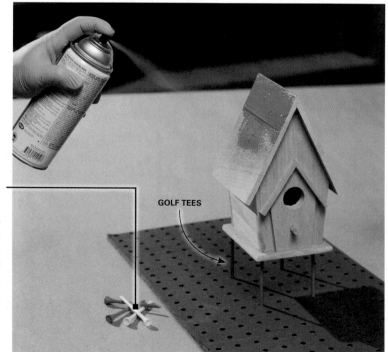

GOLF TEES

Golf tee paint helpers

When you're painting or varnishing small projects, it's best to elevate them for good coverage and to keep your project from sticking to the worktable. Use an old piece of pegboard and some golf tees. The pegboard keeps the tees in place, and you can arrange them as necessary for different size projects.

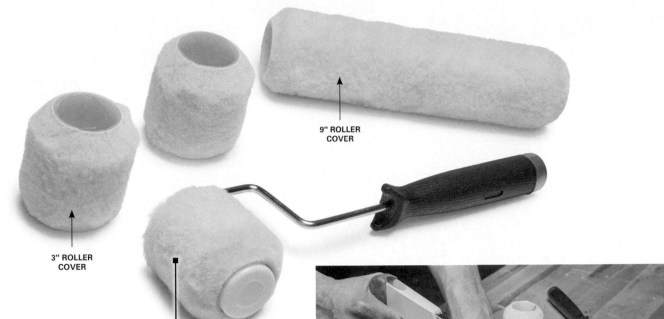

9" ROLLER COVER

3" ROLLER COVER

Make mini roller covers

Next time you're in the paint department, pick up a 3-in. roller frame, the type that takes the same diameter cover as a standard 9-in. roller. You can then cut any 9-in. roller cover into three 3-in. covers to fit it. A 3-in. roller is perfect for painting trim or small stuff like a mailbox, but not every store carries 3-in. covers. This little trick will also cut the cost of the 3-in. roller covers in half.

Mark the 9-in. roller covers 3 in. in from each end. Cut into equal pieces with a hacksaw, holding the cover steady with a bar clamp. Trim the rough edges of the nap with scissors.

Clamp

Cardboard sawhorses

Use cardboard appliance boxes as collapsible sawhorses. They're lightweight and plenty strong for many tasks. They hold heavy workpieces like doors without wobbling and fold up flat in seconds. You can cut them to a comfortable working height with a utility knife.

Disassemble if you can

Before you start painting, examine your project. If you can take it apart without too much trouble, do it! You'll have much better luck getting even coverage, seeing what you're doing and avoiding runs. But don't just dismantle the piece willy-nilly. Mark the parts for easy reassembly.

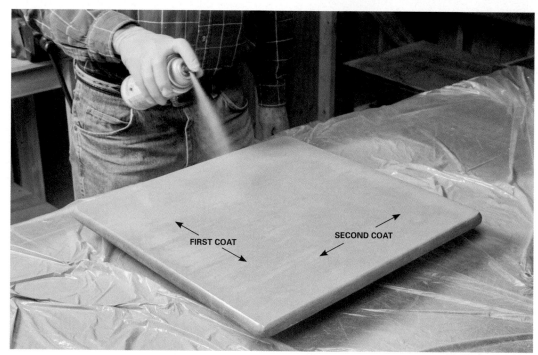

FIRST COAT

SECOND COAT

Apply coats in different directions

To achieve the most even coverage, it's a good idea to put on subsequent coats in different directions. Changing directions will help you get into all those nooks and crannies and reduce the chance of zebra stripes.

ALWAYS clean out the nozzle

Even though nozzle-cleaning directions are on every single can of spray paint, it's an easy step to skip. After use, hold the can upside down and press the nozzle until no more pigment shows in the spray, and then wipe the tip with a rag or paper towel. If you skip this step, you could end up with a nozzle completely clogged with dried paint or a partial clog that'll affect the spray pattern next time.

Dust: Public enemy no. 1

For a flawless finish on small parts, paint them inside a cardboard box. If you have larger projects, create a poly booth. In basements, dust will shake down from the floor joists, especially if someone is stomping around upstairs, so staple painter's plastic to the ceiling. Damp-mopping the floor will keep your feet from stirring up dust. Don't use a fan to speed up drying time. Wear clean clothes and a hat to keep hair out of the finish. An hour or so before you paint, shut off furnaces, the a/c and ceiling fans to let the dust settle.

Swap plugged nozzles

Most nozzles have a universal fit. If you end up with a plugged nozzle and have other cans of spray paint with good nozzles, just swap the bad one for a new one. They lift right off and push on. If you don't have any good nozzles, remove the plugged one and soak it in nail polish remover, acetone or even mineral spirits.

NEW NOZZLE

PLUGGED NOZZLE

Start with a tack coat

If you're spraying a vertical surface, it's always smart to apply a "tack" coat before applying the first full coat. A tack coat is a light mist that you allow to set for five minutes. The texture of the tack coat will help hold the paint in place and reduce runs.

Need a custom-color spray paint?

If you want to paint radiators, electrical cover plates, a shelf or anything else to match your wall or trim color, go online and search for "custom spray paint." You'll find many companies (myperfectcolor.com is one) that can custom-mix just about any color you want, provided you know the paint manufacturer and color name. If you want a different shade of an existing color, choose one of the other shades from the paint swatch you got at the home center or paint store and have that color custom-mixed.

Spray anything

The Spra-Tool is a simple product—a plastic jar plus an aerosol can. You just pour the liquid into the jar and pull the trigger. We had great results with thin liquids like stain, shellac and household cleaners. With thicker material—polyurethane and latex paint—we had to add thinner to achieve a smooth coat. In some cases, we added more thinner than the paint manufacturer recommended. (Using too much thinner can affect the paint's durability, but we didn't have a problem.) Still, we got smooth, perfect finishes—fast. The Spra-Tool kit (about $14) is available at some home centers and online.

Read the directions!

This sounds obvious, but few people bother to read the directions on the can. If the manufacturer says to apply a tack coat or start with a primer, there's probably a good reason for it. One of the most important pieces of information is the drying time between coats. Often, you can apply a second coat soon afterward. But if you miss that window, you may have to wait a long time to apply the next coat.

Directions: Use outdoors, or in well-ventilated area, when temperature is above 50°F (10°C) and humidity is below 85% to ensure proper drying. Do not apply to surfaces that exceed 200°F. Avoid spraying in very windy, dusty conditions. Cover nearby objects to protect from spray mist.

Remove loose paint and rust with a wire brush or sandpaper. Lightly sand glossy surfaces. Clean with soap and water, rinse and let dry.

Shake can vigorously for one minute after mixing balls begin to rattle. Shake often during use. Hold can upright 12-16" from surface and spray in a steady back-and-forth motion, slightly overlapping each stroke. Keep the can the same distance from the surface and in motion while spraying. Apply 2 or more light coats a few minutes apart.

May recoat within 1 hour or after 48 hours. Dries to the touch in 2-4 hours, to handle in 5-9 hours, and is fully dry in 24 hours, at 70°F (21°C) – 50% relative humidity. Allow more time at cooler temperatures. When finished spraying, clear spray valve by turning can upside down and pushing spray button for 5 seconds. If valve clogs, twist and pull off spray tip and rinse it in a solvent such as mineral spirits. Do not stick a pin or other object into the stem. Throw away empty can in trash pickup. Do not burn or place in home trash compactor.

ACTIVATED
CARBON
RESPIRATOR

Hang 'em high

If the project parts are small enough, you can suspend them for painting. You'll be able to paint all sides at the same time and have everything at eye level. Use coat hangers, wires, thumbtacks, screws—whatever you have on hand. Wear an activated carbon respirator when you spray-paint, especially if you're painting indoors.

Many *light* coats

It's common knowledge that you should apply several light coats rather than one or two heavy ones. But few have the discipline to follow this simple advice. When you're spraying, resist the temptation to fill in thinner areas on one pass to completely cover the surface. Or welcome to dealing with runs—yet again.

Authentic-look hardware...for less!

When I bought my 1923-vintage house, the two exterior doors were original, as were the doorknobs. Unfortunately, the previous owners had installed shiny new brass dead bolts and escutcheon plate—a bad mismatch. Instead of scouring local antiques stores to find replacements, I decided to try painting the brass.

After removing the hardware, I scuffed the brass finish with fine sandpaper. Then I sprayed on a coat of primer and a few coats of Rust-Oleum's hammered-finish spray paint. The hammered finish provided the aged bronze look I was after. I was amazed at how well the repainted hardware matched the old doorknobs, and the paint job has held up, inside and out, for more than 10 years. So here's my advice: Don't replace ugly metal hardware. Save money by refinishing it with a metallic spray paint.

— Gary Wentz

Self-cleaning paintbrushes

Just hang your brush in a jar of solvent: water for latex paint, and mineral spirits or paint thinner for oil-based. Using a clamp, suspend the brush in the jar with the bristles fully submerged almost to the ferrule, but not touching the bottom of the jar. Finish will slide off the bristles and settle on the bottom of the jar.

If you're using paint thinner or mineral spirits, set the jar outside to keep fumes out of your house. Be sure it's away from children and pets. After a day or two, remove the brush and give it a thorough rinse in clean solvent.

SPRING CLAMP

FERRULE

FINISH SETTLES IN THE BOTTOM OF THE JAR

Patch, prime, patch, prime...

You've done a great job of patching and smoothing over all those pesky cracks, holes and dimples in your walls and ceiling, and you've rolled on the primer. So does that mean you're ready for the topcoat? Not so fast. Take a closer look at the surfaces with a portable work light. Chances are, you still have small imperfections you'll want to touch up with spackling or joint compound. Better to take care of these now because they'll really stand out after the final coat of paint goes on.

JOINT COMPOUND

STIR STICKS

Make your own stir sticks

Forgot to grab stir sticks at the store when you picked up the paint? If you have a band saw and a hunk of 2x4, you can make your own! Take a 2-ft.-long 2x4 and draw a perpendicular line in the middle. Next, "rip" several 3/16-in.-thick strips on the band saw up to the pencil line. Then, to release the stir sticks, chop the 2x4 at the pencil line. This method keeps your fingers a safe distance from the saw blade.

Baby wipes for small messes

Keep a package of baby wipes handy whenever you paint a room. They're great for wiping up small drips before you accidentally walk through them and track paint all over the house. It beats keeping a bucket of water and rags around any day!

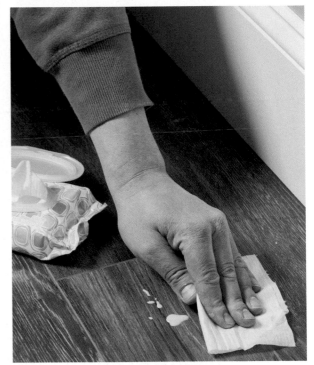

Paint walls or trim first?

We asked our Facebook followers whether they preferred to paint trim or walls and ceilings first, and boy, are people divided on this! We got more than 300 comments from DIYers and pros, but no clear consensus. However, we did learn some new tricks:

■ Paul G. paints in this order: "Hands, jeans, cat, kid, then finally the walls and trim."

■ And our keep-it-simple award goes to Brian G.: "I paint everything the same color, so it doesn't much matter."

Touch-up paint bottle

When there's only a little bit of latex paint left in the can and you want to save it for touch-ups, put a half-dozen marbles in an empty water bottle and pour in the leftover paint. When you're ready to do a touch-up, shake the bottle and the marbles mix the paint. A roll of tape with a rag draped over it helps hold the bottle steady while you pour the paint into it. Just be sure to use a funnel or you'll have a mess on your hands.

MARBLES

Shelter baseboards from splatter

When you're rolling paint onto walls or ceilings, a fine mist of paint settles on unprotected trim. For baseboards, forget about covering them completely. Just cover the top of each one with a "shelter" made from painter's tape. A single overhanging strip of 1-1/2-in. or 2-in. tape catches roller splatters just like the roof overhang on a house keeps rain off the siding. Tape doesn't stick to dusty surfaces very well, so be sure to vacuum or wipe down your baseboards before masking. Also press the tape down hard with a putty knife to prevent paint from bleeding underneath. For the best results, use "self-sealing" tape.

SELF-SEALING TAPE

Take photos of paint can lids

Have you ever thrown away a paint can and later wished you hadn't because you couldn't remember the name of the color you painted the bedroom? Paint can lids usually have labels with color information printed on them. Take photos of your paint can lids, print them and tuck them away for future reference or keep them on your phone.

Splurge on self-sealing tape

With regular painter's tape, you run the risk of "paint bleed"—paint creeps underneath the tape, leaving a ragged line where a wall meets trim or another wall or ceiling. We like self-sealing tapes like FrogTape and ScotchBlue Edge-Lock tape because they're specially designed to prevent paint bleed, giving you crisp, straight lines. They cost a lot more than regular masking or painter's tape, but they're worth it.

Angled or straight bristles?

We asked our Facebook followers whether they preferred paintbrushes with straight or angled bristles for tasks like cutting in around windows or painting trim. Most said they preferred angled, but we did hear from a handful of straight-bristle brush fans. And lots of people use both. As Lea D. told us, "Angled for corners and cutting in, and flat for all-over coverage."

Wet your brush for easy cleanup

After a long painting session, paint builds up and dries on the bristles near the ferrule, and it's tough to clean off. To prevent this, wet the bristles with water before you paint and dab off the excess on a paper towel. For oil-based paints, use paint thinner.

Waste-free painting

I have several rental properties that are always in need of repainting. Instead of throwing out leftover paint, I put it to use. I gather all my partial cans of interior latex—any color or sheen—and dump them into a 5-gallon bucket. Next, I mix the paint with a power-driven paint mixer to get a uniform color. It usually turns out off-white with an eggshell sheen. If the color is too dark, I lighten it by adding a can of white paint. Then I pour the paint into another 5-gallon bucket through a strainer bag. I lift out the strainer bag to remove any debris and pop on a lid to keep the paint fresh.
— Gary Wentz

STRAINER BAG

PAINT MIXER

EGG CARTONS

Egg carton supports

Whenever you need to paint something small, like a picture frame, and want to raise it off the table a bit to paint the edges, break out some handy egg cartons. Just cut a couple in half and use them to support the frame's edges. You can reuse them several times or just throw them away when you're done.

Don't fill the rim

Pouring paint from a can always results in paint in the rim. When you tap the lid back on, paint splatters everywhere. To prevent this, just put a strip of painter's tape across the rim of the can before you pour.

Painting tool drying cage

An inverted tomato cage makes a great drying rack for rollers, brushes, pads, rags and whatever is wet after painting cleanup. The stuff dries quickly outdoors, and there's room for everything!

Quick paint touch-ups

If you have touch-up work that's not worth dirtying a paintbrush, try makeup rounds. These smooth pieces of cotton are about the size of a silver dollar and they won't shed. You can use them to apply dabs of stain, oil or paint. We've even used them to touch up nail hole patches. You can find them near the cosmetics at drugstores and discount stores.

Free and easy paint tray

For small paint jobs, a 4-in. paint roller works great with an old gallon-size iced tea jug serving as a disposable roller tray. Just cut out part of the plastic to create a place to dip the roller. It even has a built-in carrying handle. When you're done, just throw the jug away.

Nozzle cleaner

When you're done spray-painting, pour a couple ounces of paint thinner into a small container. Remove the nozzle, shake it in the covered container, then reattach the nozzle to the can.

Self-stick paint shield

Glad Press'n Seal plastic wrap goes on fast and stays right where you put it. Paint can seep under the edges, though, so it's no substitute for masking tape in spots where you need a sharp edge.

PLASTIC WRAP

Solutions for old paint

There could be the makings of a minimalist masterpiece in your garage. If you have old, nearly empty cans of paint that have been in storage for a couple years, chances are you'll never use them. Just take old rosin or kraft paper that you've used to protect flooring and dump the paint over the paper out in the yard. The paint will dry into a flexible mat, and then you can either frame your art and hang it in your living room or roll it up and toss it into the trash.

Pro secrets
for a speedy,
great-looking
paint job

Faster, better painting

Meet the pro

Jay Gorton got his first painting lessons
more than 30 years ago when he
worked for his father-in-law painting
houses in the Minneapolis area. Since
then he's perfected his trade and
grown a business from a one-man
operation to a team of more than 30
painters at times. Most of his work is in
high-end new construction where he
specializes in glass-smooth enamel
finishes, faux-finished walls, and
antiqued and distressed woodwork.
It's from his background in this high-
quality production painting that Jay
gathered these tips.

Prep varnished wood carefully

Every surface should be cleaned before it's painted, but painting over clear finishes like varnish or polyurethane requires extra care to ensure that the new paint bonds well. Thorough sanding is one way to prepare the surface. But a liquid sander/deglosser is easier and faster. Jay uses Klean-Strip Easy Liquid Sander Deglosser, but other types are available.

Read the instructions on the container and follow them carefully. Some types of "liquid sandpaper" require you to paint over them before they dry. Others, like the one Jay is using, should dry first. Follow the sander/deglosser with a coat of bonding primer. Ask for it at the paint department. Most major paint manufacturers sell it. Valspar Bonding Primer is one example.

Paint twice as fast with this extra-wide roller

An 18-in.-wide roller setup like this may not be for everybody. Painters use them for the obvious reason that they can paint twice as fast as they can with a standard 9-in. roller.

If you have a lot of large, unbroken walls and ceilings, the investment in a large paint pail, 18-in. roller cage and 18-in. cover makes sense for you, too. You'll definitely save a bunch of time. Plus, because the roller is supported on both edges instead of just one, it's easier to apply consistent pressure and avoid roller marks left by paint buildup at the edge of the roller.

You'll find 18-in. roller equipment at most home centers and paint stores.

Caulk every crack

Rather than trying to decide which cracks are large enough to require caulk, just caulk everything. It's actually faster because you don't have to waste time deciding what to caulk and because you're not constantly starting and stopping. Caulk every intersection between moldings and between moldings and walls or ceilings. You'll be amazed at how much better the final paint job looks when there are no dark cracks showing.

Replace your roller tray with a pail

If you're like most homeowners, you have a paint tray that you use to roll walls. And if you've done much painting, you've probably stepped in or spilled the tray at least once. Plus, as you know, trays are awkward to move around, especially when they're fully loaded with paint. A paint pail solves these problems and more. Pails hold more paint than trays, and you'll find them easy to move around and tough to step in! As an added bonus, if you use the plastic lining tip we show here, you can practically eliminate cleanup. You'll find paint pails at home centers and paint stores.

1 Line the pail to simplify cleanup Use thin painter's plastic to line the pail. Cut a piece of plastic and drape it into the pail. Add your paint and then run a band of masking tape around the perimeter to hold the plastic in place.

2 Drain the leftover paint back into the can When you're done painting, just bundle up the plastic and pull it out. If there's leftover paint, hold the plastic over your paint can and slit the bottom with a utility knife to drain the paint back into your paint can.

A quicker way to mask windows

Unless you're a really good painter, it's quicker to mask window glass than to try to neatly cut in with a brush, especially if you use the masking method we show here. The three photos below show the technique. If you're going to spray-paint the window trim, cover the glass entirely by attaching a piece of paper under the first strip of masking tape. Precut the paper so it's about 1-1/2 in. narrower and shorter than the glass size.

1 Tape both sides of the glass, letting the ends run wild. Push the tape tightly into the corners with a flexible putty knife.

2 Slice off the excess with a utility knife.

3 Finish by taping the top and bottom.

Patch with glazing putty

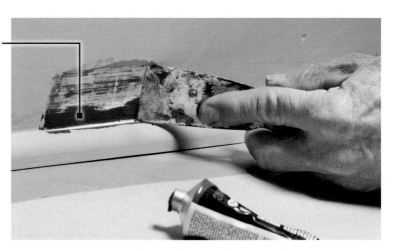

If you've done much auto body repair, you're probably familiar with glazing putty. On cars, glazing putty is used to fill small scratches and imperfections before painting because it spreads easily and dries quickly and is easy to sand. These same properties also make glazing putty ideal for filling shallow damage in trim. You'll find glazing putty in auto parts stores, hardware stores and some well-stocked paint stores.

Look for a shed-resistant, woven roller

If you're picky about how your walls look when you're done rolling on the paint, then you'll want a way to avoid leaving a trail of roller fuzzies behind. Look for rollers that are labeled "shed resistant woven." They cost a little more than some covers, but the smooth, lint-free finish is worth it.

Keep a mini roller and screen handy

A mini roller is great for all kinds of painting tasks. If you fit it with a woven sleeve to match the nap on your large roller, you can use it to touch up and to paint areas where your big roller won't fit.

Buy a small screen and just drop it in your gallon paint can so it'll be handy when you need it. If you use a plastic screen like the one shown, you can push it down into the can and still get the paint can cover on. Then when you need to do a little touch-up, just take off the lid and start rolling. Put a foam cover on your mini roller for painting doors and woodwork.

You'll find a large selection of mini rollers at hardware stores, paint stores and home centers.

Speedy, accurate masking

The key to perfect masking is to keep the tape straight and tight to the wall. Here's a tip to simplify the job. Stick about 6 in. of tape to the molding. Then, with the tape roll held tight against the wall, unroll about 6 more inches of tape. Rotate the roll down until this section of tape is stuck and repeat the process. The trick is to keep the roll of tape against the wall. It takes a little practice to master this technique, so don't give up. Once you learn to tape this way, your speed and accuracy will increase dramatically.

Drop-cloth substitute

Drop cloths can be a hassle. They slip on hard floors, get bunched up under ladders and are difficult to fit tight to baseboards. Eliminate the hassle and save time by using rosin paper instead. You can buy a 160-ft.-long roll of 3-ft.-wide heavy masking paper. Roll it out, leaving about a 1/2-in. space along the wall for the tape. Then cover the edges with tape to keep it in place. You'll find rolls of masking or rosin paper at home centers and paint stores.

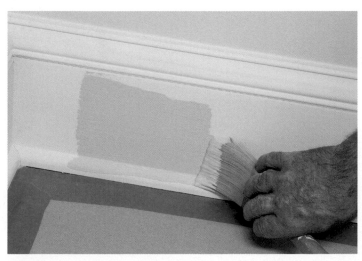

Don't start in corners

It's natural to load your brush with paint and stick it into the corner to start painting. But you'll end up with too much paint in the corner, where it's difficult to spread out. Instead, start laying on the paint about 4 to 6 in. from inside corners, and then spread the paint back into the corner with the brush. You'll get a nice, smooth paint job without excess paint buildup at inside corners.

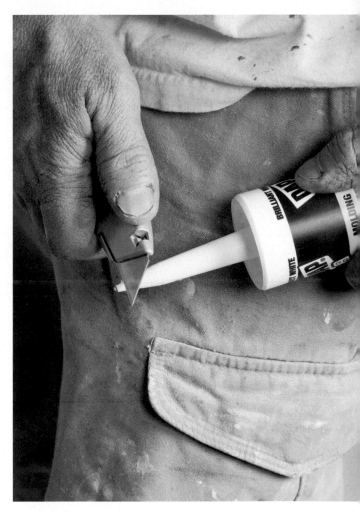

Fast caulking

A common mistake is to cut off too much of the caulk tube tip, leaving a hole that's way too big for most interior caulking work. When you're filling small cracks to prepare for painting, cut the tip carefully to keep the hole tiny—about 1/16 in. in diameter. The tiny hole lets out just enough caulk to fill typical small- to medium-size cracks.

For larger cracks, make a second pass or keep a second caulk gun on hand, loaded with a tube that has a slightly bigger hole. Keep the caulk gun moving quickly along the crack as you squeeze the trigger. This, combined with the small opening in the tip, will give you a nice caulk joint that needs very little cleanup. A quick swipe with a dampened fingertip will leave a paint-ready joint.

Paint a panel door

Paneled doors are the ultimate painter's challenge. A large area broken up by shaped surfaces is just plain tough to cover before the paint becomes sticky and unworkable. And since doors are a prominent feature, ugly mistakes like brush marks or drips are noticeable. Even though I had painted dozens of them over the years, I still felt a twinge of anxiety whenever I saw "paint door" on my to-do list. So I set out to find easier ways to get better results. I tried different tools, used different paints and watched professional painters. Here's what I learned. — **by Gary Wentz**

Gary Wentz is editor in chief at Family Handyman

Before you start

The actual work involved in painting a door typically amounts to three to five hours, depending on the condition of the door and how fussy you are. But add in the drying time and it's a full-day project. So if you're painting a door you can't live without—like a bathroom or exterior door—get started first thing in the morning so it can be back in service by day's end.

While you're picking a paint color, also think about sheen: With a flat finish, scuff marks and handprints are hard to wipe away. High gloss is easy to clean but accentuates every little flaw, so your prep and paint job have to be perfect. Satin and semigloss are good compromise choices. Also check the operation of the door. If it rubs against the jamb or drags on the carpet, now's the time to sand or plane the edges. If you have several doors that need painting, start with the least prominent one. It's better to make learning mistakes on the inside of a closet door than on your entry door.

Prep tips

Pros often paint doors in place. But from prep to painting, you'll get better results if you remove the door. Working in your garage, shop or basement, you can control lighting and drying conditions better. And laying the door flat minimizes runs in the paint job. Here's what to do after you remove the door:

■ Clean the door with a household cleaner. Almost any cleaner will do, as long as it cuts grease. Areas around doorknobs are

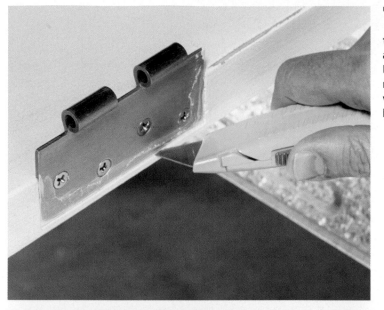

1 Remove all the hardware Slice through paint buildup around hinges and latches. Otherwise, you might splinter surrounding wood as you remove hardware.

HARD RUBBER SANDING BLOCK

2 Sand it smooth On flat areas, level out old runs and brush marks with a hard sanding block. For the shaped profiles, you'll need a combination of sanding pads, sponges and scraps of sandpaper.

> **CAUTION**
> If your home was built before 1979, check the paint for lead before you sand. For more information, go to epa.gov/lead.

3 Remove the sanding dust A vacuum with a brush attachment removes most of the dust. Wipe off the rest with a damp rag.

4 **Sand after priming**
Sand out any imperfections in the prime coat. Shine a light across the surface at a low angle to accentuate imperfections. If you find any spots that need an extra dab of filler, mark them with tabs of masking tape.

5 **Paint the edges and wipe off the slop**
Brush or roll paint onto all four edges. Immediately wipe any paint that slops onto the face of the door with a rag or foam brush. You don't have to completely remove the paint, but you do have to flatten it to prevent ridges.

6 **Brush around the panels** Work the paint into the corners and grooves, then drag the brush over the paint to smooth it. Wipe away any slop around the panel as shown in Photo 5.

especially prone to greasy buildup.

- Remove all the door hardware to get a neater paint job and save time. If you're dealing with more than one door, avoid hardware mix-ups by labeling plastic bags that will hold the hardware for each door.

- Fill dents and holes with a sandable filler such as MH Ready Patch. You'll probably have to fill deep dents twice to compensate for shrinkage.

- Remove old paint from the hardware. Start with a product intended to remove paint splatter such as Goof Off Pro Strength Remover or Goo Gone Painter's Pal. You can use paint strippers, but they may also remove clear coatings from the hardware or damage some types of finishes.

Sanding tips

If your door is in good shape, all it needs is a light sanding with sandpaper or a sanding sponge (180 or 220 grit). That will roughen the surface a little and allow the primer to adhere better. But most likely, you'll also need to smooth out chipped paint and imperfections from previous paint jobs. This is usually the most time-consuming, tedious part of the project. Here are some tips for faster, better results:

- Paint often sticks to sandpaper, clogging the grit and making it useless. So be sure to check the label and buy sandpaper intended for paint. You may still get some clogging, but you'll get less. This goes for sponges and other abrasives too.

- Start with 120 or 150 grit. You can switch to coarser paper (such as 80 grit) on problem areas, but be sure to follow up with finer grit to smooth out the sanding scratches.

- On flat areas, a hard sanding block will smooth the surface much better than sponges or other soft-backed abrasives **(Photo 2)**.

- Try a finishing or random-orbit sander on flat areas. It might save you tons of time. Then again, the sandpaper may clog immediately from heat buildup. It depends on the type and age of the paint.

- Buy a collection of sanding sponges and pads for the shaped areas. Through trial and error, you'll find that some work better than others on your profiles.

- Inspect your work with low-angle lighting **(see Photo 4)**.

Tips for a perfect workspace

- After the messy job of sanding is done, set the door aside and prep your workspace. For priming and painting, you want a work zone that's well lit and clean. Sawdust on your workbench will end up on brushes; airborne dust will create whiskers on the paint. The conditions in your work area should allow paint to dry slowly. Slower drying means more time for you to smooth the paint before it becomes gummy and more time for the paint to level itself.

7 Roll, then brush the panels Coat the panels quickly with a roller. Then smooth the paint with a brush. Be careful not to touch the profiles surrounding the panel.

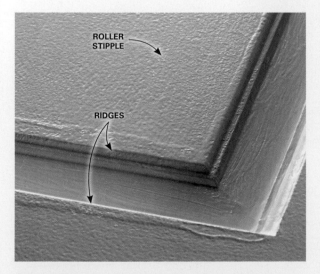

8 Roll the rails and stiles Roll the door in sections, coating no more than one-quarter of the door at a time. Then brush out the paint. Be careful not to slop paint over the edges around the panels.

ROLLER STIPPLE

RIDGES

The wrong paint Some paints show brush marks, ridges and roller stipple no matter how skillful or careful you are. Others go on smoothly and then level out beautifully, even if you're not a master painter.

Water-based alkyd is best

If you want a smooth finish, choose a paint designed for that. Some paints, even good-quality paints, just aren't formulated for smoothness. Smooth paints are usually labeled "enamel" or "door and trim." But the label alone doesn't tell you enough; some brands of "enamel" are much better than others. Advice from the store staff, and the price, are the best indicators. Super-smooth paints often cost $25 to $30 *per quart*! But I'm happy to spend an extra 10 bucks per door for first-class results.

Among the paints I've used, one category stands out for smoothness: water-based alkyds. These paints dry slowly for extra working time and level out almost as well as traditional oil-based alkyds. After applying them with a high-quality roller, I was able to skip the brush-out step shown in **Photos 7 and 9** and still got perfect results. Cleanup is as easy as with any other water-based paint. The disadvantages of water-based alkyds are a very long wait before recoating (16 to 24 hours) and a high price tag. Here are two I've used: Benjamin Moore Advance Waterborne Interior Alkyd and Sherwin-Williams ProClassic Interior Waterbased Acrylic-Alkyd Enamel. To find a dealer in your area, go to benjaminmoore.com or sherwin-williams.com.

9 **Brush with the grain** Brush across the joints where door parts meet. Then drag your brush in a straight line along the intersection. That way, any visible brush marks will look more like a wood grain pattern and less like sloppy brushwork.

The ultimate smooth finish

Even the most skilled painter can't match the perfection of a sprayed-on finish. There are two types of sprayers: "airless" and "HVLP" (high-volume, low-pressure). Both can apply a flawless coat in minutes, but HVLP is more forgiving; it produces a finer spray, which reduces your chances of blasting on too much paint and creating runs. Many HVLP sprayers won't spray acrylic/latex paint. For a model that will, expect to spend $100 to $150, well worth it if you have a house full of doors to paint. Aside from finish quality, a sprayer will also save you hours of brushwork if you have several doors to paint. For more on both airless and HVLP sprayers, go to familyhandyman.com and search for "paint sprayers."

Here's how to prep your space:

- Clean everything. Vacuum work surfaces and sweep the floor.
- Minimize air movement for less airborne dust and slower drying. Close doors and windows. Turn off forced-air heating or cooling.
- Don't rely on overhead lighting; you may even want to turn it off. Instead, position a work light 4 to 5 ft. above the floor. This low-angle light will accentuate any drips or ridges.
- Have all your tools and supplies ready, including a pail of water to dunk your paint tools in as soon as you're done.
- If you're working in the garage, unplug the garage door opener so it can't be opened while you work. An opening door raises dust.

Priming tips

You can "spot-prime" a door, coating only patched dents or areas you sanded through to bare wood. But priming the whole door is best; the new paint will stick better and you'll get a more uniform finish. Here are some tips for this critical step:

- Your choice of primer is just as important as your choice of paint. At the paint store, ask for a primer that's compatible with your paint, levels out well and sands smoothly.
- Have the primer tinted, based on the color of your paint.
- Apply the primer with just as much care as the paint and following the same steps **(see Photos 5 – 9)**. Also check out the painting tips in the next section.
- For an ultra-smooth paint job, apply two coats of primer. With a thick build of primer, you can sand the prime coat glassy-smooth, without sanding through to the old paint.
- Lightly sand the primer with 220-grit, inspecting as you go **(Photo 4)**. A couple of quick passes is all it takes. If you're not in a rush to get the door back in service, let the primer dry overnight before sanding. The longer it dries, the better it will sand.

Painting tips

Painting a door is a race against time. You have to lay down the paint and smooth it out before it becomes too sticky to work with, or so stiff that brush marks won't level out and disappear. Keep moving. Don't stop to answer the phone or get coffee. Minutes count. In warm, dry conditions, even seconds matter.

- Consider a paint additive to slow down drying and improve leveling. Your paint dealer can recommend one that's compatible with your paint.
- Start with a dust-free door; wipe it down with a damp rag just before painting.
- Spend at least $10 to get a quality brush for a smoother finish. Pro painters disagree about the size and type to use. I prefer a 2-in. sash brush.
- Don't use cheap roller sleeves or you'll get fibers in the finish. I use a mini roller and get good results with microfiber, mohair and FlockFoam sleeves. Foam sleeves also leave a smooth finish, but they hold very little paint, which slows you down.
- Paint all four edges of the door first (**Photo 5**). Here's why: when painting edges, some paint inevitably slops onto the faces of the door. It's better to have that happen *before* the faces are painted.
- Brush on a light coat. A heavy coat of paint covers better and sometimes levels out better, but runs are more likely and brush marks are deeper. So start out lightly, then lay it on a little thicker as your brush skills improve. Roll on the paint where you can. Rollers lay on paint much faster than a brush, giving you a few more precious minutes to work the paint before it begins to stiffen.
- Brush out rolled paint. Brushed paint usually levels out better than rolled paint, and any brush marks are less noticeable than roller stipple. *But you might be able to skip the brush-out step altogether.* With top-quality enamel and roller sleeves, roller results can be super smooth. This depends in part on drying conditions, so try it on a closet door or a primed scrap of wood first.
- Plan to apply at least two coats and lightly sand between coats with 220-grit to remove any dust nubs.

My favorite painting tricks

Over the years, I've spent a lot time observing and interrogating pro painters. Here are three pro tips that I've used over and over again:

LAG SCREW

Make the door flippable

Drive one screw into one end and two into the other. That lets you coat both sides of the door without waiting for the first side to dry. Drill pilot holes and drive 5/16 x 5-in. lag screws about halfway in. Smaller screws can bend and let the door drop just as you're finishing the final coat. (I learned this the hard way.)

Wet the floor

Two benefits for the price of one: A wet floor prevents you from kicking up dust that will create dust nubs in your finish. Better yet, it raises the humidity, which extends the time you have to smooth out the paint and gives the paint more time to level out. In my informal experiments, raising the humidity doubled the working time of the paint. (I also discovered that slick floors get even slicker when wet, which can lead to Three Stooges–style paint accidents. Be careful.)

Keep a pair of tweezers handy

Pluck out paintbrush bristles or rescue stuck insects without messing up the paint. This works great with other finishes too. Don't return the tweezers to the medicine cabinet. Buy a new pair (another lesson learned the hard way).

CHAPTER 4

MAGNET STICK

Workshop Tips

CAT
LITTER
POUCH

Rust prevention pouch

It's difficult to keep your tools free of rust if your
toolbox is in an unconditioned garage or in the bed of
your truck. Moisture in the air invades those spaces in a
hurry, causing tools to rust. To absorb the moisture and
prevent rust, put a scoop of silica crystal cat litter in a
rag and then tie it shut. Drop a pouch in every
toolbox and replace them once a year.

Small-parts sander

If you like to make wooden toys and other iintricate wood projects, use emery boards—the kind for filing fingernails—to sand small parts. Emery boards come in different sizes, and some are more abrasive than others, so keep an assortment on hand.

Space-saving workbench

Old doors laid across sawhorses make great temporary workbenches, but they take up a lot of space when you're not using them. Instead of full-size doors, use bifold doors with hinges so you can fold them up when you're done working. They're also easier to haul around in the pickup for on-the-road jobs.

PLASTIC SHELVING UNIT

Plywood cutting station

When cutting full sheets with my circular saw, use plastic shelving units as sawhorses. The height is just right and by using three of them, you can make cuts in any direction and the plywood is fully supported. And because the shelving units are made of plastic, you can cut right into them without worrying that they'll damage your saw blade.

Pallet dolly

I had a truckload of lumber to transport down a long hallway to my shop, and I wasn't looking forward to carrying it an armload at a time. Then I noticed the pallet it was on. I didn't have a pallet jack, but I did have a set of casters. After I installed some reinforcement blocking, it took just a few minutes to attach a 4-in. caster to each corner of the pallet. Now it's my all-around heavy-stuff mover. — Brad Holden, **senior editor**

Sanding disc cleaner

Sandpaper loses its effectiveness when it's clogged with sawdust or pitch. Gum eraser-type sandpaper cleaners work really well, but if you don't have one, the sole of an old sneaker works too. Turn on your sander and slide the rubber sole along the disc or belt, using just enough pressure to remove the sanding debris.

Convenient bench clamps

Trigger-style bar clamps make perfect workbench hold-down clamps. First, punch out the split-tube stop at the end of the clamp's bar and then slide the trigger head off. Slip the bar through a bench-dog hole and reinstall the trigger head. If your bench doesn't have dog holes, just drill a hole wherever you need it.

No-wait glue

If you don't like waiting for the glue to reach the bottle's tip when you're in the middle of a big glue-up, here's what you can do. Turn the bottle upside down in a can that sits on your workbench. The glue will be ready to flow whenever you need it.

Around-the-shop curve guides

When you need to draw a curve on a project, instead of reaching for a ruler and a compass, start looking around your shop. There are dozens of round objects available for tracing a perfect curve or radius—anything from a 5-gallon bucket to a roll of tape to the dime in your pocket.

Finishing stands

When you're finishing table legs or other furniture parts, cut square 1/4-in. plywood "stands" and screw them onto each end. The table legs stay put as you apply your finish, making the job much easier than it would be if the parts were hung on a hook. And you can stand them vertically to dry.

Faster filing with less sanding

When you use metal files on soft, nonferrous metals such as aluminum or brass, the teeth clog quickly. This means frequent cleaning with a file card. To keep the teeth from getting clogged, try this old trick: Rub a piece of chalk along the teeth before using the file on the workpiece.

CHALK

No-roll pencils

Carpenter's pencils are handy because they don't roll off your workbench or countertop. But if you prefer regular pencils for precise marking, keep them from rolling off the workbench by putting a tape "flag" around the end.

Grip odd shapes

Holding a spindle or other odd-shaped part in a bench vise is tricky. To hold the part firmly without marring it, sandwich it between two pieces of rigid foam.

RIGID FOAM

Long-reach magnet

Here's a simple tool that saves your back whenever you drop screws, nuts or bolts on your workshop floor. Glue a magnet onto the end of a stick and use that to pick up whatever you dropped.

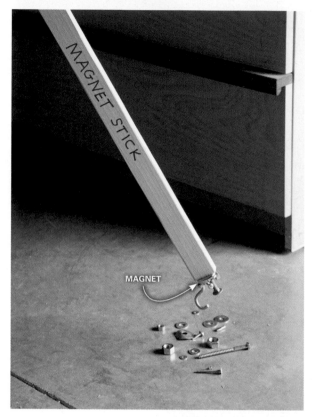

MAGNET

Blade-height gauge block

Here's a quick way to set the height of a table saw blade. Cut notches on the end of a 4x4 block at the blade heights you use most often: maybe 1/4 in., 3/8 in., 1/2 in. and 3/4 in. To use the block, position the desired notch over the blade and raise the blade until its highest point just touches the block.

Clamp with a tie-down strap

If you need to clamp boxes together, a ratchet tie-down strap can often do the job just as well as band clamps. Just make sure to protect the wood under the ratchet and hooks with cardboard.

TIE-DOWN STRAP

Use a level to extend your table saw fence

The only way to achieve a perfectly straight cut is to keep your material tight up against the table saw fence. But that's hard to do when you're cutting a large sheet of plywood on your own. Extending the fence with a 4-ft. level will make it easier to keep the plywood on a straight and narrow path as it approaches and passes through the blade. Hold the level in place with a couple clamps.

CLAMP

4' LEVEL

HOSE TO SHOP VACUUM

Less-mess tile cutting

If you're cutting tile using a grinder, build yourself a vacuum bucket. Drill a hole the same size as your vacuum's hose into the side of the bucket, near the bottom. As you're cutting tile over the bucket, the vacuum will capture most of the dust.

METAL FILE

Dedicated nail puller

Nippers are great for pulling brad nails, but the sharp edges often cut the nail as you try to pull it out. Dull a pair of nippers slightly with a metal file and mark it as your designated nail puller. Use a cheap pair; higher-quality nippers with hardened cutting edges may not file easily. Shoot a few nails into a test board to get it just right.

HANDSAW

DOWEL

Make your own pocket hole plugs

Instead of buying pocket hole plugs, use this jig to make as many as you need. Drill a pocket hole into a 2x4. Then insert a 3/8-in. dowel and slice it off flush with the face of the 2x4. After making the angled cut, push the dowel through, cut the end at 90 degrees and repeat.

600-GRIT SANDPAPER

CRAFT KNIFE BLADE

Renew craft knife blades

Don't dispose of craft knife blades when they get dull. Instead, sharpen them. All it takes is a small piece of glass or a flat surface and a piece of 600-grit sandpaper. Carefully hone both beveled faces of the blade until it cuts like new.

CARPET

No-scratch toolbox

Cut and glue a piece of carpet to the bottom of your toolbox to protect surfaces like floors and countertops from scratches. The carpet also makes it easy to slide your toolbox around rather than picking it up just to move it a little way.

Magnet in a bag

Cleaning up metal shavings around a drill press almost always results in a metal sliver or two. Using a magnet works fine, but it's no fun to get all those shavings off the magnet. So, put the magnet inside a plastic bag that's turned inside out. Attract the shavings to the bag, seal it, pull it free and throw them away without touching a single shaving.

Fiddle sticks

When you're using a belt sander, you need to make sure the piece you're sanding stays put. You can't just clamp down the board—the clamps will block the belt sander from reaching the edges. The trick is to screw boards, sometimes called "fiddles," to a corner of your workbench. As you sand, the spinning motion will push the workpiece against the fiddles, holding it in place.

FIDDLES

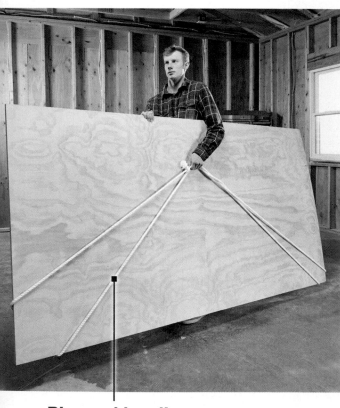

Plywood handle

Carrying a sheet of plywood by yourself is awkward and hard on your back. The best method we've found involves making a loop from an 18-ft. rope. Wrap it around the bottom two corners of the plywood sheet. The rope makes a perfect handle.

Dividing odd widths

Say you have a board that's 11-3/8 in. wide and you need to divide it into four equal parts. No problem. Angle your tape across the board until it reads a number easily divisible by four, such as 16. Then, with the tape angled, make marks at 4, 8 and 12 in.

Pencil trick for sanding

When you're sanding an edge flush to the adjacent surface, first draw a squiggly pencil line across the joint. Use the marks as a guide to help you sand flat and avoid sanding through the plywood's veneer.

No more rolling

To keep X-Acto knives from rolling off the table and stabbing you in the foot, put zip ties around them. This trick also works great for preventing short pencils from getting stuck down in narrow tool belt pockets, and carpenter's pencils from falling through the cracks when used as spacers between deck boards.

ZIP TIE

Soft-top sawhorses

Most sawhorses see rough use. If they get beat up, it doesn't matter. But if you have a few that you use for assembling projects, staple carpet scraps to them to provide a non-marring surface.

Screw organizer

When you disassemble a piece of furniture that needs to be repaired or moved to a new home, poke the screws and nails into a piece of rigid foam. Group similar fasteners together or arrange them in the order they were removed. Use a pen or marker to label the groups or make notes that will be helpful for reassembly.

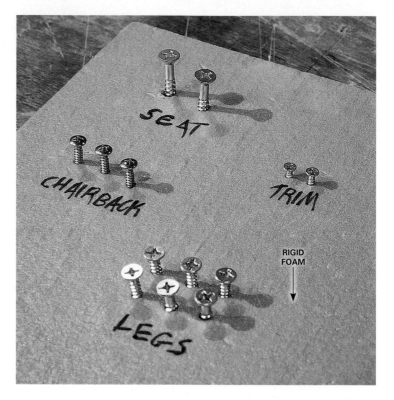

SEAT

CHAIRBACK

TRIM

LEGS

RIGID FOAM

Double-duty sandpaper

For some jobs, a single sheet of sandpaper is too flimsy; the paper backing wears out before the grit. One solution is to glue two pieces back to back with spray adhesive. And, you can use two different grits for versatility.

Sandpaper tearing blade

Cutting sandpaper will dull scissors and utility knife blades in no time. Here's a better technique: Fasten a hacksaw blade to the edge of your workbench. Slip a washer behind the blade at each of the mounting holes so a sheet of sandpaper can easily slide in behind the blade. Fold the paper to the finished size you want, then cut along the fold.

HACKSAW BLADE

Bobby pin nail holder

When you're hammering small nails or any nails in tight quarters, keep your fingers out of the line of fire with a bobby pin. It will grip even the smallest nails.

Hole-saw depth marker

The best way to avoid tear-out with a hole saw is to drill halfway through the wood and flip it over to complete the hole. But how do you know when you've cut halfway? Mark your saw with a line that's slightly more than halfway. With 3/4-in. stock, mark the saw at just past 3/8 in. Use a pencil so you can easily wipe off the line and mark a different depth as needed. This tip also makes it easier to remove the plug; more of it extends past the saw teeth so you can grab it to pull it free.

Instant hardware patina

Gun bluing (available at sporting goods stores) gives off-the-shelf hardware an attractive, aged patina. Simply dip nuts, bolts, washers or other hardware into a cup of gun bluing. When the hardware turns black, rinse it with water and dry it with a paper towel. Be sure to wear rubber gloves and eye protection.

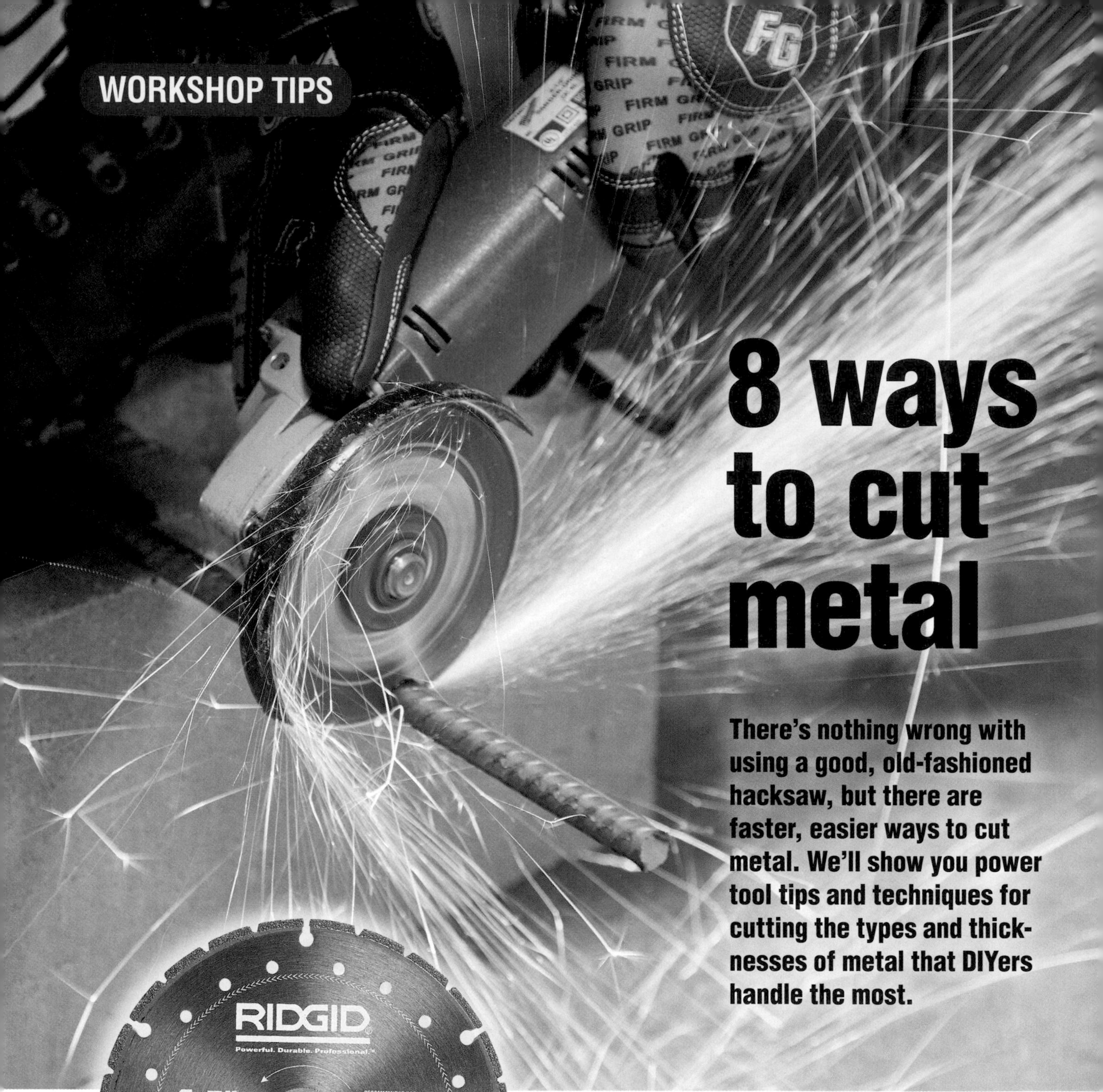

8 ways to cut metal

There's nothing wrong with using a good, old-fashioned hacksaw, but there are faster, easier ways to cut metal. We'll show you power tool tips and techniques for cutting the types and thicknesses of metal that DIYers handle the most.

RIDGID
Powerful. Durable. Professional.™

4.5"
115mm
7/8"-20mm-5/8"
Arbor/Arbre/Eje

RECOMMENDED TOOL:
MAX RPM 13,300
13,300 tr/mn. max

METAL CUTTING
DIAMOND BLADE

Always use safety guards and wear safety glasses.
Before using, read all warnings in machine
manual & blade package.
MTL45

1 Ditch the abrasive grinder discs An angle grinder fitted with an abrasive metal-cutting disc works well to cut all kinds of metal, including bolts, angle iron, rebar and even sheet metal. But the discs wear down quickly, cut slowly and shrink in diameter as you use them. Instead, we recommend using a diamond blade that's rated to cut ferrous metal. These will last much longer, cut faster and cleaner, and wear down much slower than abrasive discs. You'll find ferrous-metal-cutting diamond blades at home centers, hardware stores and online.

FERROUS-
METAL
BLADE

2 **Cut metal with your circular saw** It may not be an obvious choice, but fitted with the right blade, a circular saw is a great metal-cutting tool.

In our test, it cut through rebar like a hot knife through butter. You can cut mild steel up to about 3/8 in. thick using a ferrous-metal-cutting blade. Be careful, though! Hot metal chips will fly everywhere. Put on your safety gear, keep bystanders away, and cover anything you don't want coated with metal chips. You'll find ferrous-metal-cutting blades at home centers, hardware stores and online. There are two types: inexpensive steel tooth blades and carbide-tooth blades. Carbide-tooth blades are more expensive but will last longer.

METAL
ROOFING

NONFERROUS
BLADE

WOOD
BACKER

ALUMINUM
ANGLE

3 **Cut aluminum with your miter saw** Making accurate cuts on aluminum rods, tubes and angles is easy with a miter saw and a blade designed to cut nonferrous metal (check the label). If the motor housing on your saw is open and could collect metal chips, tape a piece of cloth over the openings to protect the motor windings and bearings while you cut the aluminum. (Remember to remove it when the saw goes back into regular service or the motor will overheat.) Trapping the aluminum with a wood backer as shown reduces the danger of flying metal shards and makes it easier to hold the metal in place for cutting. This tip is especially important when you're cutting thin-walled pieces. Without the backing board, the blade will often catch on the metal and distort it and make it unusable.

Tips for cutting metal safely

Cutting or grinding metal sends tiny chips or shards of metal everywhere. And they can be hot and sharp. To avoid eye injuries, cuts, burns and other injuries from cutting metal, follow these rules:

- Read and observe safety precautions printed on metal-cutting discs and blades.
- Wear safety glasses, a face shield and hearing protection.
- Cover all exposed skin with gloves, a long-sleeve shirt and pants.
- Allow freshly cut metal to cool before touching it.
- Wear gloves when handling metal that could have sharp edges.
- Securely clamp metal before cutting it.
- Never allow anyone near you while you're cutting metal unless they're wearing hearing and eye protection.

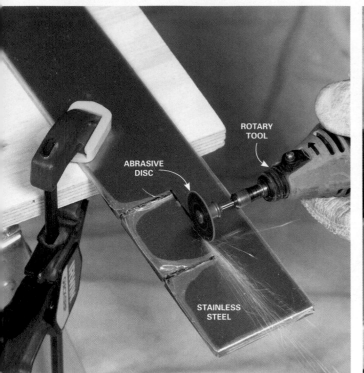

4 Cut stainless steel with a grinding disc There are many types of stainless steel, and some hard varieties are challenging to cut. For small jobs like cutting stainless steel backsplash tiles, a rotary tool fitted with an abrasive metal-cutting disc works fine. For larger jobs, mount an abrasive disc in an angle grinder.

5 Simply score and snap Siding contractors and roofers routinely score and snap aluminum siding and flashing to create straight, precise cuts. And you can use the same technique anytime you need a straight cut on aluminum or other light-gauge sheet metal, even steel. Clamp or hold a straightedge or square along the cutting marks and score a line with the tip of a sharp utility knife blade. Then bend the sheet back and forth a few times to snap it. You can use the same trick to cut steel studs. Snip the two sides. Then score a line between the cuts and bend the stud to break it.

6 Get into tight spots with an oscillating tool When access is tight, or you need to make a flush cut, an oscillating tool fitted with a metal-cutting blade will solve the problem. Corroded mounting nuts on toilets and faucets are easy to cut off with an oscillating tool. You can also use an oscillating tool to cut plumbing pipes, automotive bolts, nails and other metal objects in places where a larger tool wouldn't fit. Just make sure the blade is intended to cut metal.

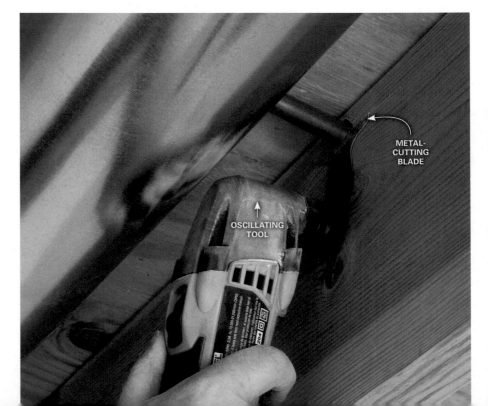

METAL-CUTTING BLADE

7 Cut smarter: use a recip saw

The next time you reach for your hacksaw, grab your reciprocating saw instead. Mount a metal-cutting blade in your recip saw and you've got the ultimate power hacksaw for cutting bolts, rods, pipes and angle iron. A recip saw with a metal-cutting blade also works great for remodeling demolition when there are nails and pipes to cut off. Here are a few tips for cutting metal with a recip saw:

- Set your saw to straight rather than oscillating if there's a choice.
- Extend blade life by keeping the saw's speed slow.
- Choose a blade with 20 to 24 TPI (teeth per inch) for thin metal, 10 to 18 TPI for medium-thickness metal, and about 8 TPI for thick metal.
- Buy bimetal or carbide-tooth blades for longer blade life.

Match the blade to the metal

With the right blade or grinding disc, you can cut almost any kind of metal. The key is to match the blade to the material.

There are two types of metal: ferrous and nonferrous. (The term "ferrous" is derived from the Latin word "ferrum," which means iron.) Any metal that contains iron is a ferrous metal and requires a ferrous-metal cutting blade. Steel angle iron, steel roofing, rebar and steel bolts are examples of ferrous-metal building materials. Most metal-cutting blades and discs are labeled for cutting either nonferrous or ferrous metal.

The two most common nonferrous metals DIYers need to cut are aluminum and copper. Nonferrous metals are usually softer and easier to cut than ferrous metals.

METAL LATH

DIAMOND BLADE

8 Cut metal lath and mesh with a grinder
Metal lath and hardware cloth can be cut with tin snips, but there's an easier way. Mount a diamond blade in your angle grinder and use it like a saw to cut the mesh. We recommend using a diamond blade that's labeled as a ferrous-metal-cutting blade, but many tradespeople use a regular masonry diamond blade with good results.

Best workbench upgrades

Our favorite ways to add storage, convenience and handy features to any workbench

To find the best ideas for simple workbench upgrades, we sampled the workbenches of our staff and pro friends. No matter what kind of workbench you have, you can add one or all of these improvements to make your bench more functional and fun to use.

The largest project here, the three roll-out drawers, only requires one sheet of 3/4-in. plywood and less than a day to build. The rest of the projects require even less time and materials. You could build any of these projects with basic carpentry tools and a circular saw, drill and jigsaw.

But a table saw will simplify the process by adding speed and accuracy. And, of course, a pneumatic trim nailer would be handy for building the shallow drawers and for tacking together the roll-out drawers before you strengthen them with screws.

① Easiest add-on drawers

These roll-out drawers are easy—you don't even have to mount them to the bench. They're just sturdy boxes that ride on 2-in. casters. Measure from the floor to the bottom shelf of your workbench and subtract 3-1/4 in. to figure the height of the boxes. Then subtract 3/4 in. from this measurement to determine the height of the drawer front, back and sides. Next, decide how many drawers you want and calculate the widths. Allow for a 1/2-in. space between drawers.

Cut the parts and screw them together. Then measure the width and length of the box and cut the bottom. Screw on the bottom and cut a handhold in the front of the drawer with a jigsaw. Finish up by screwing 2-in. fixed (not swiveling!) casters to the bottom of the drawer as shown.

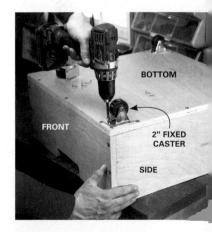

Build basic plywood boxes and screw on the casters. Carefully align the casters parallel to the box sides so the drawers roll smooth and straight.

② Our favorite convenience feature

Every bench needs easy-access storage for all the odds and ends that would otherwise clutter the benchtop. These shallow drawers, which mount directly under the benchtop, fit the bill perfectly.

There's no fancy joinery on these drawers. And the special pencil drawer slides simplify mounting. We used 22-in.-deep drawer slides and built the drawers 22 in. deep to match. The drawer slides (No. KV8250; $24 a pair) are available from wwhardware.com (800-383-0130).

1 Mount the drawers with special "pencil drawer" slides. These slides include hanger brackets, so you don't have to build extra parts just to attach drawer slides.

You can build the drawers up to about 30 in. wide, but remember to allow a few inches of space on each side for the mounting hardware. Rip strips of 3/4-in. plywood or solid lumber to 3-1/4 in. wide for the front, sides and back. Cut the sides 22 in. long and the front and back pieces 1-1/2 in. less than the desired width of the drawer. Glue and nail the sides to the front and back. Then measure the width and length of the drawer and cut a bottom from 1/4-in. plywood. Glue and nail the bottom to the assembled frame. If you're careful to cut the bottom piece perfectly square, your drawer will be square. Or you can hold one side and the drawer front against a framing square while you nail on the bottom.

Photo 1 shows how to attach the drawer slide. Line up the bottom of the slide with the seam between the drawer bottom and drawer side. If you don't have 2x4 crosspieces under your bench, add them in the location of the drawer hardware. Then prop up the drawer in the right spot and screw through the brackets into the crosspieces **(Photo 2)**. Finish by cutting drawer fronts that are 1-1/2 in. longer and 1/2 in. taller than the drawer. Attach the drawer front from the back with 1-1/4-in. screws driven through the front of the drawer box.

ADDED CROSSPIECE

TEMPORARY SUPPORT

2 Prop up the drawer and screw it to the underside of the workbench. Add crosspieces if there's nothing to screw into.

③ Best benchtop space-saver

When you want to use the whole top of your workbench, a permanently mounted vise or grinder just gets in the way. Free up space by mounting your grinder and vise to a double-thick piece of 3/4-in. plywood and hanging them on the end of your workbench until they're needed.

Cut four 20-in.-long x 12-in.-wide pieces of 3/4-in. plywood. Glue and nail them together in pairs to make two 1-1/2-in.-thick slabs. Transfer the location of the mounting holes on your vise and grinder to the plywood. Use a 1-in. spade bit to drill a 1/2-in.-deep recess at each hole location. Then drill through the plywood with a 3/8-in. bit and mount the tools with 3/8-in. bolts, washers and nuts. Position the recess on the side of the plywood opposite the tool to ensure a flush surface.

We screwed a double-thick piece of 3/4-in. plywood to the end of the workbench to make a sturdy mounting plate, but your workbench may not need this. Any strong, flat surface will work. Drill two 1/2-in. holes into each tool holder and mark matching hole locations on the mounting plate. Drill 3/8-in. holes at the marks and attach 3/8-in. bolts with nuts and washers. We recessed the nuts in the mounting plate so the tool holders would sit flush, but this isn't necessary.

3/8" BOLT

1/2" HOLE

④ Our favorite 15-minute workbench accessory

This tool tray is so simple to build that you can have it mounted in about 15 minutes, start to finish. It's a great place to keep small, commonly used tools handy but off the benchtop. And it keeps pencils and other small tools from rolling or getting knocked off the bench and landing on the floor where you can't find them.

Building the tray couldn't be simpler. Just cut a 1x4 and two 1x3s 24 in. long and nail the 1x3s to the sides of the 1x4. Cut two pieces of 1x3 5 in. long and nail them to the ends to complete the tray. Screw the tray to the end of your workbench and you'll never waste time searching for a pencil again.

⑤ Most versatile hold-down system

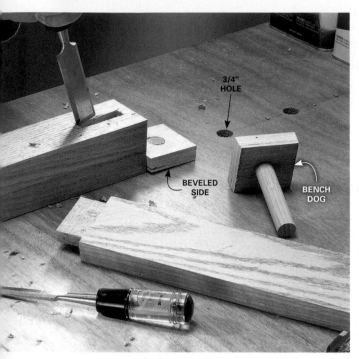

You don't need a super-expensive vise or fancy clamps to hold large projects while you work on them. An inexpensive woodworker's vise paired with shop-made bench dogs will do the trick. We ordered this Adjustable Clamp medium-duty vise online. You may have to cut and notch your workbench to make the vise fit. The goal is to align the top of the jaw flush with the top of the bench. If your workbench is less than 3/4 in. thick, reinforce it by gluing and screwing a 2x4 block underneath the vise area. Then drill 1-in. holes 1/2 in. deep to recess the mounting bolt holes, and bolt the vise to the top of the workbench.

You can extend the versatility of your woodworker's vise by drilling a series of 3/4-in. holes 4 in. apart in your benchtop. Drill the holes in a line at a right angle to the clamp jaws and centered on the sliding steel dog built into the vise. You can buy plastic or metal bench dogs to fit the holes, or make some simple plywood and dowel dogs like ours.

To make a bench dog, rip a scrap of plywood to 2-1/2 in. wide. Set your miter saw to 10 degrees and cut a 2-1/2-in. length from the strip of plywood to form a 2-1/2-in. square with one beveled side. Drill a 3/4-in. hole in the center of the plywood square and glue a 4-in. length of 3/4-in. hardwood dowel into the hole. The short side of the bevel should be on the side with the dowel extending from it. Face the beveled side of the bench dog toward the piece you're clamping. The bevel keeps the workpiece from sliding up and over the dog.

⑥ Our favorite double-duty bench stop

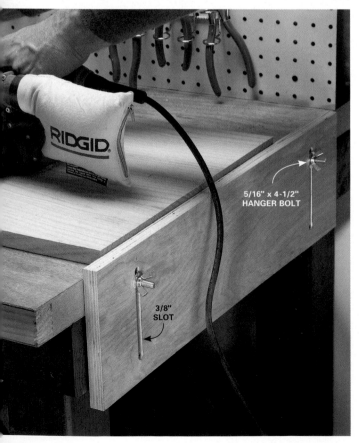

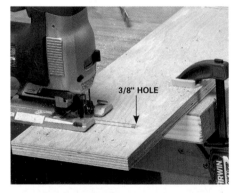

Cut slots in a piece of 3/4-in. plywood and attach it to your bench with bolts and wing nuts. Drill 3/8-in. starter holes. Then cut the slots with a jigsaw.

Here's a simple add-on that can do double duty as a stop or outfeed support for your miter saw. Elevate the sliding piece of plywood slightly above the work surface and use it to keep your work from sliding backward while you're belt sanding. Or adjust it upward to match the height of your miter saw bed and use it as a support for long stock.

Cut a piece of plywood 8 in. wide x 20 in. long. Then mark 3/8-in.-wide slots 2 in. from each end and 1 in. from the top and bottom. Drill 3/8-in. starter holes and cut the slots with a jigsaw as shown. Use the completed bench stop as a pattern to mark the bolt locations.

We screwed 5/16-in. x 4-1/2-in. hanger bolts into our thick workbench top, but you may have to use another method on your workbench. Hanger bolts have wood threads on one end and machine threads on the other. Drill a 7/32-in. starter hole. Then thread two nuts onto the bolt and tighten them against each other. Now place a wrench on the outermost nut and screw in the hanger bolt. Leave 1-1/4 in. of the bolt protruding. Remove the nuts. Mount the bench stop to the bolts with washers and wing nuts.

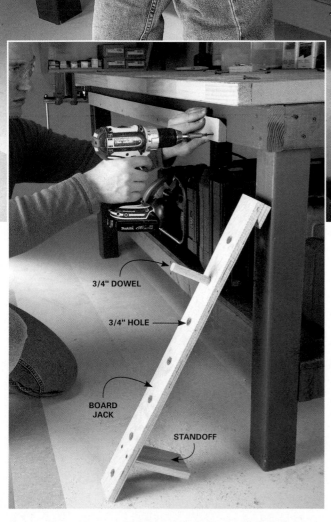

3/4" DOWEL

3/4" HOLE

BOARD JACK

STANDOFF

⑦ Simplest support for long boards

Have you ever needed to hold a long board or door on edge to work on it but struggled to find a good method? If you have a woodworker's vise, adding this board jack is an easy solution. The board jack shown hooks onto the beveled support strip and slides along it to adjust for the length of the workpiece. The 3/4-in. dowel adjusts up and down to accommodate different widths.

Start by ripping a 45-degree angle on a 1x3 board or strip of plywood. Screw the strip to the front of your workbench **(photo left)**. Then build a board jack like the one shown. Drill 3/4-in. holes every 6 in. and insert a 4-in. dowel in the hole to support your work. Adjust the length of the standoff to hold the board jack plumb on your workbench.

Mount a board jack to the front of your workbench and use it with your vise to support your work. Screw a beveled strip to the front of your workbench. Then build the board jack and hook it over the top to support your work.

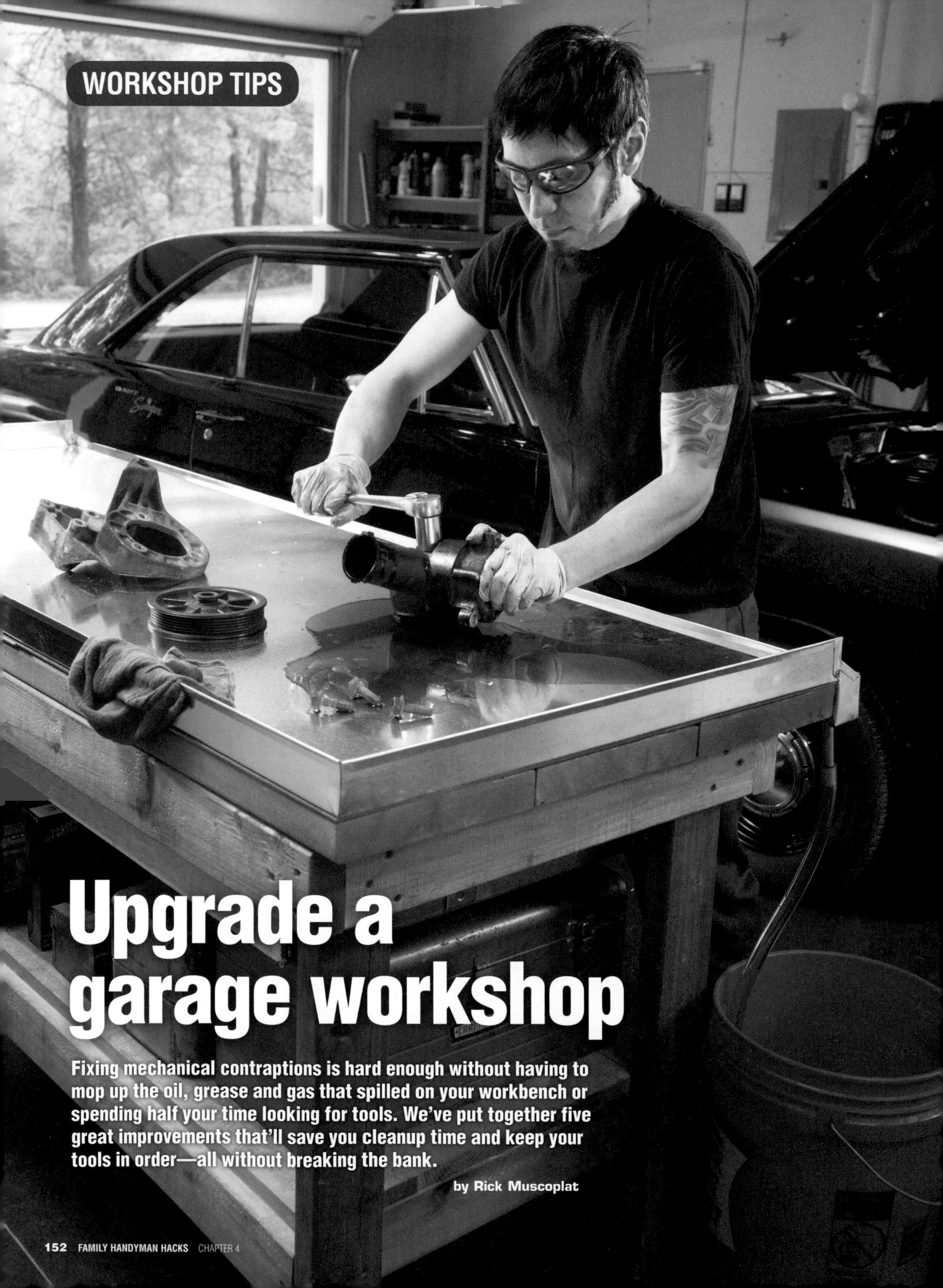

Upgrade a garage workshop

Fixing mechanical contraptions is hard enough without having to mop up the oil, grease and gas that spilled on your workbench or spending half your time looking for tools. We've put together five great improvements that'll save you cleanup time and keep your tools in order—all without breaking the bank.

by Rick Muscoplat

The always-clean workbench

This sheet metal workbench cover **(shown at left)** is one of the wisest investments you can make. It's easy to clean (just squeegee the oil into the gutter and drain bucket), and it's heavy duty enough to handle heavy car parts. All it takes is some measuring and sketching and a trip to a sheet metal shop or a local HVAC shop and steel yard. The whole thing assembles in less than an hour and costs less than $300.

Skip the steel decking if you wish, but it does prevent the top from denting and provides a more solid work surface.

GUTTER

DRAIN

Drill, countersink and screw the steel plate to any wood top. Then screw down the cover with a few pan head screws covered with a dollop of silicone. Clamp a vinyl tube onto the drainpipe and route it into a bucket.

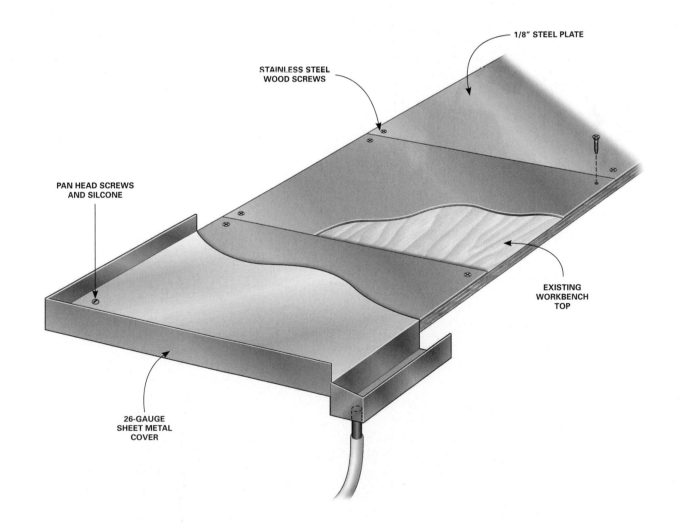

1/8" STEEL PLATE

STAINLESS STEEL
WOOD SCREWS

PAN HEAD SCREWS
AND SILICONE

EXISTING
WORKBENCH
TOP

26-GAUGE
SHEET METAL
COVER

1/2" J-HOOK

JACK HANDLE

Jack and jack-stand holder

Haven't you tripped over your jack stands enough? Build this super –simple storage rack and get them off the floor. If you have a lightweight floor jack, add mounting hooks under the holder. Screw a 2-in. PVC coupler onto the side of the rack and a 2-in. cap on the wall near the floor for the handle.

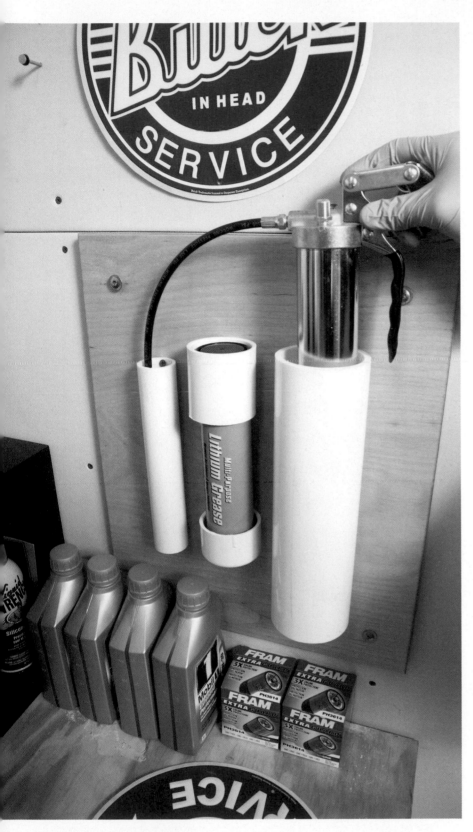

PVC drawer organizers

When you're right in the middle of a project, you don't need to waste time pawing through drawers looking for tools. So keep frequently used tools neatly stacked in your workbench drawer using this handy setup.

Cut 1- or 2-in. PVC pipe to length. Glue on end caps and then slit each pipe in half on a band saw. Screw them to the drawer bottoms and load them up!

Grease gun holster

A grease gun is big and, uh, greasy. So don't slime up your drawers or cabinets with it. Slice up a few sections of 1-in. and 3-in. PVC pipe and screw them to a plywood backer to make this slick grease gun holder. Then slap up a 2-in. coupler and cap to hold a backup tube of grease.

Testing and storing holiday lights

Test the bulbs

PROBLEM: You're putting up the outdoor lights you used last year and half of the lights won't work. You know it's cheaper to just replace them, but you hate to throw them away. You also hate to pull out every bulb to find the bad one.

SOLUTION: Most of us have experienced the frustration of uncooperative holiday lights. There's a simple way to solve the problem. First, slide back the plastic covering on the plug to check the fuse **(Photo 1)**. Some strings have more than one fuse, in which case they'll be next to each other. Replace any blown fuses. New ones are available where holiday lights are sold and at some electronics stores.

Second, test the bulbs with an inexpensive tester, available where holiday lights are sold and online. Usually, changing a problem bulb (or tightening it) will fix the entire strand. The tester will indicate which bulbs are bad and need to be replaced. (For the tester to work, the lights must be plugged into the electrical outlet correctly—the narrow "hot" blade into the narrow slot and the wide neutral blade into the wide slot.)

Some testers work by having you slide each bulb through a hole **(Photo 2)**. With other testers, you simply touch each bulb **(Photo 3)**. You can test an entire strand in a few minutes. Sometimes you have two or more defective bulbs, so only identifying one bad bulb may not fix the problem.

Keep in mind that inexpensive strings of lights aren't durable. At the end of the holiday season, take down the lights with care. Don't pull too hard on the wires. A loose bulb, broken socket or frayed wire is sometimes all it takes for the strand to malfunction.

1 Check the fuse

After taking down the lights, plug them in before storing them, to make sure they still work. Then carefully wrap the lights in their original or similar containers, making sure the bulbs don't bang together. Proper storage is key to their continued success. Wadding them up in a coil and stuffing them into a box will almost guarantee they won't work next year.

Also be aware that most holiday light bulbs have short life expectancies, about 1,000 to 1,500 hours. This means the lights are designed to last one to three seasons, depending on your usage. Newer LED lights are the exception. They can last 10 times longer than traditional lights.

BULB TESTER

BULB TESTER

2 **Check the bulbs:** Tester 1

3 **Check the bulbs:** Tester 2

Test the whole string

If you're looking for an easy way to test (and fix) the entire string of miniature lights without testing each bulb individually, try a light tester. It'll identify and oftentimes fix most problems in light sets with a few squeezes of the trigger **(Photo 4)**.

The trigger sends an electric charge through the circuit to repair internal bulb failures. (The "shunt" in the bulb is supposed to act as a bypass if a filament fails to complete the circuit. If the shunt fails, it knocks out the lights in the section. The electricity sent by pulling the trigger locates and fixes the defective shunt.)

If that doesn't work, hold down the black button on top of the tester and move the tip along the string so it beeps **(Photo 5)**. Note where the beeping stops, then replace the previous bulb.

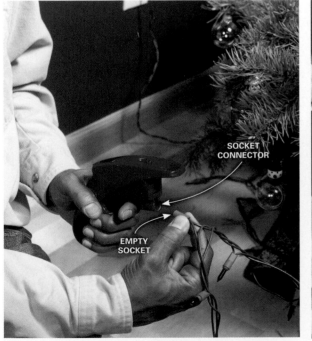

SOCKET CONNECTOR

EMPTY SOCKET

4 Remove a bulb from an unlit section, plug the empty socket into the connector, plug the string into an electric outlet, then squeeze the trigger until the lights turn on.

AUDIBLE CONTINUITY DETECTOR

5 Press down the black button, hold the tip about 1/2 in. from the string, and move it along the cord until it stops beeping (at the defective bulb).

Installing holiday lights

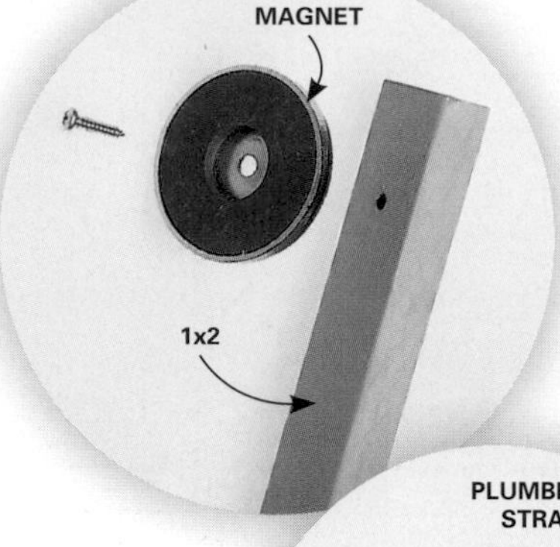

MAGNET

1x2

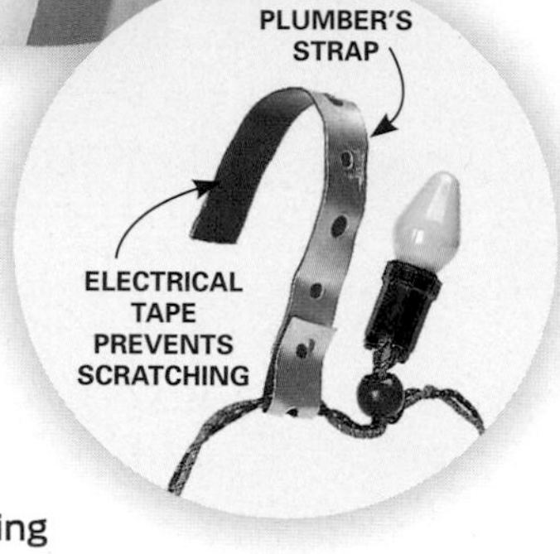

PLUMBER'S STRAP

ELECTRICAL TAPE PREVENTS SCRATCHING

Hang lights from gutters

If your house has gutters, you can hang lights from them without leaving the ground. All you need are an 8-ft. 1x2, a strong magnet and some galvanized steel plumber's hanger strap (all available at home centers).

■ Cut the hanger strap into 7-in. sections, bend the sections into hooks, and attach the hooks to the string of lights every 5 ft. or so.

■ Screw the magnet to the 1x2, and hang the hooks on the gutter one at a time. This is a bit more difficult on a two-story house: You have to screw two or three 1x2s together to reach the gutters, and "grabbing" the hooks with the magnet as they hang far above you is trickier. But it's still better than climbing a ladder.

DANGER! Stay away from power lines.

Better holiday light clips

Make inexpensive and long-lasting holiday light clips using a common staple for electrical cable wiring. Snip the staple in half and fasten it to your fascia or trim with the remaining nail. It holds the wire securely, but it's still easy to slip the wire behind the clip. These clips hold up year after year no matter how cold it gets. If you have metal fascia, use stainless steel screws so they won't rust.

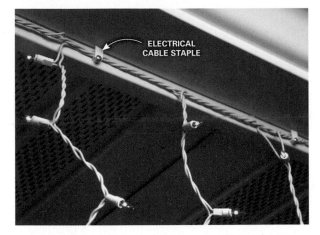

SNIPPED ELECTRICAL STAPLE

STAINLESS STEEL SCREW

ELECTRICAL CABLE STAPLE

Hook for tall trees

Putting up and taking down holiday lights in a tall outdoor tree can be tricky. One method is to use a paint roller extension pole with a hook on the end. You can use a wire coat hanger or other heavy-gauge wire. Just embed it in the pole threads, bend the wire up into a hook and secure it with duct tape to keep the hook from sliding around the pole.

COAT HANGER

Clothespin clips

Instead of poking nails into aluminum soffits and fascia when you're hanging holiday lights, clip the wires to the bottom lip of the fascia with clothespins.

Storing holiday lights

In a bucket

Test your lights before you go to the effort of stringing them on the tree. When the season is over, coil them into a 5-gal. pail to keep them tangle free for next year.

On a hose reel

To keep your holiday lights from getting tangled and make it easy to string them around your yard, roll about 30 strings of lights onto a portable hose reel that has wheels and a handle. Pull the lights around your yard and roll off as many as you need.

In a bag

This has got to be the easiest way to store strings of holiday lights. Just put each string in a separate plastic bag and write where the lights go right on the bag. No wrapping or coiling necessary.

On a spool

Here's a great way to recycle cardboard and keep your strings of holiday lights from getting tangled when you store them. Just use strips of cardboard and cut out a slot on each end to make a "spool" to keep the lights from slipping off. Wrap each light string around a cardboard spool, label it and store it in a plastic bin for next year.

On a stand

Storing lights without wrecking them is tough. After trying a lot of different methods, we think this is a winner. Just screw a dowel to each end of a wooden base cut to the size of a large plastic bin. Then wrap your lights around the dowels in a figure eight and place the stand in the bin. You'll be amazed how many light strings you can wrap around the stands without tangles or damage.

Trees

Buy a bag

Slip a tree disposal bag over the base of the tree before putting it in the stand. (Tear a slit for the trunk so the tree can get water!) The bag hides under the tree skirt until you're ready to haul the tree out the door—without leaving a trail of needles through the house. Just remove the ornaments from the tree, pull the bag up like a pair of pants, and you're on your way.

TREE BAG

WATER HEATER CATCH BASIN

Tighten stand with a drill

Tightening tree stand nuts by hand is tiring and takes forever. Here's an alternative: Cut off the little Ls at the end of the tree stand bolts with a hacksaw. Chuck the ends of the bolts into a variable-speed drill to tighten them into the trunk. You'll be out from under that prickly tree in no time. **Bonus tip:** Place an inexpensive plastic water heater tank catch basin under the tree stand to catch overfilled water.

Easy watering technique

To make tree watering easier, hang a funnel from a tree branch with a loop of clothes hanger. Then slip a plastic tube over the end of the funnel and run the tube along the trunk and into the water reservoir. To prevent overfilling, have someone watch the water level or put a finger in the reservoir and tell you when it's full.

The basics

- Check the height of the tree *before* you bring it into the house to make sure it'll fit under the ceiling. Then if you have to shorten the trunk, the sawdust will stay outside.
- Cut an inch or so off the bottom of the trunk. The fresh wood can absorb more water, so the tree will stay fresher longer.
- Check the trunk diameter by test-fitting the stand. If the tree's too big, you'll need to either get a bigger stand—or start whittling.
- Use a lopper to trim any bottom branches that don't clear the sides of the stand.

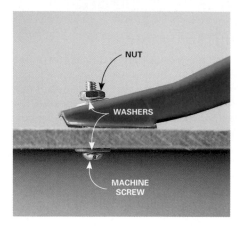

NUT

WASHERS

MACHINE SCREW

Tip-proof tree

To make a tree stand more firmly on deep, spongy carpet, set the stand on an inexpensive piece of 1/4-in. hardboard (a.k.a. Masonite). Some home centers have 4 x 4-ft. and 4 x 8-ft.sheets. To make the tree tip-proof, bolt the tree stand to the hardboard using 1/4-in. pan head machine screws. On wood or tile floors, cover the screwheads with duct tape so they don't scratch the floor.

Cat-proof christmas tree

Two or three lengths of fishing line can keep climbing cats or rambunctious kids from tipping your tree. Just tie one end of each line to the top of the tree and the other to something sturdy: a screw driven into an inconspicuous spot on the wall, moldings above windows or doors, or even a curtain rod.

PLASTIC PROTECTS FLOOR FROM SPILLS

Stand saucer

A plastic snow saucer, the kind with the flat area in the center, is great for keeping overflowing Christmas tree water from staining your floor. Place a carpet remnant under the saucer to prevent scratches on wood flooring.

SNOW SAUCER

Magic carpet

Winding the lights around the Christmas tree is always a pain. Here's a great way to rotate the tree in its stand—without scratching up your floor. Put a bath rug underneath the tree stand, fabric side down, rubber side up. Now you can easily turn the tree to string lights and place ornaments just where you want them. It makes "undecorating" the tree a breeze too. Fold the rug under the tree skirt to keep it hidden.

Tree safety

Every year Christmas trees cause fires. Here's what you can do to help prevent a tree fire. First off, choose a recently cut, healthy tree. A fresh tree holds moisture better. Grab a tree branch and run your hand over it—no more than a few needles should fall off. As soon as you get the tree home, cut 1/2 in. off the trunk and place the tree in a bucket of water until you're ready to bring it into the house. When you set the tree up to decorate it, make sure it's stable in the stand and won't tip over, and water it frequently. A 6-ft. tree needs about 1 gallon of water every other day.

When decorating, use lights rated for indoor use that don't create heat (such as LED lights). And don't overload your electrical outlet. If you want to power dozens of strands of lights and other electric decorations, plug them into different circuits around the house. If you continually blow a circuit, it's probably overloaded.

Here are some other tips:

■ Don't use electric lights on a metal tree.

■ Unplug tree lights before leaving the house or going to bed.

■ Keep the tree at least 3 ft. from candles and fireplaces.

A Christmas Tree Safety System by LifeKeeper is designed to detect low water in the tree stand and send a warning if a fire starts **(see photo)**. Place the system's low water detector in the tree stand. It'll send an audio alert and trigger flashing lights on the attached heat sensor angel if the water level gets too low.

The ornamental angel signals a remote alarm if it senses heat, warning you that a fire could start or has started. The alarm plugs into the wall. To buy the system, search "Christmas tree safety system" online.

HEAT SENSOR ANGEL

LOW-WATER DETECTOR

Labeled tree layers

Artificial Christmas trees are assembled in color-coded layers. After a few years, the colors rub off (or you lose the instructions), and putting the tree together gets confusing. Try this simple trick. When you disassemble the tree at the end of the season, do it one level at a time. Once all the branches from one level are off, duct-tape them together and number each layer with a marker. Next year, the tree will go together in a snap!

Tree in a tube

If you have an artificial Christmas tree, you know that it takes up a lot of storage space. Here's a great idea. Use two 8-in.-diameter concrete form tubes, wrap each layer of the tree in twine and store half the tree layers in one tube and half in the other. Mark the layer numbers on each tube and stow the tubes in your garage rafters.

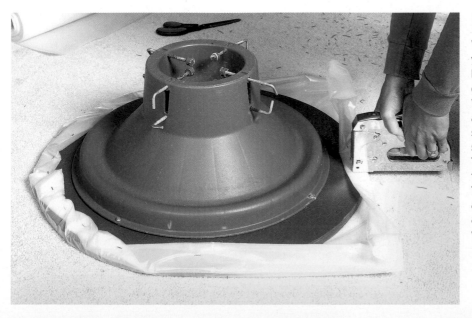

No tip, no drip

We've tried different tree stands over the years, but we've still had trees fall over—because they either were top heavy with ornaments or got tipped over by the cat. We came up with this easy solution: Cut a 2-ft.-diameter circle out of plywood, screw the tree stand to it and then staple plastic sheeting to the plywood. The wooden base gives the tree solid footing and even the cat can't topple it. The plastic helps you slide the tree around on the carpet for easy decorating and protects the carpet from any watering spills.

CHAPTER 5

Storage & Organizing Hacks

Two-tier spice drawer

"We doubled our spice and utensil storage in a couple of hours."

By Spike Carlsen

Recently we remodeled our kitchen: new cabinets, countertops, appliances, the works. Yet the first thing we show off when people visit isn't the fancy new stove, but the $20 two-tier spice tray. When

DRAWER BACK

1 Cut away the top half of the drawer back
Use a jigsaw to cut away a little more than half of the drawer back.

MOUNT SLIDE FLUSH TO DRAWER TOP

2 Install the tray slides Secure full-extension drawer slides to the top inside edges of the drawer. Install them "backward" so they extend toward the back of the drawer. It's OK if they run an inch or so beyond the back of the drawer; most cabinets have extra space in back.

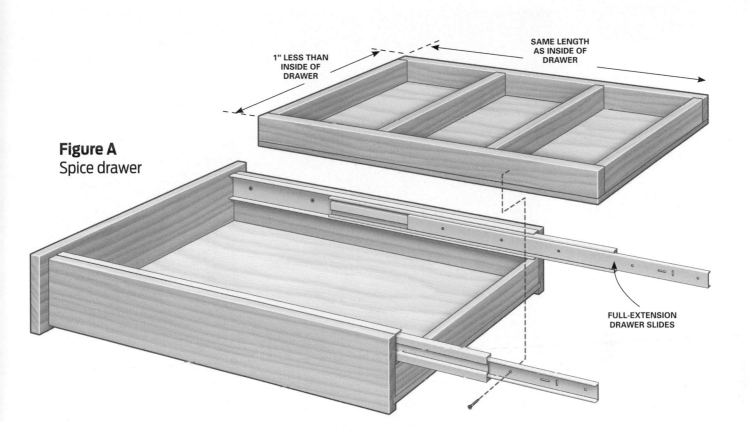

Figure A
Spice drawer

SAME LENGTH AS INSIDE OF DRAWER

1" LESS THAN INSIDE OF DRAWER

FULL-EXTENSION DRAWER SLIDES

we open the drawer, we can slide the top tray all the way back into the cabinet to access the entire bottom layer; no need to lift out a separate tray or sort through layers of stuff. It's not only a space-saver but also a smart organizer since all the spices are in one place, face up. We used the same basic design to make a two-tier utensil drawer too.

Do a little measuring before diving into this project. You can install the 1-3/4-in.-thick tray (like ours) if your drawer is at least 4 in. deep on the inside. Also, these trays are most useful if your existing drawers have (or you install) full-extension slides on the main drawer.

1/4" PLYWOOD BOTTOM

3 Build the upper tray
Since most standard drawer glides are 1/2 in. wide, build your tray 1 in. narrower (or a hair less) than the inside width of the drawer. Build your tray the same length as the inside drawer length. Install partitions according to your needs.

4 Install the tray
Attach the plywood bottom to the tray with nails or brads. Screw the tray to the drawer slides so the top of the tray is flush with the top of the drawer. Then reinstall the drawer.

Measuring cup hang-up

Free up drawer space by hanging measuring cups inside a kitchen cabinet. Position and mount a wood strip so that the cups will hang between the shelves and allow the door to close completely. Mount a second strip for your measuring spoons, then screw in cup hooks on both strips.

CLOSET ORGANIZER RACKS

ATTACH SCREWS TO BACK SIDE OF FACE FRAME

Racks for canned goods

Use closet racks as cabinet organizers. Trim the racks to length with a hacksaw and then mount screws to the back side of the face frame to hold the racks in place. The back side of the rack simply rests against the back of the cabinet. Now you can easily find your soup and check the rest of your inventory at a glance.

1x2

Easy-to-make wine rack

If you need more space for wine storage, make this wine rack using pantry shelves and 1x2s. Cut the 1x2s to length to fit the shelf depth and use a router to round over their top edges. Then space the 1x2s about 2 in. apart and screw them to the shelf. Adjust the shelf spacing so there's about 5 in. of clearance for the bottles.

TENSION ROD

Corral those container lids

To keep storage container lids organized, pop a tension rod into a drawer and stand them up along the side.

Pot & pan pullout

A solution to stooping, searching and stacking

By Spike Carlsen

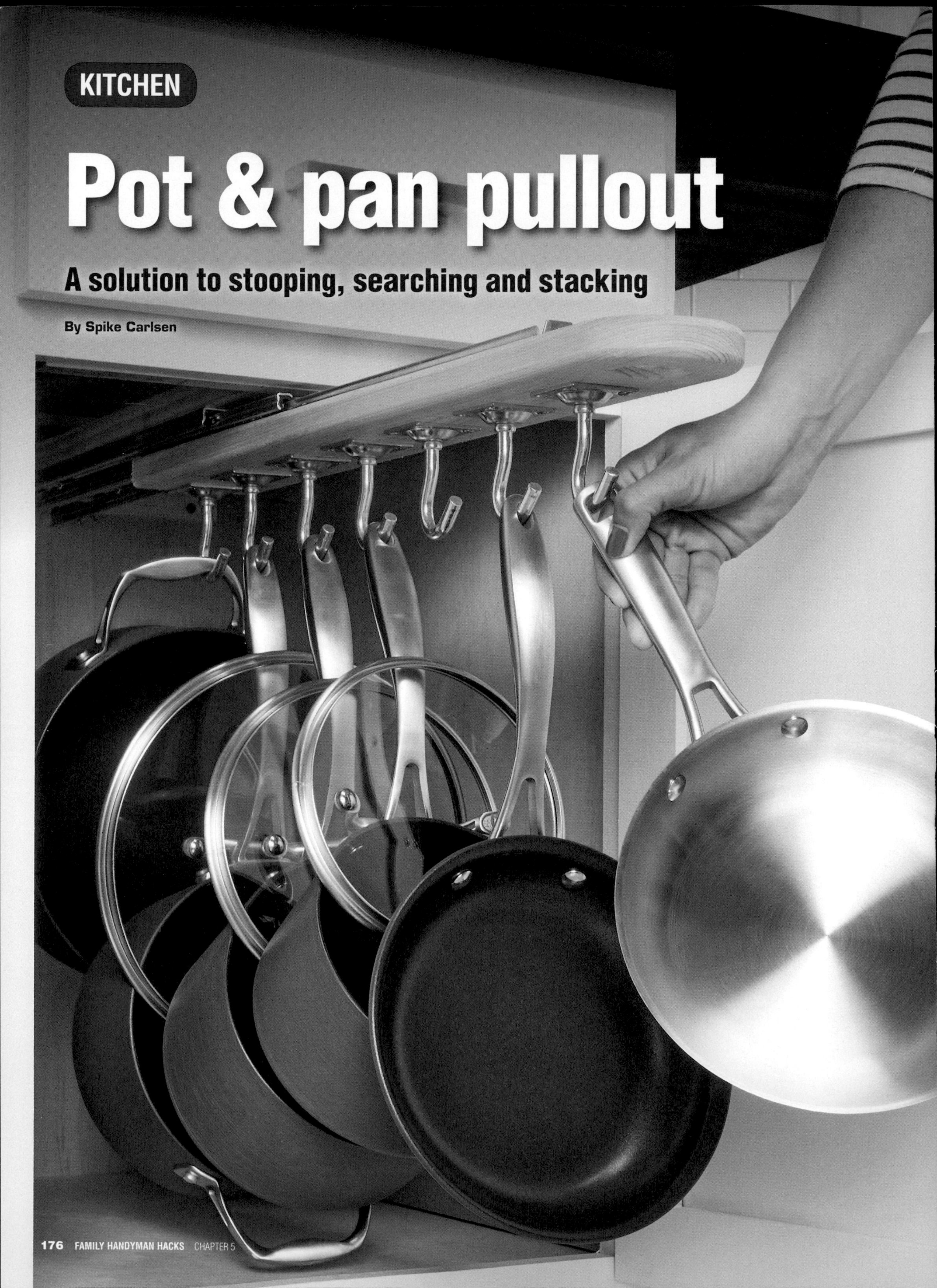

The only time our pots and pans were truly organized was when they were new in the box—since then, it's been "every pan for itself." Pots and pans are difficult to organize; if you stack them up, it's a hassle getting to the bottom ones. If you spread them out, they take up tons of valuable cabinet space.

This pot and pan pullout makes your pans easy to access and organize and—depending on your cookware—may even give you a place to stash your lids. It only takes a couple of hours, a couple of boards and a couple of drawer slides. Note: This accessory is designed to support everyday pots and pans, not extremely heavy objects or kids doing pull-ups.

FACE FRAME

1 Measure the cabinet Measure the depth of the cabinet from the back to the *inside* of the face frame. This measurement determines the overall length of the H-frame.

SUPPORT SLAT

CROSS ARM

2 Build the H-frame Screw the cross arms to the support slat. Predrill holes and countersink screw heads to prevent splitting.

3 **Mount the drawer slides** Screw the slides into place with the back ends even with the back of the H–frame.

SLIDES ARE EVEN WITH H-FRAME

How to build it

Empty your cabinet and measure the depth of the cabinet **(Photo 1)**. Build the H-shape frame **(Photo 2)**. The frame needs to be the same length as the inside depth of the cabinet, in our case 23 in. We cut our 1x4 support slat 21-1/2 in. long (two 3/4-in.-thick arms plus the 21-1/2-in. slat equals 23 in.). Predrill screw holes in the cross arms and bore countersink holes to accommodate the heads.

Screw on the two slides **(Photo 3)**. Cut the carrier the same length as the depth of your cabinet. Flip the assembly over and attach the carrier as shown in **Photo 4**.

4 **Screw the slides to the carrier** Cut the carrier to length, round the end and bore a finger hole, and then soften the edges with sandpaper or a router. Align the carrier with the back end of the slides.

MOUNT CARRIER FLUSH WITH EXTENDED SLIDES

CARRIER

Install the hooks **(Photo 5)**; we used beefy "clothesline hooks." You may want to use shorter or skinnier hooks and space them differently, depending on the sizes of your pans.

Attach the H-frame in the center of the cabinet opening **(Photo 6)**. Load up your pots and pans; you may want to readjust the spacing of your hooks based on how the pans fit. Then get cooking.

5 **Add the hooks** Secure the hooks to the carrier. Fiddle around with your pots and pans beforehand to determine the most efficient spacing.

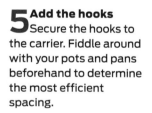

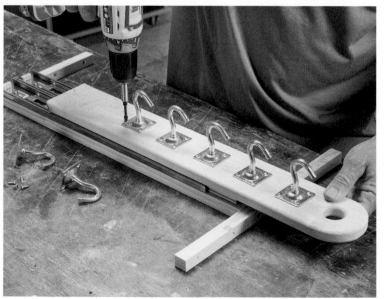

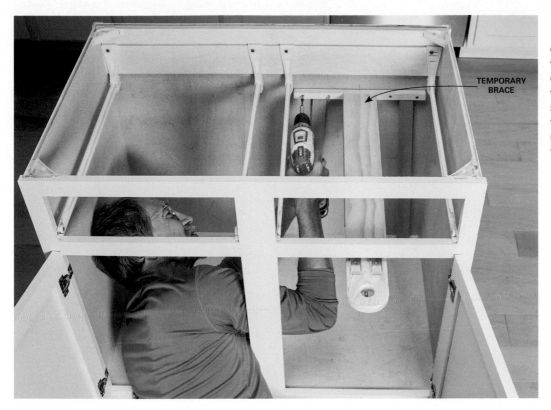

6 **Install it!** Position the bottom of the cross arm even with the top of the cabinet opening and attach it with screws. Then secure the back end at the same elevation, using temporary braces to prop it up.

TEMPORARY BRACE

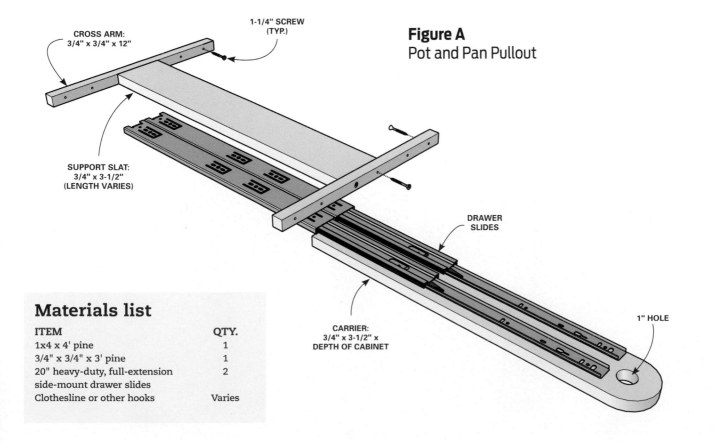

CROSS ARM:
3/4" x 3/4" x 12"

1-1/4" SCREW
(TYP.)

Figure A
Pot and Pan Pullout

SUPPORT SLAT:
3/4" x 3-1/2"
(LENGTH VARIES)

DRAWER
SLIDES

CARRIER:
3/4" x 3-1/2" x
DEPTH OF CABINET

1" HOLE

Materials list

ITEM	QTY.
1x4 x 4' pine	1
3/4" x 3/4" x 3' pine	1
20" heavy-duty, full-extension side-mount drawer slides	2
Clothesline or other hooks	Varies

One-hour drawer organizer

Our kitchen drawers used to have pans crammed in however they'd fit. And it always seemed like the one we needed was at the bottom of the pile. This simple drawer organizer makes everything neat and easily accessible.

To make one, cut a piece of 1/8-in. pegboard to fit into the bottom of the drawer. Next, cut 1/2-in.-diameter dowels 6 to 8 in. long. Drill pilot holes in the dowel ends, and then attach them in rows from underneath using 1-in. screws. I used three dowels per row to accommodate any size pan. — **Spike Carlsen**

DOWEL

PEGBOARD

Trash-bag dispenser

You can build a simple dispenser for your trash bags using 1/2-in. pipe and a few fittings. Screw a floor flange to the cabinet, thread in a 3-in.-long pipe nipple, and then thread a 90-degree elbow onto the nipple. Cut the vertical pipe so it's a bit longer than the width of the roll of bags. Thread the vertical piece into the elbow and slip on the roll.

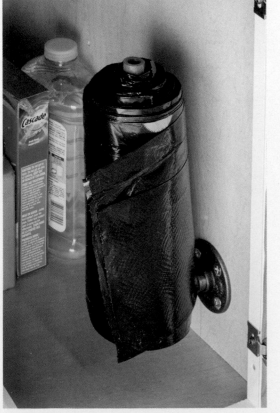

Gutter shelves

Vinyl rain gutters are fairly inexpensive and great for storing small items. They come in 10-ft.-long sections, so you can cut them up with a power miter saw or hacksaw and make several shelves out of them. Just snap an end cap on each end, drill a couple of holes and attach them to your cabinets with wood screws and finish washers. For heavier stuff, attach them with fascia gutter brackets, which you'll find at the home center right next to the gutters.

Cabinet Dividers

Adjustable slots organize cookware for space-efficient storage

By Spike Carlsen

Cookie sheets, cutting boards, cooling racks, serving trays, pizza peels... Most of us have a disorderly pile of large, flat cookware—and the thing we need is always at the bottom of the stack. This simple system of dividers brings order to the chaos. It requires minimal skills and materials and goes together fast, which allows you to spend more time cooking and less time searching and sorting.

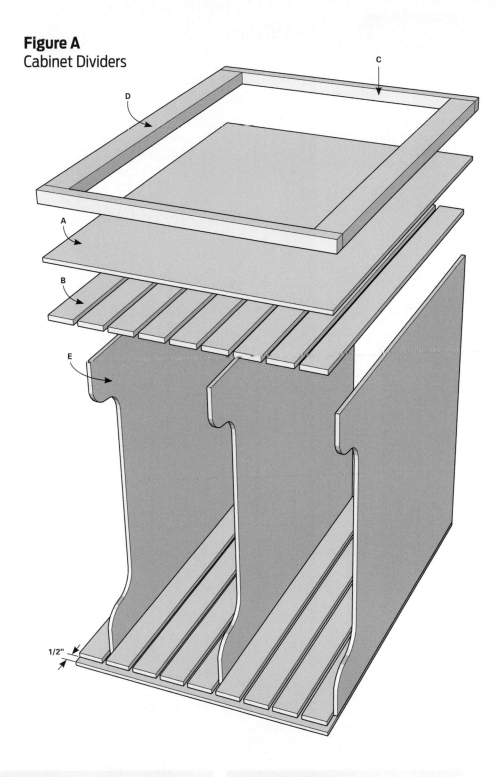

Figure A
Cabinet Dividers

Cutting list

KEY	QTY.	MATERIAL	PART
A	2	1/4" plywood*	Top/bottom panels
B	10–20**	3/8" x 1-1/2"	Slats (mull strip)*
C	2	3/4" x 3/4" pine*	Frame front/back
D	2	3/4" x 1-1/2" pine*	Frame sides
E	4–6**	1/4" plywood*	Divider panels

Notes:
*Dimensions determined by cabinet width and length
**Quantity determined by cabinet width

Materials list

ITEM	QTY.
1/4" x 4' x 8' AC or better plywood	1
3/4" x 3/4" x 4' pine	1
3/4" x 1-1/2" x 4' pine	1
3/8" x 1-1/2" x 8' mull strip, available in the trim aisle at home centers	Varies

1 Measure inside

Measure the width and depth inside the cabinet. Subtract 1/8 in. from those measurements and cut the top and bottom panels to that size.

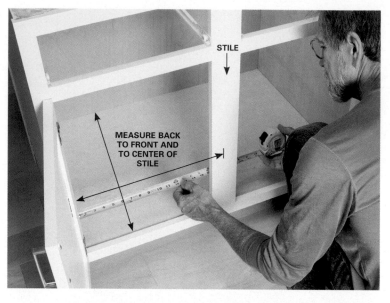

STILE

MEASURE BACK TO FRONT AND TO CENTER OF STILE

2 Tack the slats to the panels

Fasten the slats with glue and 1/2-in. brads. Space the slats with a scrap of 1/4-in. plywood and a credit card.

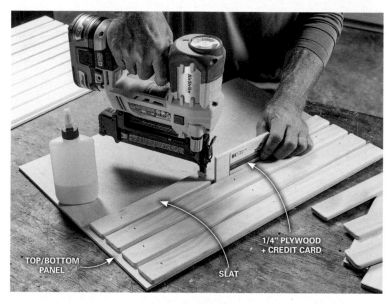

TOP/BOTTOM PANEL

1/4" PLYWOOD + CREDIT CARD

SLAT

3 Assemble the top frame

Build a frame the exact dimensions of the top/bottom panels. This frame provides a mounting surface for the top panel.

How to build it

Measure the width and depth of your cabinet **(Photo 1)**, then cut two 1/4-in. plywood panels (A) to fit. If you have a double-wide cabinet (like ours), cut the plywood so it extends at least halfway beyond the vertical center stile. Tip: If you have a double cabinet, you can cut the plywood extra wide, install the divider strips, then cut the plywood to final width so you wind up with full-width divider strips on both ends.

Cut the slats (B) 1/2 in. shorter than the plywood and use a sander or sandpaper to lightly round the ends. Glue and nail the divider slats into place **(Photo 2)**, using a scrap piece of 1/4-in. plywood and an old credit card as spacers; this extra wiggle room will allow you to slide the divider panels in and out more easily. To prevent brad nails from poking through the plywood, adjust the depth setting of your nailer and drive brads at a slight angle.

Build the top frame (C and D) the exact size of your plywood panels **(Photo 3)** and predrill the mounting holes on each end. Install this frame with the bottom edge even with the top of the cabinet opening **(Photo 4)**. Screw the front in place first. Before screwing the back, make sure it's at exactly the same height as the front.

Attach the panels (A) to the bottom of the cabinet **(Photo 5)** and to the upper frame. Measure between the panels to determine the height of the dividers (E). Cut one divider panel to size **(Photo 6)** then "test slide" it through several of the openings. If all the openings are equal, use your first divider panel as a template for cutting out the remaining ones **(Photo 6)**. We created a 2-in. indent on the end of the divider panels to allow easier access to the trays and other items stored between them.

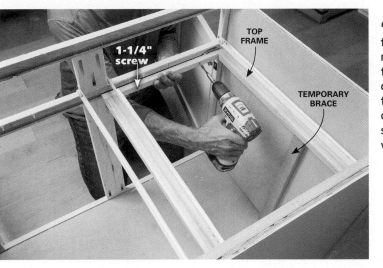

4 **Install the top frame** Screw the frame to the cabinet, making the bottom edge flush with the top of the cabinet opening. Have the frame propped up with a couple braces cut from scrap wood while you work.

5 **Install the top and bottom panels** Secure the panels to the cabinet bottom and to the upper frame using nails or screws.

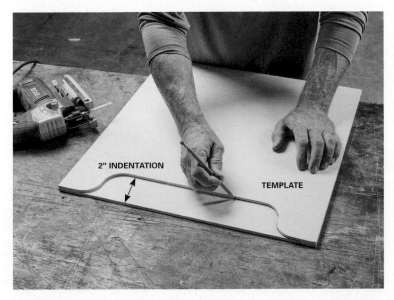

6 **Measure, cut and install the divider panels** Cut one panel to size, then test-fit it in several of the openings. Use that panel as a template for making the remaining divider panels.

Wine rack towel holder

If you have very little space to store fresh towels in your bathroom, use a wine rack. The wall over the toilet is pretty much wasted space, and the wine rack fits there perfectly. Plus, it looks really cool!

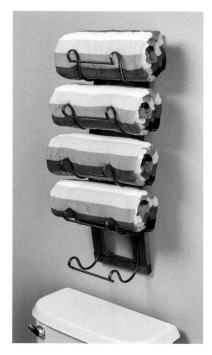

Under-sink archives

Don't file away the manuals for your kitchen and bath fixtures. Instead, slip them into a zip-top plastic bag and hang the bag in the cabinet under the sink. They'll always be right where you need them. Toss in paint samples and spare cabinet hardware too.

His-and-hers shower shelves

If you need more than shampoo and a bar of soap in the shower, here's how to provide space for all your vital beauty potions: Get a couple of those shelves that are designed to hang from a shower arm and hang them on cabinet knobs. Use No. 8-32 hanger screws to screw the knobs into studs or drywall anchors.

Easy storage for hair appliances

This PVC wye fitting looks like it was designed to store hair appliances! The 4-in. opening is perfect for a hair dryer, and the 2-in. one is just the right size to hold a curling iron or straightener. The fitting is stable enough to sit on a vanity top without tipping over. If you don't like the look, either spray-paint it or mount it inside a cabinet with a couple of screws.

WYE FITTING

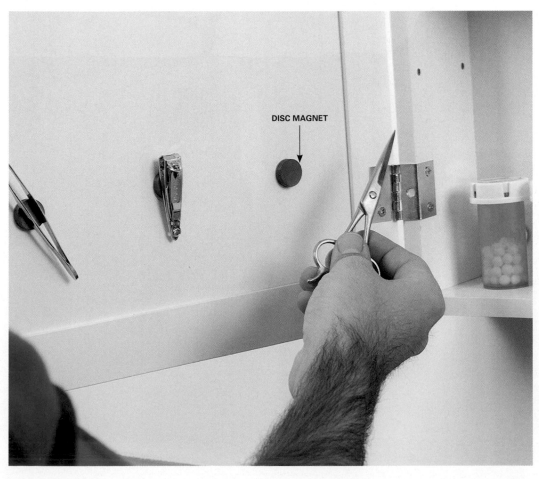

Medicine cabinet magnets

Nail clippers and tweezers tend to get buried in the medicine cabinet. So hot-glue a few magnets to the back of the cabinet door to hang these small items in plain sight. Use cheap disc magnets from the hobby store; the more expensive rare-earth magnets are too strong.

DISC MAGNET

Kitchen tray in the bathroom

A silverware drawer insert works just as well in the bathroom as it does in the kitchen. The various compartments are perfect for organizing toothbrushes, toothpaste, razors, clippers, lip balm and more.

SILVERWARE TRAY

Toilet paper shelf

Create a practical toilet paper cubby and shelf with a deep "shadow box" picture frame from a craft store. All you need to do is paint it (we used white enamel) and hang it around your toilet paper holder. It provides two convenient shelves for small items.

Under-sink organizer

To tame the clutter under your bathroom sink, make this organizer from scraps of 3-in. PVC. Cut the pipe into short lengths and then glue them to 1/2-in. plywood with polyurethane construction adhesive. Space the pipe pieces to accommodate liquid soaps, shampoos and other bottles and leave spaces between the pipe sections for odd-shaped spray bottles. Now things will be organized and they don't topple over every time you reach for something.

Expand bathroom storage with shelves

In a small bathroom, every single square inch counts. These shelves make the most of wall space by going vertical. The version shown here, made of cherry, cost about $100. But you can build one for less if you choose a more economical wood like oak or pine. All you need is a 6-ft. 1x4, a 6-ft. 1x6 and a 6-ft. 1x8.

Cut the middle spacers and the shelves 12 in. long. Cut the bottom spacer 11 in. long to allow for a decorative 1-in. reveal. Cut the top spacer to fit (the one shown was 7-1/4 in.). Measure 1 in. from one edge of the backboard and draw a guideline for the shelves and spacers along its length. Nail the bottom spacer in place, leaving a 1-in. reveal at the bottom edge. Center the first shelf by measuring 3-1/4 in. in from the edge of the backboard and nail it in place. Work your way up the backboard, alternating between spacers and shelves **(Photo 1)**.

On the back side, use a 1/8-in. countersink bit to drill two holes, one at the top and one at the bottom of each spacer. Drill two holes spaced 1 in. from each side of the backboard into each shelf ledge. Drive 1-1/4-in. drywall screws into each hole **(Photo 2)**. Paint or stain the assembled unit. If you'd like to clearcoat it, use a wipe-on poly or spray lacquer—using a brush would be really tough. Mount the unit on the wall with two 2-1/2-in. screws and screw-in drywall anchors. Drive the screws where they won't be seen: right below the bottom shelf and right above the top shelf.

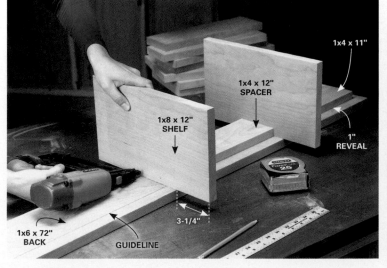

1 Nail the spacers and shelves in place, starting at the bottom and working your way up. Place the bottom spacer 1 in. from the lower edge of the backboard.

2 Strengthen the shelves by driving screws through the backboard into the shelves and spacers. Drill screw holes with a countersink bit.

We step into our bathrooms every morning to get ready for the day. We pull out hair dryers, curling irons and trimmers, untangle their cords and fumble around for the outlet to plug them in. Then we unplug them and stuff them in a drawer, just to untangle them all again the next morning. What a waste of time! But this cabinet rollout has built-in outlets to eliminate those hassles and get you on your way.

Plugged-in bathroom storage

Your gear is always ready to go!

By Mike Berner

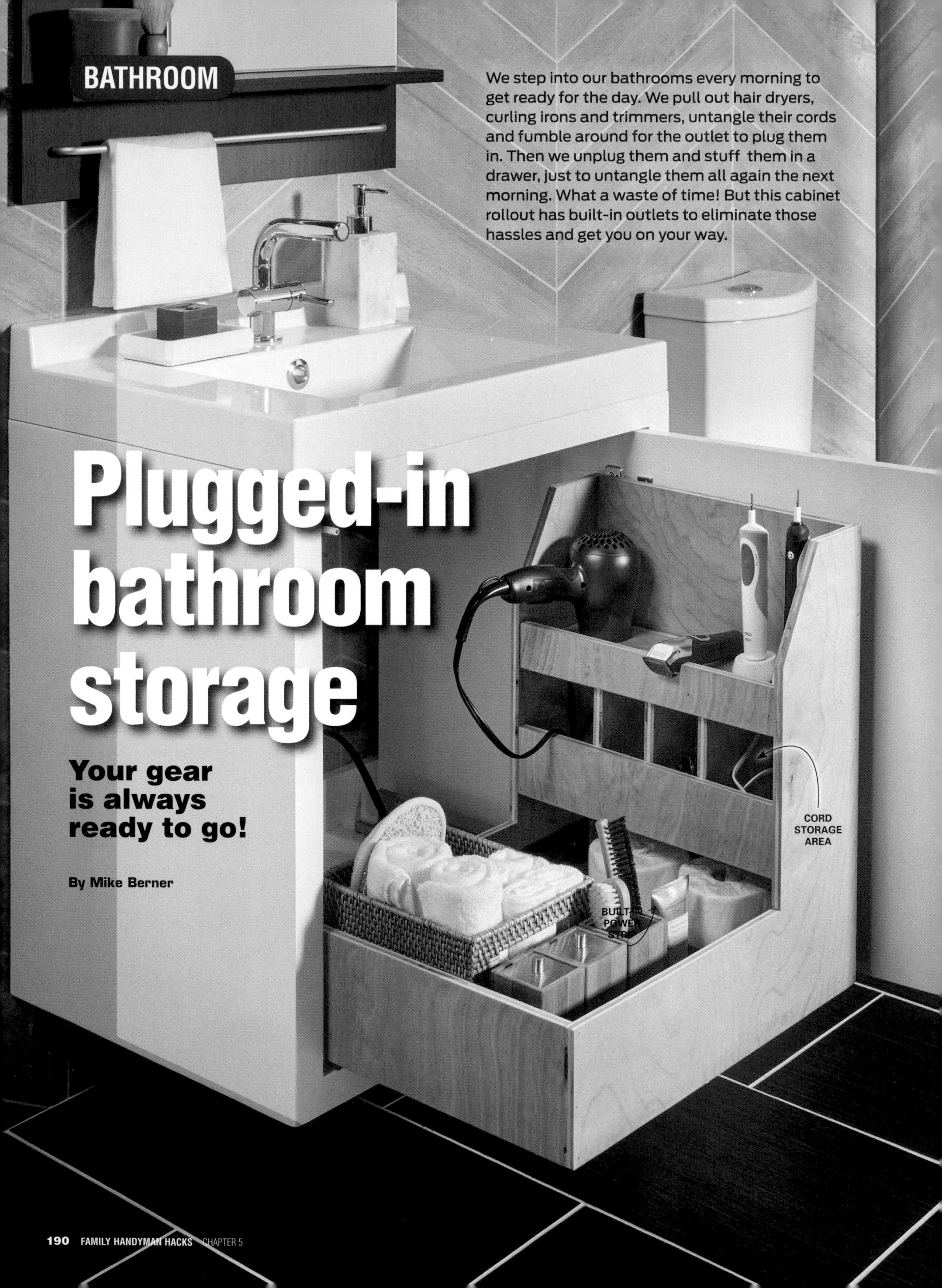

CORD STORAGE AREA

BUILT-IN POWER STRIP

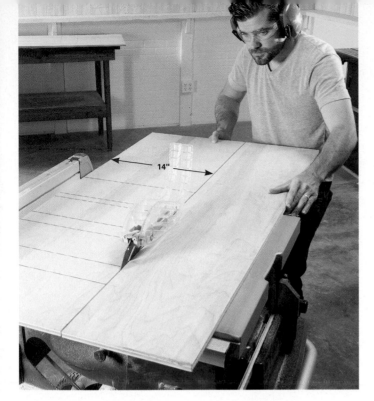

1 Start with two rip cuts Set the table saw fence to 19 in. to cut the width of the drawer front and back pieces. Then make another rip at 14 in. for the drawer sides and shelf parts. This approach keeps similar parts the exact same length and helps keep the drawer square and easy to assemble. Crosscut the front, back and tall side at 20 in., then crosscut the remaining parts.

2 Cut the front and back You can cut the front and back of the L-shaped drawer with a jigsaw or circular saw. But here's how to make straighter cuts using a table saw: Mark the cutouts on both sides of the front and back. Set the fence to 6 in. to make the first cut for the depth of the shelf. When you're 3 in. from the end of the cut, stop, turn the saw off and wait for the blade to stop. Do the same with the second part, then flip both parts, set your fence to 5-3/4 in. and make the second cut the same way. Finish the cuts with a handsaw or jigsaw.

3 Size the bottom Cut the grooves as shown in Figure A. Glue and nail the front and one side together. Slide the bottom into the grooves and mark 5/16 in. inside the front of the drawer and 3/16 in. beyond the side. Then adjust the fence to the marks and cut the bottom to size. Glue and nail the sides, front, and back together, leaving the bottom panel floating in the grooves.

4 Fit the power strip Find a spot where there will be enough room for the drawer to close once the power strip is installed. Trace the power strip on your drawer, then drill a 1/4-in.-diameter hole in each corner. Fit a jigsaw blade into one of the holes and connect the holes. Insert the power strip and secure it with two screws.

Figure A
Powered vanity rollout

OVERALL DIMENSIONS:
20" High x 19" Wide x 15" Deep

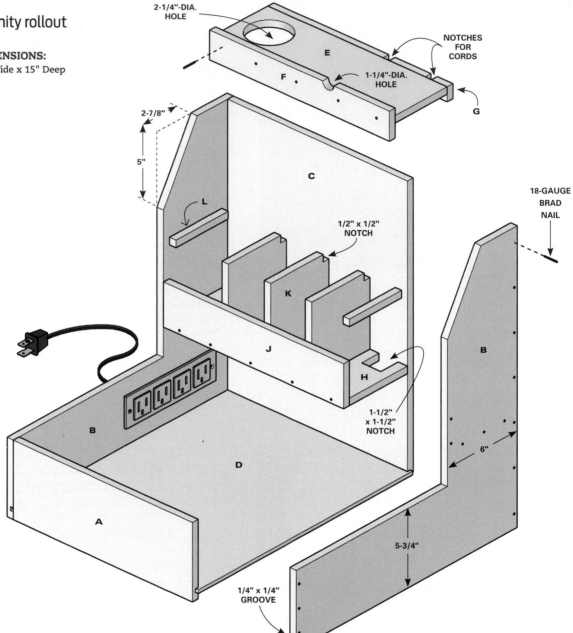

2-1/4"-DIA. HOLE

NOTCHES FOR CORDS

1-1/4"-DIA. HOLE

G

E

F

2-7/8"

5"

L

C

1/2" x 1/2" NOTCH

K

18-GAUGE BRAD NAIL

B

J

H

B

6"

1-1/2" x 1-1/2" NOTCH

B

D

5-3/4"

A

1/4" x 1/4" GROOVE

1/2"

Cutting list

KEY	NAME	DIMENSIONS
A	Drawer side	1/2" x 5-3/4" x 14"
B	Drawer front/back	1/2" x 20" x 19"
C	Drawer side	1/2" x 20" x 14"
D	Bottom	1/4" x 18-7/16" x 14-7/16"
E	Shelf	1/2" x 4-1/2" x 14"
F	Shelf front	1/2" x 2" x 14"
G	Shelf back	1/2" x 1" x 14"
H	Cord shelf	1/2" x 5" x 14"
J	Cord shelf front	1/2" x 3" x 14"
K	Cord dividers	1/2" x 5" x 5-1/4"
L	Shelf cleats	1/2" x 1/2" x 4-1/2"

Materials list

One sheet of 1/2" x 4' x 8' birch plywood
(it's more economical to buy a full sheet)
One sheet of 1/4" x 2' x 4' birch plywood
UL-listed furniture power strip
BLUM Tandem Plus drawer slides
18-gauge 1" brad nails
Polyurethane

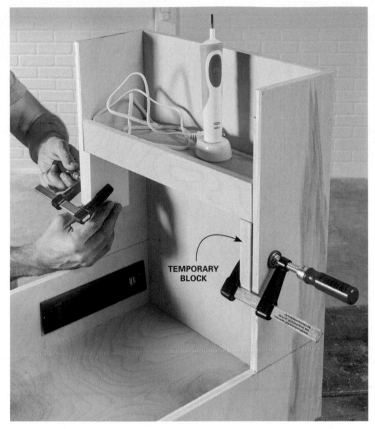

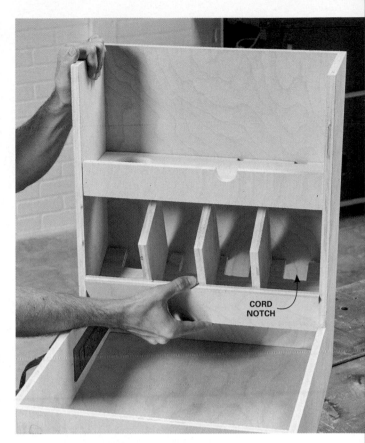

5 **Customize the shelf** Determine the height of the shelf by placing the tallest appliance on it and adjusting it up and down to fit. Clamp blocks against the drawer to hold it in place, then mark its position and glue and nail the shelf cleats into place. Use the appliances to map out where and how they will be held. I used a 2-1/4-in. hole saw to make a hair dryer holster and a 1-1/4-in. Forstner bit to cut a half-moon shape for my beard trimmer. I made notches for the charging cords with a pull saw and a chisel.

6 **Build storage for your cords** The cord storage shelf separates each set of cords so they don't get tangled. The dividers are spaced between the appliances and fastened with glue and 18-gauge brad nails. I cut 1-1/2-in. square notches for the plugs with a jigsaw to provide a path for the plugs to get to the power strip. The removable appliance shelf allows easy access to the cords when needed, and the opening in front lets you shove cords in when they're not in use.

Choose the right power strip

The power strip you choose should be UL-listed for this specific purpose. I used a furniture power strip that has a switch to cut the power when the appliances aren't in use. It's UL-listed to be attached to furniture and plugged into a permanent receptacle. I found it online for $21.

7 Cut notches for the slides Flip the drawer over, hook the slides over the side lip on the bottom and mark where each slide meets the back. Use a handsaw, coping saw or jigsaw to cut the notches to fit the slides. The notches should be 1/2 in. deep and flush with the inside edge of the drawer.

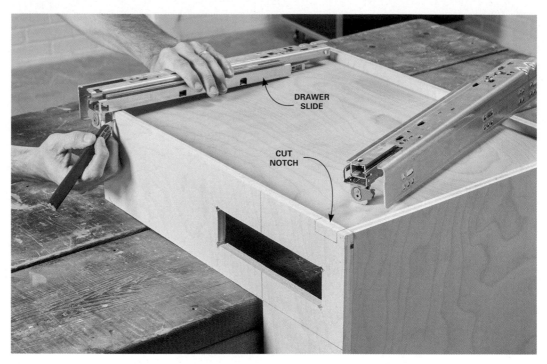

DRAWER SLIDE

CUT NOTCH

Adding an outlet under the sink

This project requires an outlet inside the vanity. If there's power above your sink that shares a stud bay inside your vanity, it's an easy job. First switch off the power to the circuit at the electrical panel. Remove the existing outlet and send a few feet of cable to a new single-gang box behind the vanity and make the connections to a new outlet. If there's a stud between the old outlet and the spot for the new one, the job becomes more complicated. To learn more, search for "add an outlet" at familyhandyman.com.

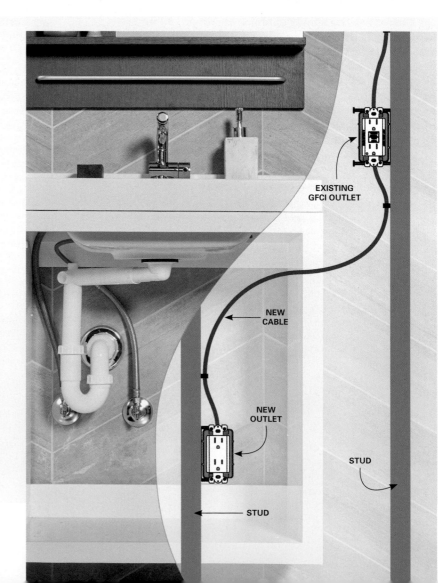

EXISTING GFCI OUTLET

NEW CABLE

NEW OUTLET

STUD

STUD

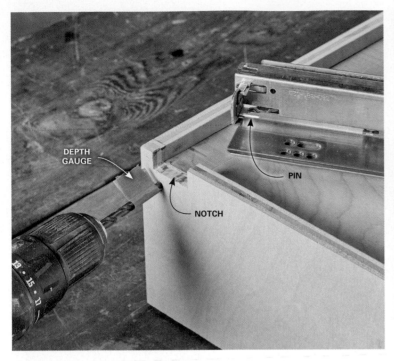

8 **Drill the pin hole** The pin that keeps the drawer slide in place requires a 1/4-in.-diameter hole. Put the slide in place and mark the back of the drawer where the pin hits. Drill a hole just deep enough to fit the pin without going through the back. Then apply your choice of finish to the drawer.

9 **Fasten the locking devices** Fit the locking devices into the front corners on the underside of the drawer. Drill angled pilot holes for the screws and fasten the devices in place. The locking devices hold the drawer on the slides and allow you to easily remove the drawer.

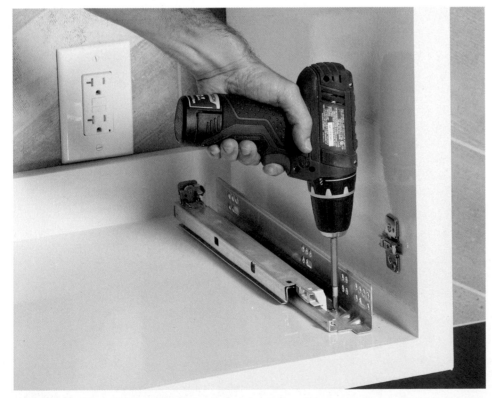

10 **Attach the slides** Screw the first slide to the side of the cabinet opposite the hinges, then measure the inside of the drawer and add 1-5/8 in. to determine the location of the second slide. Draw a parallel line and screw the slide to the bottom of the cabinet inside the line.

Don't fear fancy drawer slides

I used Blum Tandem Plus drawer slides ($32 online), which can be mounted to the side or bottom of a cabinet. They're completely hidden when the drawer is open, which gives it a high-end look. They're much easier to install than they look. You'll need to build the drawer to match the length of the slides, which require a 1/2-in. recess underneath the drawer. I chose the 15-in. slides to fit into the 18-in.-deep vanity and allow room for the inset door and the power strip.

Beautiful built-in cabinet

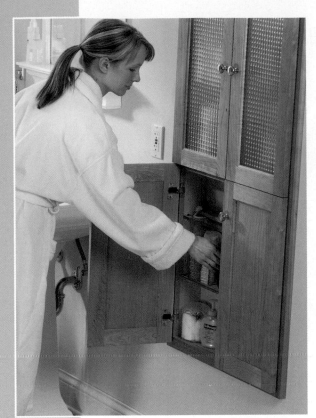

Create the perfect space to keep all your bath products organized and easy to reach

By Jeff Gorton

If you're short on bathroom storage space, this built-in cabinet could be just the ticket. It's large and spacious, yet the shallow depth allows easy viewing and access to all of the contents. No more digging around in drawers or the dark corners of linen closets to find what you need. And since it's recessed into the wall, you won't lose any valuable floor space.

This project is a great introduction to basic cabinet-building skills. It's a simple box with a face frame attached to the front. You buy the doors in the style that best fits your bathroom décor and mount them to the face frame. We ordered the doors complete with 35mm holes to accept the concealed "euro-style" hinges. These hinges are great for novice cabinetmakers because they allow you to adjust the doors for a perfect fit.

We'll walk you through the entire cabinet assembly process. Then we'll show you how to cut a hole in your wall and safely remove a stud to create a recessed space for the cabinet. Even with little woodworking experience, you should be able to complete the cabinet in a day. Applying the finish and installing the cabinet will take another five or six hours.

You could cut the cabinet sides and face frame parts with a circular saw and saw guide, but you'll get tighter-fitting joints if you use a power miter saw or a table saw with a miter gauge. We used a pocket hole jig and pocket screws to assemble the face frame pieces and attach it to the box. If you don't own a pocket hole jig, glue and nail the face frame to the cabinet box with finish nails.

We ordered these cherry cabinet doors and received them in about three weeks (see the Buyer's Guide on p. 205 for ordering information). Oak doors would be less expensive than cherry. We ordered the patterned glass and glass shelves from a local glass company. The Blum Compact 33 hinges and mounting plates are available online. We've listed sources in the Buyer's Guide.

1 Cut the cabinet box pieces (A and B) to length. Mark the location of the center divider on the side pieces and drill screw-clearance holes. Also drill holes for the adjustable shelf supports using a pegboard jig.

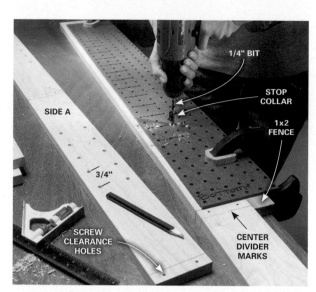

SIDE A

1/4" BIT

STOP COLLAR

1x2 FENCE

3/4"

SCREW CLEARANCE HOLES

CENTER DIVIDER MARKS

2 Screw the sides to the top and bottom through the predrilled clearance holes. Then line up the middle horizontal divider with the marks and screw it in.

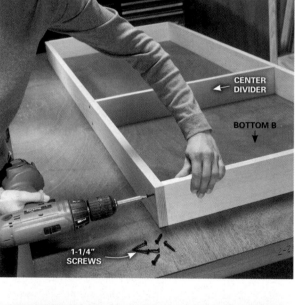

CENTER DIVIDER

BOTTOM B

1-1/4" SCREWS

3 Align one edge of the 1/4-in. plywood back with the side of the cabinet. Predrill the screw holes and screw it into place with 1-in. screws. Then square the cabinet and screw the other three edges and center divider.

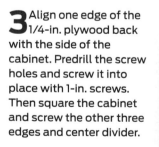

1/4" PLYWOOD BACK

1" SCREWS

Choose the cabinet location carefully

Before you order doors or start building the cabinet, make sure you have a good spot to install the cabinet. Exterior walls are out. There's likely to be insulation in them, and there may be structural issues to deal with as well. Look for a space that's about 26 in. wide and 68 in. high. After you've found a potential location, use a stud finder to locate the studs, then mark them with masking tape. Position the cabinet so that you only have to remove one stud. You can put your cabinet at any height. The top of our cabinet lines up with the door, 80 in. above the floor.

Then make sure the spot you chose doesn't have any hidden obstructions. The easiest method is to cut two 6-in. square inspection holes in the drywall, one on each side of the stud you'll be removing. Then look in with a flashlight to make sure there aren't any electrical wires, plumbing pipes or heat ducts in the way. A less invasive but also less thorough method is to poke a bent wire clothes hanger through a hole in the wall and probe around. You'll have to do this in several places, though. If space is tight, you may have to adjust the cabinet dimensions to fit it in. When you've found a location, order the doors and hinges. If the door sizes are different from ours, adjust the cabinet sizes to fit them. The doors overlap the face frame 3/4 in. on all sides.

Build the box first

Start by cutting the 1x4 cabinet sides (A), and top, center and bottom (B) to length. Then use a square to mark the location of the center divider on the sides **(Photo 1)**. Drill 5/32-in. screw-clearance holes through the sides at these marks and at the top and bottom. Complete the side pieces by drilling the shelf pin holes. Make a drilling jig by screwing a 1x2 fence to a strip of pegboard (make sure the pegboard has 1/4-in. holes). Position the edge of the 1x2 fence 3/4 in. from the center of the first row of holes. Use a 1/4-in. brad point bit to drill the holes. Tighten a drill stop collar onto the bit to limit the depth of the holes to the thickness of the pegboard plus 1/2 in. Notice that we skipped every other set of holes to create holes that are 2 in. apart. Be careful to mark the bottom of the jig and align it the same for both sides to ensure that the holes line up.

Screw the sides to the top, bottom and middle piece with 1-1/4 in. screws **(Photo 2)**. Then cut 1/4-in. plywood for the back and attach it with 1-in. screws **(Photo 3)**. Make sure the plywood back is perfectly square. Then align the cabinet edges with it to square the cabinet.

Assemble the face frame and attach it to the cabinet box

Start with 1x2s that are milled accurately with square edges. Home centers and lumberyards usually stock a few species of hardwood 1x2s, but cherry may be a little harder to find. Check hardwood lumber suppliers or call a local cabinetmaker to find a source. Sight down the boards to make sure they're perfectly straight. Then use a miter saw or table saw to cut the pieces to length, making sure the end cuts are perfectly square. Arrange the face frame parts with the best-looking face down and make a pencil mark on the back of each piece. Using a pocket hole jig with a stepped drill bit, drill a pair of holes in both ends of the rails **(Photo 4)**. Drill on the back, or marked, side. Complete the face frame by clamping the joints one at a time and joining them with 1-1/4 in. pocket screws **(Photo 5)**. If you haven't used a pocket hole jig before, practice on scrap wood. You'll quickly get the hang of it.

Drill pocket holes around the outside of the cabinet box and attach the face frame with pocket screws **(Photo 6)**. The face frame is sized to overlap the interior of the cabinet box by 1/8 in. Make sure this overlap is even all the way around, then clamp it before you attach the face frame. If you don't own a pocket hole jig, you can nail the face frame to the box with 6d finish nails and fill the holes later with putty in a matching color.

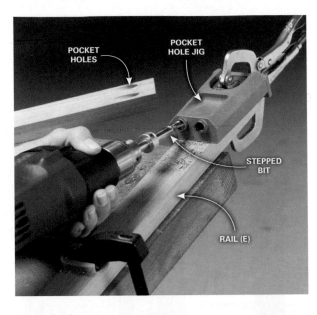

4 Cut the face frame parts to length (D and E; Figure A). Drill pocket screw holes on the back side of the rails (E) with a special stepped bit and pocket hole jig.

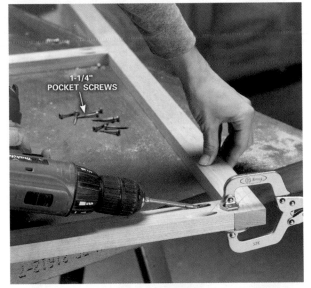

5 Align the face frame parts (D and E). Clamp them and join them with pocket screws.

6 Drill pocket screw holes on the outside of the cabinet box (parts A and B). Center the frame on the cabinet box (it should overlap the inside 1/8 in.), clamp it and attach it with pocket screws.

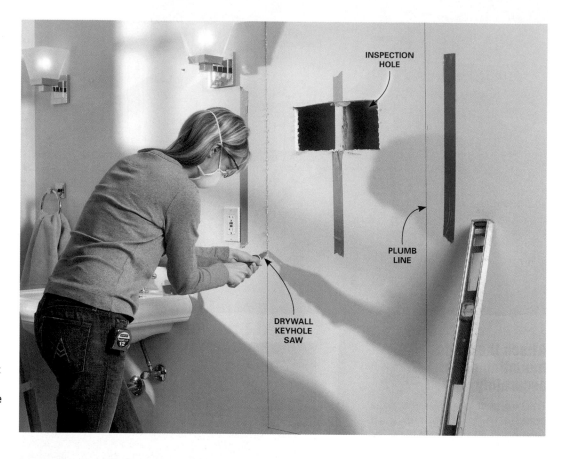

INSPECTION HOLE

PLUMB LINE

DRYWALL KEYHOLE SAW

10 Mark the cutout dimensions on the wall. Cut along the lines with a drywall keyhole saw.

CUT THROUGH STUD

3-3/4"

11 Draw horizontal lines 3-3/4 in. above and 1-1/2 in. below the opening at the stud location. Cut through the stud at these lines with a reciprocating saw or handsaw. Also cut the stud in the middle to simplify removal.

Cut the hole for the cabinet

In most cases, you'll have to remove a stud to make a wide enough opening **(Photos 10–12)**. **Photos 13 and 14** show how to add a header to support the cutoff stud. The metal angle brackets support the new header. The sill and side pieces aren't structural but provide backing for the drywall and a place to attach the cabinet.

Use a level and pencil to mark the cutout dimensions on the wall **(Photo 10)**. Mark the outline 1/4 in. taller and wider than the cabinet box dimensions. Cut the drywall along the lines with a drywall saw and break it out.

The next step is to cut out the stud to make room for the header **(Photos 11 and 12)**. Make a short level line 3-3/4 in. above the top of the cutout opening and centered over the stud. This is where you'll cut the stud to allow room for the header to fit under it. Make a similar line 1-1/2 in. below the bottom of the cutout. Cut through the stud at each spot **(Photo 11)**. If you're careful to control the depth of the blade, you may be able to cut through the stud without cutting through the drywall on the opposite side. But don't worry. If you do cut through, the thin slot will be easy to patch.

Remove the cutout section of stud by hitting it hard with a hammer on the edge nearest you to twist the nails or screws loose from the drywall on the opposite side **(Photo 12)**. Measure the distance between the remaining wall studs and cut two 2x4s 3/16 in. shorter than the measurement. Build the 2x4 header by sandwiching scraps of 1/2-in. plywood or 1/2-in. strips of wood between the 2x4s and nailing them together with 12d nails. Slide the header up against the cutoff stud **(Photo 13)** and hold it temporarily in place with a screw through the drywall. Level the header and support it by screwing metal angle brackets (Simpson No. A-33) to the studs with Simpson Strong-Drive screws **(Photos 13 and 14)**. Cut a 2x4 the same length as the header for the sill, level it and attach it to the studs with 2-1/2 in. screws driven at an angle. Complete the framing by cutting 2x4s to fit between the header and sill on each side of the cabinet and securing them with angled 2-1/2 in. screws **(Photo 15)**. Predrill to keep the sides from slipping back too far **(Photo 15 inset)**.

Finish up by mounting the cabinet

It's easiest to sand and finish the cabinet before mounting it to the wall. Apply stain if you desire and three coats of polyurethane varnish. Then just slip the cabinet into the opening, level it, and screw it into the framing on each side **(Photo 16)**. Don't overtighten or you'll pull the frame out of square. Remount the doors and adjust the hinges so the spaces between the doors are even **(Photo 17)**. We ordered the top doors to accommodate 1/8-in. glass. They came with a clear plastic strip that we slid into a slot to hold the glass in place. Make sure to get recommendations from your door supplier for securing the glass in the door you order.

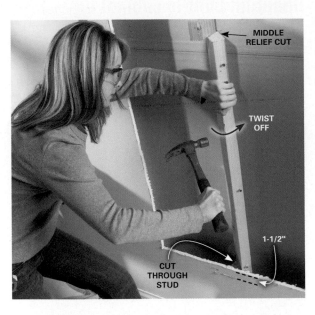

12 Pound on the corner of the cutoff stud to twist it away from the drywall. Pull it out of the opening.

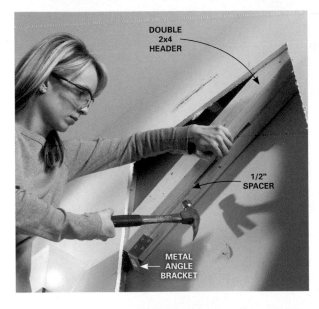

13 Nail together the double 2x4 header and screw a metal angle bracket to one end. Slide it into position against the cutoff stud, and level the header.

14 Screw the metal angle bracket to the stud. Screw another special angle bracket to the opposite end of the header and to the stud.

15 Nail a 2x4 sill to the cutoff stud. Level it and drive angled screws into the studs at each end. Cut 2x4s to fit between the header and the sill and fasten them even with the drywall edges with angled screws.

16 Slide the cabinet into the opening and level it. Secure it with trim screws driven through the sides into the framing. Conceal the screws by driving them into shelf pin holes.

Ordering cabinet doors

The advantage of building your own cabinet with custom-made doors is that you can choose any door style you want and have it made of oak, maple or cherry to match the existing cabinetry or woodwork in your house. The terminology for door styles can be a little confusing, though, so it's best to choose the style you like from pictures or illustrations provided by the door manufacturer. The manufacturer we used has illustrations on its site to help you choose. We chose cherry frame-and-panel doors with a flat plywood panel on the lower doors, and upper doors machined for glass panels. We ordered door frames with square outside edges and a 1/4-round

"bead" on the inside edge. Don't forget to ask the manufacturer to bore 35mm holes for the hinges. If you plan to use Blum Compact 33 hinges like ours, ask that 2-1/2 to 3mm be left from the edge of the door to the edge of the hole.

We measured the glass recess in the back of the upper cabinet doors after they arrived and deducted 1/8 in. from both the width and the height. Then we used this dimension to order the 1/8-in. thick cross-reeded glass from a local glass shop. Glass has to be tempered for safety within 2 ft. of a door or in a shower area. Expect to spend about four times as much for tempered glass.

17 Reinstall the doors and adjust them until the space between the doors is even. Loosen the base plate screws to move a door up and down. Loosen the hinge screw to adjust the doors sideways.

Editor's note

I've cut a lot of holes in walls over the years, and most of the time things have gone smoothly. But not always. I've accidentally cut electrical wires and plumbing pipes because I failed to check the wall cavity first. But the worst thing I remember is the thumping and tinkling sound made by dozens of collectible glass kitty cats as they fell off shelves and shattered on the floor in the adjoining room. That's right. I forgot to check the opposite side of the wall I was beating on. You can't be too careful when it comes to wall tearout.

— Jeff

Bath cabinet shopping list

ITEM	QTY.
1x4 x 6' birch or maple (A, B)	3
1x2 x 6' cherry (D, E)	3
4x8 x 1/4" birch plywood (C)	1
12" x 42" cabinet doors (F)	2
12" x 24" cabinet doors (G)	2
Pieces of patterned glass for doors	2
Blum No. 033.360NI Compact 33 face frame hinges	10
Blum No. 130.1100.22NI 3/4" overlay mounting plates	10
3-3/8" x 22-3/4" x 3/8" polished-edge glass shelves	5
Shelf supports	20
1-1/4" drywall or cabinet screws	12
1" drywall of cabinet screws	24
1-1/4" pocket screws	30
1-1/4" trim head screws (mount cabinet)	4
Cabinet handles	4
Polyurethane finish	1 qt.

Buyer's guide

Get Blum Compact 33 hinges (part No.B033.360NI) and mounting plates (part No. B130.1100.22NI) from Woodworker's Hardware (800-383-0130; wwhardware.com).

Buy the Kreg pocket hole kit and an extra pack of 1-1/4 in. pocket screws from amazon.com.

Order cabinet doors from Maple Craft USA at maplecraftusa or call 800-756-8077.

Customized garage

By Elisa Bernick

Create your own custom storage system in one weekend

You can drop a lot of cash on garage storage systems. Shelves, tool racks, special hooks, and other odds and ends can really add up. Our homemade system gives you the versatility of those store-bought systems without the big price tag. Our materials cost for the whole system you see here, covering 16 ft. of wall, was about $250. It'll be even cheaper if you have scrap plywood and other common materials lying around.

This system is so simple and fast to build that even a beginning DIYer can complete it in a weekend. You'll find everything you need at home centers or hardware stores. And the system is completely customizable to your specific garage and gear—you can easily move or add accessories by driving in a few screws. Transform your cluttered garage into one so organized you'll be the envy of the neighborhood.

Start with struts

Each of these storage accessories hangs from a simple framework of vertical struts, which are just 2x2s screwed to the garage wall studs. If you use struts, you can hang something on the wall without hunting for studs, and you can screw shelf brackets and accessory hangers to the sides of them. Of course, if you have bare stud walls, you can skip the struts. We used 2x2s rather than 2x4s because they cost slightly less and have fewer knots. Just be sure you screw them in every 16 in. for extra strength. Most home centers sell 2x2s in 8-ft. lengths.

Shorten or lengthen the struts to suit your garage. If you go with 6-footers like we did, you can use the leftover 2x2 scraps to build some of the accessories described here. It doesn't matter if the struts are centered 16 in. or 24 in. apart. Just make sure they're plumb by using a level.

wall

Screw 2x2 struts to each wall stud. Snap a chalk line to align the tops of the struts and mark the stud locations with masking tape. Drill pilot holes or use "self-drilling" screws to avoid splitting the struts.

TAPE MARKS STUD

CHALK LINE

2x2

Yard tool rack

Weed trimmers and leaf blowers can slide around if you prop them in a corner, and fall off the wall if you try to hang them from a hook. Solve the problem with this custom storage rack, which uses 3/4-in. plywood for the brackets, top and back. Cut two 8-in. x 11-in. brackets to support the top and back of the rack. Our rack is 34 in. long and 12 in. deep—customize the dimensions to fit your yard tools. To determine the best shape for your slots, measure the diameter of your tools and cut basic slots in the top of the rack. Then play with the shape of your slots to get a snug fit.

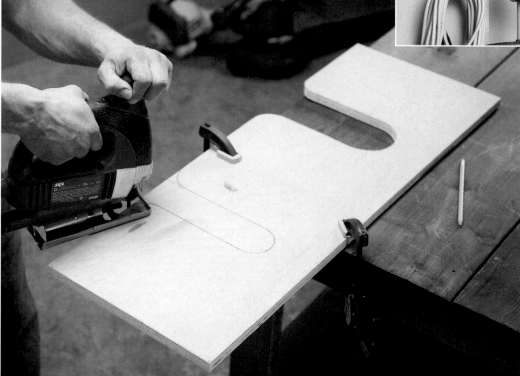

Cut basic slots in the top of the rack and test-fit the tool. Enlarge the slot or change its shape until the tool hangs securely.

Strong, low-cost hooks

Plumbing hooks are designed to support pipes, but they make great storage hooks too. We used them to hold ladders, sports gear and wheelbarrows. You can easily cut them to length if space is tight. They're sized for pipe ranging from 1/2 in. to 4 in. and cost 25¢ to 80¢ apiece.

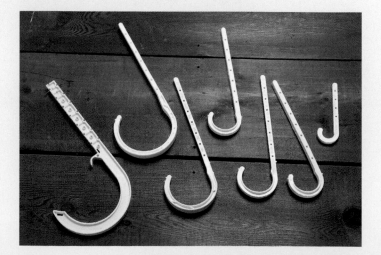

Shelf brackets

Metal shelf brackets seem inexpensive (around $1 each), but the cost can add up quickly if you're installing several shelves. So why not make free brackets from plywood scraps? We created a simple, flexible and inexpensive shelving system using 3/4-in. plywood brackets screwed to the vertical framework. We used 3/4-in. plywood rather than 1/2-in. because it gives you a wider surface to screw into when attaching the shelves to the brackets.

For shelves, we used 3/4-in. birch plywood, but you could use 1x12s or melamine-coated particleboard, or you

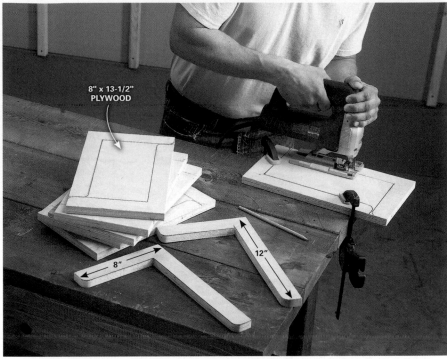

Cut shelf brackets from scrap plywood. Cut the scraps into rectangles first, using a table saw or circular saw. That keeps time-consuming jigsaw cuts to a minimum.

could edge-band the plywood for a more finished look. Screw a bracket at each strut to support the shelves. You can put shelving across the entire length of the wall or stack shorter shelves on top of each other (or do both, as we did). The 1-1/2-in.-wide brackets are surprisingly strong and will easily hold 100 lbs. or more.

Vinyl gutter storage bins

Ten-foot lengths of vinyl gutter screwed to the 2x2 framework are a perfect place to store long items like hockey sticks, fishing rods, dowels, wood trim and corner bead. Items like these often end up leaning against a wall or taking over an entire corner only to tumble over or get wrecked because they're not really supposed to be stored on end.

Shorter sections of vinyl gutter and sturdy window box liners (available at home and garden centers) attached the same way work well for storing hard-to-hang items like gloves, hose nozzles, fertilizer spikes and sprayers. And people who refuse to hang stuff back up on the wall can just toss it into the bin. If the gutter end caps don't fit snugly, apply PVC cement, silicone or gutter adhesive and press firmly.

Vinyl gutters are surprisingly sturdy —you can even store a few sections of rebar and metal pipe in them without a problem. Metal gutter is also an option. It's the same price, but it's harder to cut and too flimsy for heavier items.

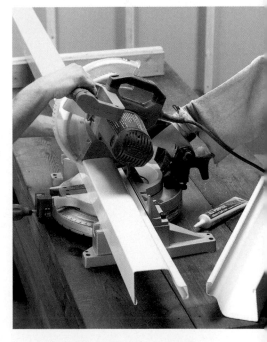

Cut vinyl gutter sections to length with a miter saw. You can use a handsaw, but you'll need to mark the cut carefully to get it square.

Long-handled tool storage

Typical brackets for storing long-handled tools stack the tools one on top of another. This is definitely an efficient use of wall space, but it's frustrating to move other tools out of the way to reach the one you're after. Or you end up devoting an entire wall to hooks that hang individual items.

Here's a better solution. Screw a pair of 3/4-in. plywood brackets to a chunk of scrap 2x2. Attach several 16d finish nails to the side of each bracket and screw the bracket assembly to the 2x2 framework. Drill holes into each of your tool handles, and you can easily hang and retrieve individual rakes and shovels without using up a lot of wall space.

**5/8"
COUNTERSINK
BIT**

Drill holes in your tool handles. Then taper the holes with a countersink bit so the tools will slip easily on and off nails.

Slip the bracket over the strut and screw it into place. Be sure to drive nails into the bracket's outside edge before you install it. Leave 1-1/2 in. of the nails exposed to hang tools.

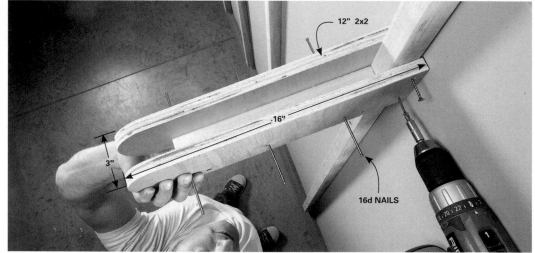

12" 2x2

16"

3"

16d NAILS

Wheelbarrow storage hub

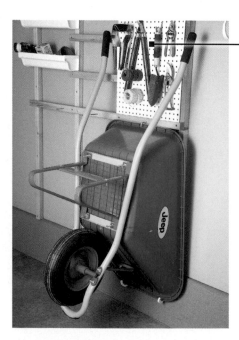

Here's a slick way to get your wheelbarrow off the garage floor: To start, screw two plumbing hooks to the wall (we used 1-1/2-in. hooks). Tilt the wheelbarrow onto the hooks and up against the wall. Drill a pilot hole and then drive in a screw hook to hold the wheelbarrow upright. To release the wheelbarrow, just turn the hook.

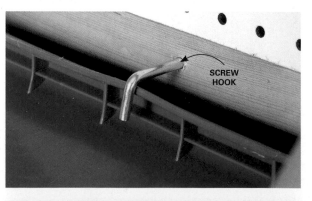

**SCREW
HOOK**

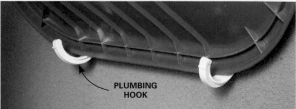

**PLUMBING
HOOK**

Hose and sprinkler bucket

Storing hoses and cords on thin hooks or nails can cause them to crack or lose their shape. Five-gallon buckets fitted with a scrap of 3/4-in. plywood in the bottom and then screwed to the wall make great multipurpose holders. The plywood can be any shape, but to give it a more finished look, cut a circle slightly smaller than the diameter of the bucket.

Mount the bucket by driving screws through the plywood. Without plywood, the screws will pull through the bottom of the bucket.

Sports gear rack

Specialty gear hooks and bat racks run $15 to $25 a pop. Vinyl-covered utility hooks only cost $2, but they only hold single items. Each of these inexpensive sports gear hangers will hold several bats and racquets.

Each set of hangers is made from a pair of lag screws covered with CPVC sleeves to protect the gear. Customize the hangers by spacing them closer or wider apart depending on what you want to hang.

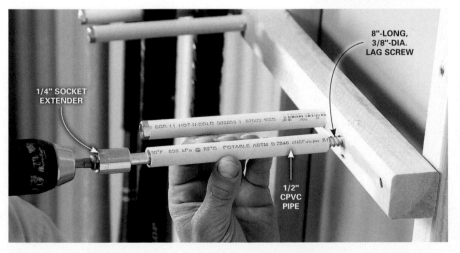

Screw a scrap of 2x2 to the face of a vertical 2x2 to hold the hangers. Slip a 6-in. length of 1/2-in. CPVC or PVC pipe over an 8-in.-long, 3/8-in.-diameter lag screw. This CPVC sleeve will prevent the lags from scratching the sports gear.

Kid-friendly ball corral

This sturdy ball corral holds a herd of balls and lets kids easily grab the balls at the bottom without unloading all the ones on top. It's built from 3/4-in. plywood and 2x2s. We made our ball corral 24 in. wide x 33 in. high x 12 in. deep.

The hooks on Bungee cords can be a safety hazard for kids and adults alike. So cut the hooks off the cords (or use elastic cord available at camping, sporting goods and hardware stores). Thread the cord through predrilled holes and secure with knots. Drill the holes slightly larger than the cords to make threading them easier.

We added plumbing hooks and short gutter troughs on the outside of the corral to make it easy for kids to stash smaller balls, helmets and mitts.

Storage pockets for skinny things

Saw off short pieces of 1-1/2-, 2- or 3-in. PVC plumbing pipe with 45-degree angles on one end. Screw them to a board to hold paintbrushes, pencils, stir sticks and just about any other narrow paraphernalia in your garage. Mount them by drilling a 1/4-in. hole in the angled end, and then drive a 1-5/8-in. drywall screw through the hole into the board.

Between-the-studs shelving

Store small containers—spray paint, putty cans, glue bottles—right in the wall! Screw shelf brackets (6-ft. lengths are available at home centers) to the studs, then install shelves, cut from standard 1x4 boards, on adjustable clips. The boards fit perfectly; there's no need to saw them to width.

Double-duty shelf brackets

Shelf brackets designed to support clothes hanger rods aren't just for closets. The rod-holding hook on these brackets comes in handy in the garage and workshop too. You can bend the hook to suit long tools or cords. Closet brackets are available at home centers and hardware stores.

5/16"
THROUGH BOLT

BLOCKING

WYE

ELL

Overhead garage storage

Stow bulky items overhead by cementing together a simple rack from 2 in. PVC pipes and fittings. Bolt the straight pipe to the ceiling joists to support heavy loads, and screw the angled pieces from the "wye" connectors into the cross brace to stabilize the whole rack. The PVC's smooth surface makes for easy loading and unloading.

Under-joist shelf

Create extra storage space by screwing wire closet shelving to joists in your garage or basement. Wire shelving is see-through, so you can easily tell what's up there. If you want to store anything round up there, install the shelf with the hanging rod up so you are less likely to get conked on the head.

Long-term storage

One way to get rid of clutter in your storage shed or garage is to do what's shown here. Screw 16-in. scrap 2x4s at a slight upward angle to each side of a wall stud. They will hold a wide variety of yard tools.

Electrical box toolholders

Junction boxes can hold a lot more than switches and wiring. Nail or screw them wherever you need handy holders for small stuff. They come in several different sizes and shapes.

Cannery row hardware storage

Don't recycle those steel or aluminum cans quite yet. Set aside a few months' worth of fruit and soup cans and put these cannery rows to work organizing all of the small hardware in your shop.

All you need are some homemade wood clips and a chunk of 3/4-in. plywood screwed to a wall. To make the clips, rip a 3/4-in.-thick board into 1-3/8-in.-wide strips. Saw or rout a 3/8-in. x 1/4-in. rabbet along one edge.

Drill 1/8-in. screw holes every 3/4 in. and then cut off 3/4-in.-wide clips. To mount the clips and cans on the plywood, screw on a clip, notch end down, then set a can on the clip and screw on a second clip overlapping the can's rim about 1/4 in.

That's it! Keep adding clips and cans until every screw, bolt, nail and nut has a can to call home. Label the cans, and keep one loaded with surplus clips and screws for adding on.

3/4"

1/4"   3/4"

3/8"

1-3/8"

3/8" RABBET BIT

Magnetic toolbox labels

If you are tired of trying to figure out which toolbox drawer has the tool you're looking for, buy magnetic business cards at an office supply store. Peel the film off the front, stick a piece of card stock on top of it (old business cards work great) and label each drawer.

Shoe pocket storage

Hanging shoe bags are great for closets, but they can also cut the clutter in your garage, workshop or laundry room. Shoe bags are available at discount stores.

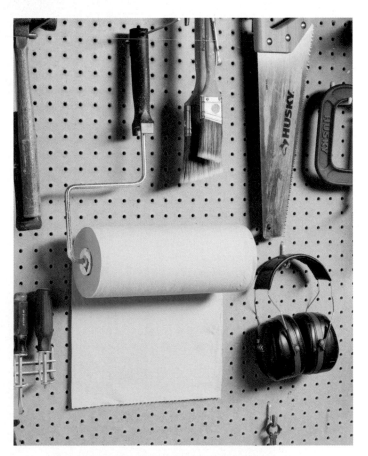

Instant paper towel holder

If you need a way to hang paper towels in your workshop, find an old 9-in. paint roller, hang it on a nail and put a roll of paper towels on it. You can move it around wherever you want. And best of all, it's free!

Mate hose ends for storage

Apparently, an empty garden hose makes a cozy home for various critters. We've heard that hoses have housed snakes, frogs and most frequently, ants. When that happens, if you hook up your oscillating sprinkler to the hose, it will immediately be plugged with ants! Yuck! Here's how to avoid this: In the fall, drain your hoses and mate the ends before storing them for the winter. If you forget to mate the ends, or if you haven't used the hose for a while in the summer, make sure to run water through the hose before connecting it to the sprinkler.

File by grit

Tired of digging through a drawer full of sandpaper and turning over each sheet to figure out the grit, Solve that problem with a handy sandpaper organizer made from a plastic file box. Each hanging file contains a different grit, and you can write the grit numbers on the tabs so you can instantly find the sandpaper that you're looking for.

Eyeglass-case hardware storage

If you have a drawer full of old eyeglass cases that you don't use anymore, repurpose them to store small things like drill bits and screws. Stick a case in your shirt pocket when you're working and toss it into a toolbox when you're done. It's much easier than digging around for small stuff in the bottom of your tool apron.

Flexible paper towel storage

Need out-of-the-way storage for paper towel rolls? One simple solution uses four eye hooks and two bungee cords. Attach two eye hooks low and two higher up. Stretch the bungee cords from the lower hooks to the upper hooks and let the cords hold the paper towels neat and tidy.

Garden hose roundup

Store garden hoses coiled up in a garbage can, with sprinklers right in the middle. When spring comes, you've got everything in one place.

Picture hanger tape holder

If you use your tape measure a lot, you want to know where it is at all times. So, screw a "sawtooth" picture hanger on the edge of your workbench and always return your tape measure to that spot when you're done using it.

SAWTOOTH
PICTURE HANGER

Easy chair storage

Here's how to store your lawn and folding chairs so they're out of your way. Take two pieces of 1x4 lumber (any scrap lumber will do) and create some simple, cheap and useful brackets on the wall. Cut each board 7-3/4 in. long with a 30-degree angle on both ends. Fasten pairs of these brackets with three 2-in. screws to the side of the exposed wall studs, directly across from each other, and you've got a perfect place to hang your chairs.

Rake rack

Don't throw away that old rake. When the handle breaks on an old rake, repurpose it for use as a rack to store garden hand tools. It fits the gardening theme and keeps what you need in plain sight!

Easy flag storage

Storing an American flag in a dusty corner of the garage doesn't feel very respectful. So to keep it clean and protected while it's put away, store it in a length of PVC drainpipe hung on the wall. The pole-mounted flag slides inside the pipe, which you can loosely cap on each end.

Reader photo

Fishing rod saver

Protect your fishing rods with pool noodles! Cut a slot down the length of a noodle and slip it over the fishing rod to prevent damage.

POOL
NOODLE →

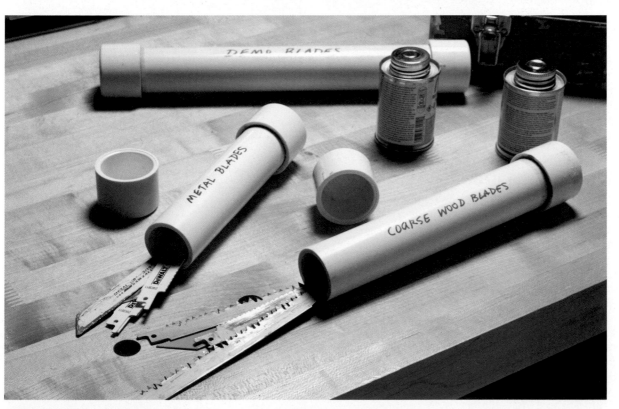

Blade storage tubes

If your reciprocating saw gets used a lot, and the tool case becomes a mess, try this. Make blade storage tubes from 1-1/4-in. PVC waste pipe and end caps. Just cut the pipe to length, glue one end and then label and store the blades. The open end gets friction-fitted with the cap. Now you can find the right blade at a glance.

Garden tool hideaway

A mailbox near your garden provides a convenient home for tools. Small mailboxes like this one are sold at hardware stores and home centers. King-size models are also available.

Yard tool holders

To make it easier to carry yard tools like rakes and shovels around your property, make tool holders from PVC pipe for your tractor cart. Glue on end caps and attach the holders to the cart with U-brackets. Drill a hole in each end cap so water can drain out.

Reader photo

Yard tool organizer

Create a simple long-handled tool hanger out of two 1x4s. On the first one, drill a series of 2-in. holes along the edge of the board. Center each hole about 1 in. from the edge. That leaves a 1-1/2-in. slot in the front that you can slip handles through. Space the holes to accommodate whatever it is you're hanging. Screw that board to another 1x4 for the back and add 45-degree brackets to keep it from sagging. If you wish, pound nails into the vertical board to hang even more stuff. No more tripping over the shovels to get to the rakes!

2" HOLE

PVC tool holder

Build this rack to store your tools on the wall. Use a jigsaw to cut a 1-1/4-in.-wide notch the length of a 2-in.-diameter PVC pipe. Cut several 3-1/2-in.-long, 1/8-in.-wide holes behind the notch. Use 1-1/4-in. drywall screws to attach these pieces to a 2x4 screwed to the wall.

Wheelbarrow rack

Hang your wheelbarrow on the garage wall to free up floor space. Center a 2-ft. 1x4 across two studs, 2 ft. above the floor. Tack it into place, then drive 3-in. screws through metal mending plates and the 1x4, into the studs. Leave about 3/4 in. of the plate sticking above the 1x4 to catch the rim. Rest the wheelbarrow on the 1x4 as shown, and mark the studs 1 in. above the wheelbarrow bucket. Drill pilot holes and screw ceiling hooks into the studs. Twist the hooks so they catch on the wheelbarrow lip and hold it in place.

MENDING PLATES

CEILING HOOK

Bucket-lid blade holder

Do you get tired of your extra saw blades banging around in the drawer every time you open it? If so, attach them to a 5-gallon bucket lid with a bolt and a thumbscrew. Now they'll stay put, and the lid protects your hands when you're digging around for other stuff.

MAGNET

5-GALLON
BUCKET LID

1/4"
CARRIAGE
BOLT

A safe chuck key holder

Some people hang the chuck key for their drill press on a string taped to the press. That works fine until the day they bump it and the string catches the moving chuck and sends it flying. It's better and safer to use a magnet to keep the chuck key handy.

Wire dispenser

A plastic crate is a great place to store anything on a spool. Just slip the spools onto a piece of metal conduit and secure the conduit with washers and bolts. There's even space below the spools for tools or scraps of wire.

Travis Larson

Build shallow drawers

I have a pretty organized shop with lots of drawers, and here's my tip. If you're going to build drawers, build lots of shallow ones and very few deep ones. Here's why. Just about everything you store for a shop is fairly thin—hand tools, blades, fasteners, sandpaper, etc. If you have a ton of shallow drawers, you can dedicate each one by category. Plus, it's easier to find what you need when it's not buried under 8 inches of other junk in the same drawer.

— Travis Larson

Keep track of screw bits

It's common now for a box of screws to include a bit—for star or Torx heads, for example. But small bits always seem to disappear just when you need them. So next time you buy a box of screws, store them in a glass jar and glue a magnet to the inside of the lid. The magnet holds the bit, and you don't have to dump out all the screws to find it.

Reader photo

In-line workshop

Place your planer, router table and radial arm saw all in a line and at the same height with roller stands on each end. This allows you to take a long piece of stock and cut, rout or plane it all on one worktable.

Mark Hardy

WOOD BLOCK

Tool bucket

A 5-gallon bucket comes in handy out in the garden—and not just for collecting weeds. You can load it up with all your gardening tools and carry them easily from place to place. If it starts to rain, protect the tools with the lid. But here's the best part—it doubles as a portable stool when you need to rest or do some pruning. The only problem is that the lid can be hard to pry off. Solve that by cutting off all but two of the plastic tabs. The lid will go on and off in a snap.

Garage storage

Cardboard concrete-forming tubes are inexpensive ($10 at any home center) and provide a great place to store baseball bats, long-handled tools and rolls of just about anything. Rest the tubes on a piece of 2x4 to keep them high and dry. Secure each tube to a garage stud with a plumbing strap.

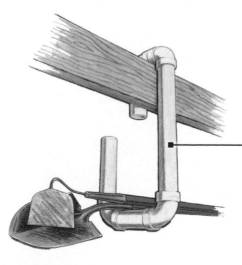

Storage hooks

Get ladders, tree pruners, kids' bikes and other unwieldy items off your garage floor with these inexpensive PVC hooks. For heavy items, you could make the hook out of steel pipe.

HOOK-AND-LOOP
TAPE

Extension cord smarts

To prevent tangled extension cords, use hook-and-loop tape to keep long cords organized. Wind the cord in 10-ft. loops and wrap each coil with hook-and-loop tape. That way you can easily unwrap only what you need for a given job. It keeps the work site safer and you don't have to unwind and rewind 50 ft. of cord when you only need 11.

Sheet metal drawer liners

If you're one of those people who uses old kitchen cabinets in your workshop, here's a tip for you. It's a bad idea to throw oily, greasy tools into those drawers, where the wood soaks up everything. Instead, take some careful measurements of the width, depth and height to any HVAC shop. For about $20 per drawer, you can get custom liners for each one. The interiors will look like new, and you'll be able to clean them as needed.

Hang-it-high helper

With this extension pole, you can hang objects in high, hard-to-reach areas. Attach a spring clamp to the end of an ABS or PVC drainpipe, and use the end of the clamp as a hook to lift items on or off a hook or nail.

SPRING CLAMP

1-1/2" ABS PIPE

Simple spiral hose storage

Here's a handy tip for storing your spiral hoses so they don't end up tangled. Just wrap them around the handle of a rake or shovel. The long-handled tool does double duty!

Save your lawn products

Leave a bag of fertilizer or weed killer open for long and it'll soak up moisture from the air and won't go through a spreader. Even grass seed could use an extra layer of protection from a moisture-wicking concrete floor. Place opened bags of lawn products in large resealable plastic bags. The products will be free of clumps or pests when you need them.

Garden gear caddy

An old golf bag, especially one on a cart, is perfect for storing and hauling garden tools. Get them all to the garden in one trip and park them in the caddy shack when you're done. Fore!

Hang-it-all hooks

Those plastic hooks that plumbers use to support pipes make convenient hangers for just about anything. They're strong and cheap and they come in a range of sizes. Find them in the plumbing aisle at home centers and hardware stores.

Twin closet shelves

By Spike Carlsen

I tossed my hat onto the closet shelf the other day and discovered a whole lot of unused real estate up there. Made me think, if one shelf is good, two would be better. And the upper shelf could be 15 in. deep instead of 12 in. because there's no closet rod hanging out below. The deep baskets (I bought these at Michaels; michaels.com) help with the organization; cabinet knobs make for easier access. We show a two-tier shelf; you can install three if your closets (and you) are tall enough.

4-1/2"-TALL BLOCKS

4"-TALL BASKET

Secure blocking to the existing shelf Buy your baskets, then cut spacer blocks 1/2 in. wider than the baskets are tall. Cut the ends of the blocks at an angle to accommodate the wider top shelf. Screw blocks to the bottom shelf, spacing them 1/2 in. farther apart than the baskets are wide. Then install and secure the top shelf.

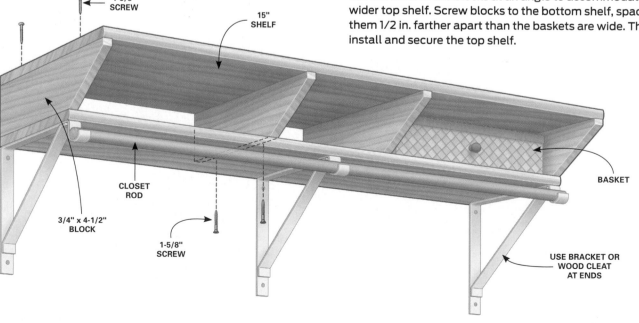

1-5/8" SCREW

15" SHELF

CLOSET ROD

3/4" x 4-1/2" BLOCK

1-5/8" SCREW

BASKET

USE BRACKET OR WOOD CLEAT AT ENDS

Sliding tie and belt rack

You can make this super-handy rack to hang all of your belts, ties, necklaces, etc. All you need is a little plywood, dowels and a full-extension 12-in. drawer slide. Drill holes in the wood and pound in the dowels (use a dab of glue if they're loose.) Attach the drawer slide to the side of your closet shelf and the rack. If you need even more hanging room, add a block of wood to the side of your shelves to offset the slide, and attach dowels to both sides of the rack. The drawer slides come in pairs, so you might as well make two of these racks!

S-hook hang-up

Turn any closet into a useful hang-up storage space by adding S-hooks to wire shelving. This provides tidy storage for mops, brooms and other cleaning tools.

S-HOOK

Add a closet rod and shelf

This project will save you hours of ironing and organizing. Now you can hang up your shirts and jackets as soon as they're out of the dryer—no more wrinkled shirts at the bottom of the basket. You'll also gain an out-of-the-way upper shelf to store all sorts of odds and ends.

Just go to your local home center and get standard closet rod brackets, a closet rod and a precut 12-in.-deep melamine shelf. Also pick up some drywall anchors, or if you have concrete, some plastic anchors and a corresponding masonry bit. Follow the instructions in **Photos 1 and 2**.

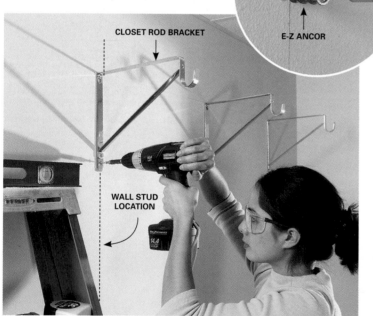

CLOSET ROD BRACKET

E-Z ANCOR

WALL STUD LOCATION

1 Draw a level line about 78 in. above the floor and locate the studs behind the drywall. Fasten at least two of your closet rod brackets to wall studs (4 ft. apart) and then center the middle bracket with two 2-in.-long screws into wall anchors (inset).

You can get these great-looking Lido Rail chrome brackets and rod at home centers or buy them online.

MELAMINE SHELF 3/4" x 12" x 72"

2 Fasten a 12-in.-deep Melamine shelf onto the tops of the brackets with 1/2-in. screws. Next, insert your closet rod, drill 1/8-in. holes into the rod, and secure it to the brackets with No. 6 x 1/2-in. sheet metal screws.

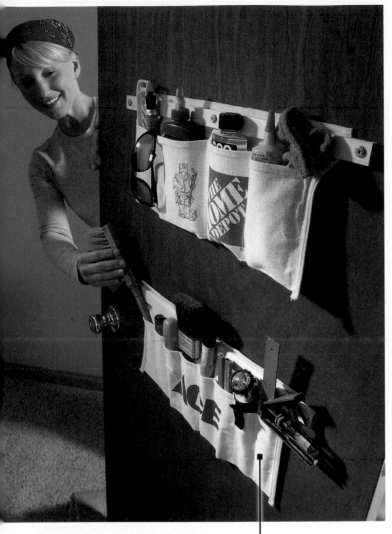

Wire shelving "corral"

If you store your gift wrap propped against the wall in the hall closet, some of the rolls can fall over and get lost behind other things or end up wrinkled or torn. Here's a better idea: Use plastic shelf clips and a small section of wire shelving to create a wrapping paper "corral." The rolls stay neatly organized and are easy to reach. You could corral other tall items too, like hockey sticks, bats and umbrellas.

Tool-apron storage

Tool aprons can be modified to store nearly any household item. Just sew a variety of pocket widths in the aprons, then mount the aprons by screwing a wood strip through the top of each and into a closet door. For hollow-core doors, use hollow anchor fasteners to hold the screws firmly to the door.

Turn a shelf into a clothes rack

Sometimes you just need another place to hang clothes, like on the shelf over your washer and dryer. Turn the edge of that shelf into a hanger rack by predrilling some 3/4-in. plastic pipe and screwing it to the edge of the shelf.

Closet nook shelves

Salvage the hidden space at the recessed ends of your closets by adding a set of shelves. Wire shelves are available in a variety of widths. Measure the width and depth of the space. Then choose the correct shelving and ask the salesperson to cut the shelves to length for you. Subtract 3/8 in. from the actual width to determine the shelf length. Buy a pair of end mounting brackets and a pair of plastic clips for each shelf.

Make the most of the recesses at the ends of your closet with wire shelving.

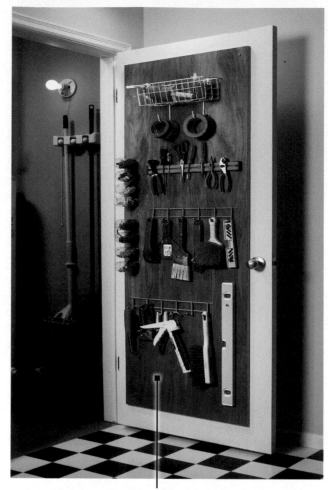

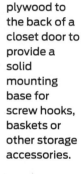

Screw 3/4-in. plywood to the back of a closet door to provide a solid mounting base for screw hooks, baskets or other storage accessories.

Back-of-door organizer

The back of a door that opens into a utility room or closet makes a handy hanging space. The trouble is that most doors don't offer a good mounting surface for hardware. The solution is to screw a piece of 3/4-in. plywood to the back of the door. Add construction adhesive for hollow-core doors. Cut the plywood 3 or 4 in. shy of the door edges to avoid conflicts with the doorknob or hinges. Now you can mount as many hooks, magnets and other storage gizmos as you like.

Closet glove rack

If you don't have radiators, finding a good spot to dry wet hats and mittens can be tough. Tossing them into a plastic bin gets them out of the way, but they never dry and it's no fun putting on damp mittens in the morning. This simple back-of-the-door glove and cap rack allows wet things to dry and keeps easily misplaced items organized. Just string clothespins on aluminum wire (it won't rust) and stretch it between screw eyes on the back of a closet door. This also works great out in the garage for drying garden and work gloves.

18-GAUGE ALUMINUM WIRE

Shoe-storage booster stool

Build this handy stool in one hour and park it in your closet. You can also use it as a step to reach the high shelf. All you need is a 4 x 4-ft. sheet of 3/4-in. plywood, wood glue and a handful of 8d finish nails. Cut the plywood pieces according to the illustration. Spread wood glue on the joints, then nail them together with 8d finish nails. First nail through the sides into the back. Then nail through the top into the sides and back. Finally, mark the location of the two shelves and nail through the sides into the shelves.

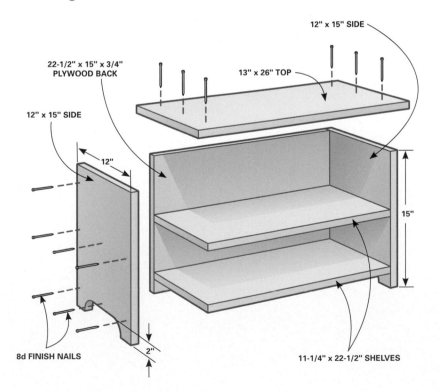

22-1/2" x 15" x 3/4"
PLYWOOD BACK

12" x 15" SIDE

13" x 26" TOP

12" x 15" SIDE

12"

15"

8d FINISH NAILS

2"

11-1/4" x 22-1/2" SHELVES

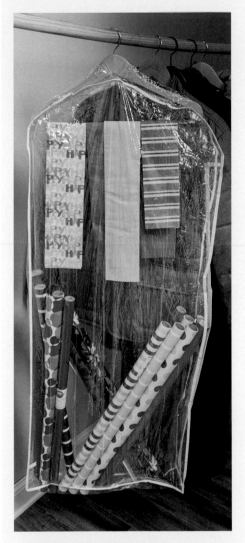

Gift wrap organizer

If you've stored rolls of wrapping paper under a bed or in the corner of a closet, you know how dusty and crumpled the paper can get.

One solution is to use a clear garment bag, hung in a closet. Rolls of paper, flat-folded paper and tissue, ribbon, tape, scissors—everything can go in one place where you can see it and it's protected from dust and rumpling.

CHAPTER 6

Safety & Security Hacks

Secret hiding places

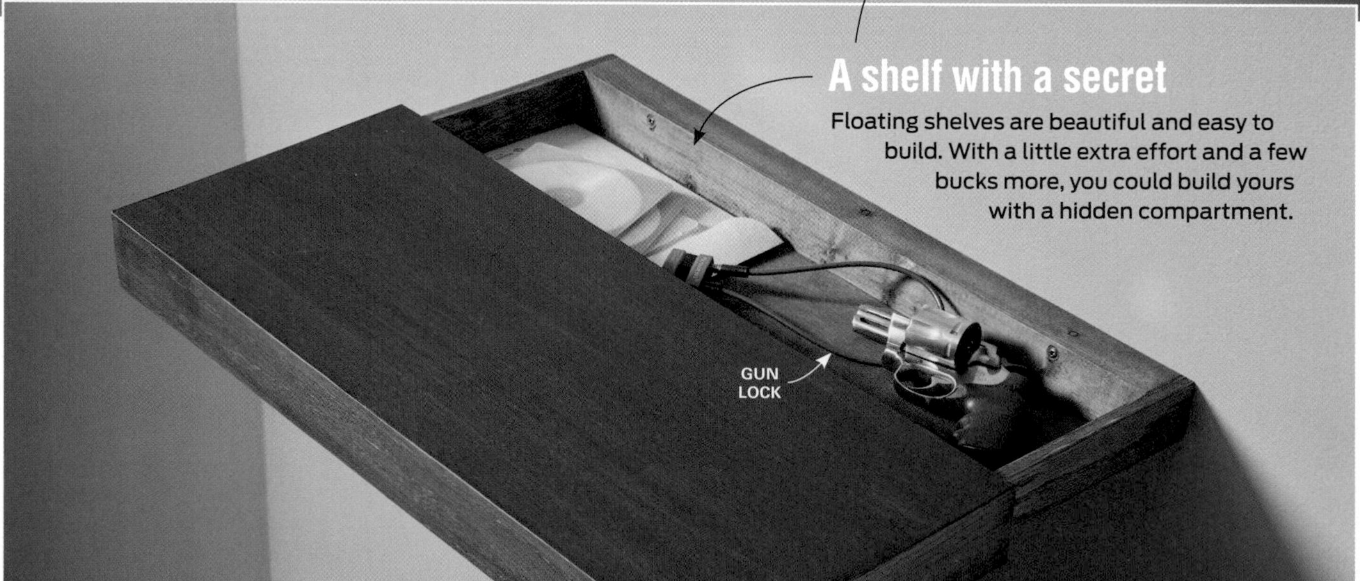

A shelf with a secret

Floating shelves are beautiful and easy to build. With a little extra effort and a few bucks more, you could build yours with a hidden compartment.

GUN LOCK

TIP
To learn how to make floating shelves, visit tfhmag.com/floatingshelves

Make a treasure map

Having several hiding places makes sense . . . unless you forget where they are! Avoid this misfortune by making yourself a map of your various treasure sites. That way you only need to remember one location—the place where you hid the map.

You can't take it with you

Prepare for the worst, and make sure your valuables are not lost forever by including all your secret hiding places in your will.

Sneaker subterfuge

Some shoes have a removable sock liner (the foam pad your foot rests on). Pull out the sock liner and slide in some cash. What thief is going to want to dismantle your stinky shoes? This is also a good place to hide emergency cash on your person while you're on vacation. Unless your sneakers are nice enough that someone would want to steal them too.

SOCK LINER

Secret in the ceiling

You can stash treasures above the suspended ceiling tiles in your basement. At that height, would-be thieves can't get at them without a ladder. Keep your goodies in a plastic container to protect them from bandits of the rodent variety. And don't stash anything heavy that could cause a ceiling tile to sag.

Who'd suspect an ironing board?

Many ironing boards have tubular legs with plastic caps on them. Pull the cap and you've got yourself a perfect little hidey-hole. Slide in a wad of paper towels first so your secret stays near the opening and doesn't rattle around.

Key magnet

It's a good idea to keep a spare key hidden somewhere on your vehicle. But don't use a magnetic key box because it can fall off, and it's not easy to find a place big enough to stick them to mostly plastic modern cars. Instead, bolt your spare key to a magnet, the kind with metal on one side and a hole in the middle. It fits perfectly in a little nook near the rear bumper, and it'll be there for years without falling off.

Tissue coverup

Stick a flat box of tissues in a full-size tissue box holder and you've just created a convenient little hiding spot. You could buy a one-size-fits-all box like this, or a regular box holder and set the box of tissues on a couple of blocks.

Password protection

If you keep a list of your passwords on a sheet of paper near your computer, be sure to protect your list from bad guys and nosy coworkers by putting it in a file folder. Lay the folder flat on the bottom of a file cabinet drawer under the other hanging folders. It's unlikely anyone will find it there.

A safe safe

It's a good idea to protect your valuables in a fireproof safe. The problem is that these smaller safes are as easy to grab as a briefcase; some even have a handle on them. But, you can hide it in a suitcase!

SPRINKLER HEAD
KEY HIDER

Stow a key in your yard

If you have an irrigation system, install a phony pop-up sprinkler head near the front door and hide a key in it. You could dismantle an extra sprinkler head or buy a fake one designed to hold a key. They cost less than $5 at home centers and discount stores.

SMOOTH-EDGE
CAN OPENER

Kitchen cabinet cache

There are tons of ways to hide stuff in a kitchen cabinet. Bury a zipper-top bag full of jewelry at the bottom of a half-full oatmeal box. Open a cereal box at the bottom and shove in some cash. Or try a "smooth-edge" can opener that cuts through the top in such a way that the top often fits snugly right back in place after you've stashed your cash.

Hide a key in the keypad

If your kids can't keep track of their house key, you may have considered installing a remote keypad for the garage door opener. Of course, that works great until you lose power and your child is left out in the cold . . . literally. You can solve this problem if the key fits right behind the nine-volt battery inside the keypad. A key in a keypad!

Family album

Nobody ever looks at those old photo albums, but they never get thrown away either. That's why they're the ideal place to store a little emergency cash.

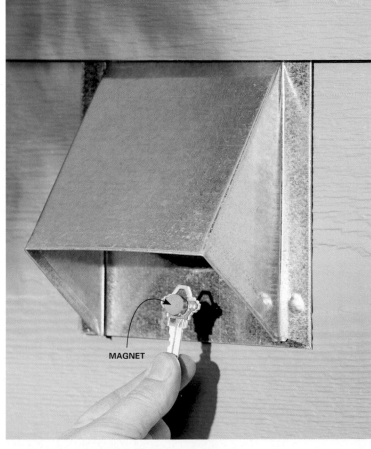

MAGNET

Good venting is key

Stick a magnet to a spare house key using hot glue, and tuck the key up out of sight inside the dryer vent hood. If your vent hood is aluminum or plastic, glue a magnet to the inside of the hood as well as the key.

"Litterally" buried

Put small containers of valuables in a tub of cat litter (unused!) and then pour the cat litter back into the tub.

Sitting pretty

Dining chairs often have space under the seat for a drop-down hinged panel.

HINGED PANEL

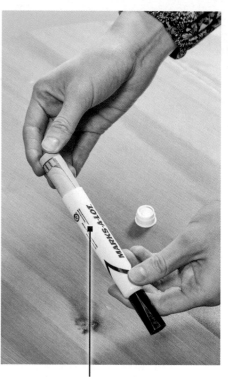

It's magic, all right

Pop the end cap off a marker and remove the ink cartridge. Just right for a spare roll of cash.

Spare tire

Pick up a spare wheelbarrow wheel and tire (about $20 at a home center). Deflate the tire, tuck in your goods and reinflate it.

A roll in the roll

Take apart the spring bar that holds your toilet paper. Roll up a stack of bills, stash them inside and reassemble the bar.

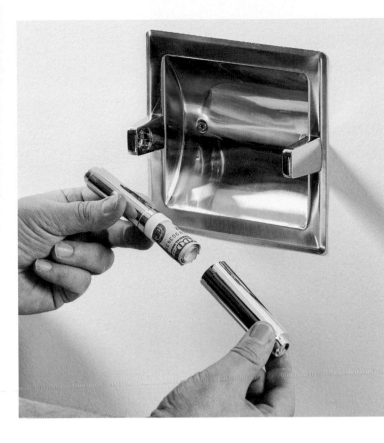

Secret cash stash

Keep some emergency cash rolled up in a clean, empty sunblock tube. Tuck it in a drawer or medicine cabinet where you can easily grab it when you need it.

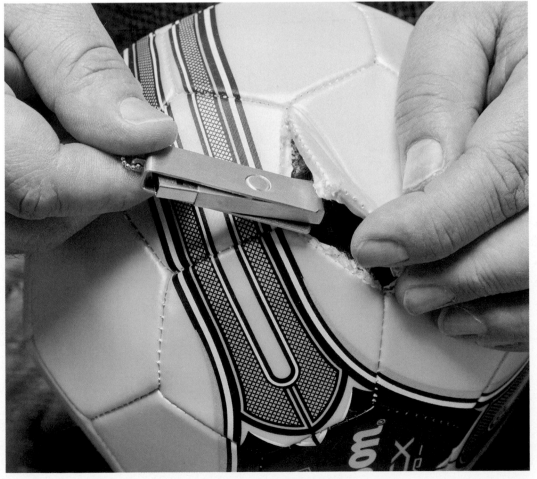

Don't kick this ball!

A soccer ball makes a perfect spot for little items. Let some air out of the ball and cut one of the seams using a utility knife. After inserting your items, tuck the seam back into place.

Slip a box inside a box

Store a container of valuables inside a larger bin full of unappealing stuff. Label it accordingly.

FAMILY JEWELS

WINTER CLOTHES

HARD DRIVE

Time well spent

Store a few small items in a wall or mantel clock, as long as the clock itself isn't worth stealing! Tape them to the back or put them in any open cavities.

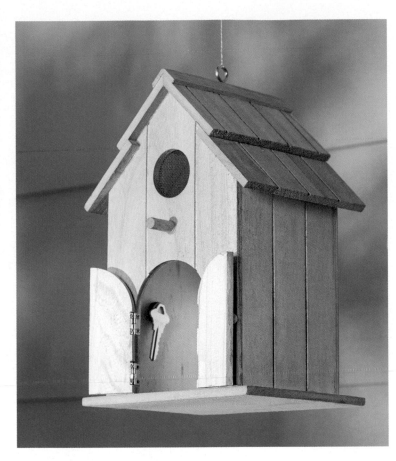

Key house

An unoccupied birdhouse makes a handy spot for a spare key. Screen off the bird entrance to keep out tenants.

Slit open a tennis ball

Slice open a tennis ball and you've got yourself a little vault just like those rubber squeeze coin purses from the '70s. Don't store the ball in the garage with the other balls or it could get tossed across the yard for your dog.

Not IN the drawer

Drawers don't go all the way to the back of a cabinet, and there's typically a little space on the underside too. Put cash or important papers in an envelope and tape them to the back or underside of a drawer.

EMERGENCY CASH

Depositing checks with an Apple®, Android, or Windows supported mobile device is fast, easy, and secure.

Together we'll go far

Tips for everyday life

MAIN WATER SHUTOFF

Turn off the water supply before going on vacation

Water damage from undetected plumbing leaks will quickly ruin ceilings, floors and walls, leading to repair bills in the thousands. This is especially true if you're away on vacation. Yes, such a leak is unlikely, but insurance companies report hundreds of these incidents every year. Look for the main valve near the water meter and turn it clockwise to close it. If it's stuck, leaks or doesn't turn on again, hire a plumber to replace it. The ice maker in your refrigerator may freeze up while you're gone, so shut it off too or thaw it with a hair dryer when you return.

Use metal tubing rather than plastic for ice maker supply lines

If you've had mice in your home, use a copper (type L) or braided stainless steel line rather than a plastic supply line for the ice maker in your refrigerator. Mice like to run behind refrigerators and occasionally chew holes in plastic lines, causing a leak that can ruin floors and ceilings before you detect it. Plastic tubes also can harden over time and crack. Find metal ice maker lines at home centers and wherever appliances are sold.

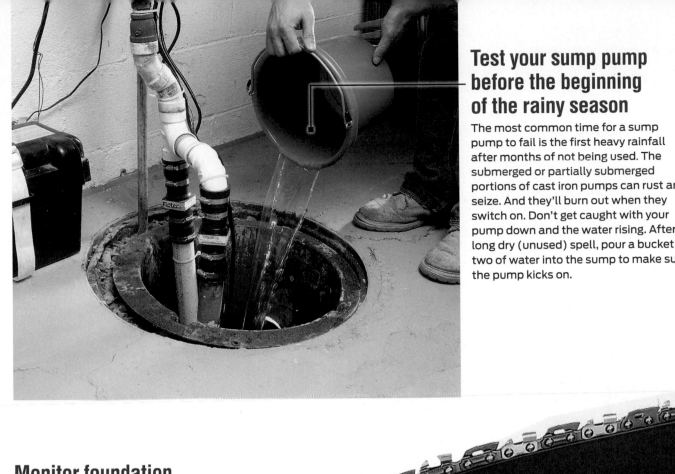

Test your sump pump before the beginning of the rainy season

The most common time for a sump pump to fail is the first heavy rainfall after months of not being used. The submerged or partially submerged portions of cast iron pumps can rust and seize. And they'll burn out when they switch on. Don't get caught with your pump down and the water rising. After a long dry (unused) spell, pour a bucket or two of water into the sump to make sure the pump kicks on.

Monitor foundation or wall cracks

Hairline cracks in a concrete foundation are normal, but cracks that continue to widen spell trouble. They'll eventually cause shifting and cracking in the walls above, tilt floors and move doors and windows so they won't open and close. The movement is glacially slow. To help you spot it, measure and record the gap size. Check it every few months. If the cracks widen, call in a foundation specialist to assess the foundation. Solutions can be expensive, but the cost of ignoring the problem is greater. A major foundation fix can cost thousands.

Trim trees around the house so dead branches won't crash down on the roof

Insurance companies get a flood of tree-related claims after major storms. You can't prevent all of these incidents, but many you can, if you trim out overhanging branches and dying trees just waiting to fall. Major tree trimming is dangerous and not a do-it-yourself project. Call in a tree service to trim all tall trees around your home every few years. Don't procrastinate. Spending a few hundred dollars now could save you several thousands in roof repairs later.

Once a year, inspect your foundation for termite tunnels

Pull out your flashlight and walk around your home, examining the foundation, both inside and out, to inspect for termite tunnels. Much of the damage termites do is invisible, inside walls and floors. Take the time to look for telltale sawdust and tunnels, because termites can do major damage before you even know they're there. If you spot signs of termites, call in a professional exterminator.

Buy no-burst hoses for your clothes washer

If your current hoses are more than five years old, replace them with no-burst hoses. The supply hoses to your clothes washer are always under pressure, just like the supply pipes in your water system. However, eventually the rubber will harden, crack and leak. If undetected, the leak can cause extensive water damage. An inexpensive solution is to buy no-burst hoses. These high-quality hoses are less likely to leak and they'll keep any leak from becoming a torrent. They are available at home centers, hardware stores and appliance stores.

Put splash pans under washers and water heaters to catch leaks

Once upon a time, water heaters and clothes washers always sat on concrete floors near drains, where spills and leaks wouldn't hurt anything. Now they often sit on framed wood floors, sometimes on the second floor, where spills, overflows, broken hoses or slow drips can cause stains, rot and other potentially expensive water damage. You can buy special pans at home centers and appliance dealers that catch slow leaks and mild overflows. Some have drain holes where you can connect a tube that leads to a floor drain. They won't stop burst water lines or massive overflows, but they're cheap insurance against water damage caused by minor spills and leaks.

Add 6-ft.-long downspout extensions

A 1-in. rainfall drops about 650 gallons of water on an average roof. And your downspouts concentrate all that water in only a few spots. If dumped too close to the house, the water will undermine your foundation, causing it to leak, shift or crack—very expensive to fix. Downspout extensions will prevent most major problems, including wet basements, cracked foundation walls, and termite and carpenter ant infestations.

WATER HEATER STRAP

Strap your water heater if you live in an earthquake-prone region

Earth tremors can tip water heaters and break the gas lines that lead to them, causing either water damage, or worse, an explosion and fire. Water heater straps can prevent this disaster. (They're required in California and other regions.) In earthquake-prone regions, you can find them at home centers and hardware stores. Otherwise, order them online.

Install surge protectors to protect your electronics and prevent data loss

Electronic devices are sensitive and highly vulnerable to momentary power surges, especially powerful ones induced by lightning. Losing a computer is bad enough, but losing photos, music and other irreplaceable stuff on your hard drive is often much worse. Insulate your data from this danger by plugging devices into a surge protector. Better surge protectors will have the following ratings printed somewhere on the box: meets UL 1449 or IEEE 587; clamps at 330 volts or lower; can absorb at least 100 joules of energy or more; and handles telephone lines and video cables as well.

SURGE PROTECTOR

Earplug tether

If your earplugs are never around when you need them, and you often go without rather than search, try this. Tether your earplugs to your cap! There's no longer an excuse for skipping the hearing protection.

Stuck on safety

There is no good excuse for not wearing eye protection when using power tools. To help you remember, glue some small magnets to several pairs of safety glasses and stick them on all the power tools that have metal housings. It will be fast and easy for you to grab the glasses when you need them.

Nonslip ladder

If you use a multi-position ladder for repairs, you've probably experienced trouble getting good footing. One solution is to apply anti-slip tape to the rungs. Its heavy-duty grit really helps grip your boots. Clean the rungs and then just cut the tape to size with a utility knife and straightedge and apply it to the rungs and press the tape in place.

Slide-proof ramps

If your vehicle ramps slide forward as you drive onto them, secure them to a piece of plywood. You can use 3/4-in. plywood, some 2x4 blocks, lag screws and bolts. Now as you drive onto the plywood, the weight of the car holds the ramps in place so they don't skid away on contact. Drill a hole in the plywood so you can hang the ramps on the wall.

Tips for safely working alone

By Travis Larson

Increase productivity and limit aggravation with a crew of clamps, jigs, ropes and duct tape!

Working alone isn't much fun, especially when you're trying to do the work of two. No one's around to hold the other end of the tape, support the other end of the board, or hand tools or materials up to the roof. And to top it all off, there's no one to visit with either.

We can't help you with the loneliness (get a dog), but we can offer some commonsense tips to make solo work as painless, safe and productive as possible. The idea is to creatively use clamps, blocks, nails, sawhorses and scrap building materials in new, different ways. Once you start thinking like this, you'll be surprised at how much you can safely accomplish by yourself.

Bring everything with you so you don't waste time climbing up and down ladders

When you have a job to do in an attic, in a crawlspace or on a roof, concentrate on assembling all the tools and materials you need to save trips back and forth to the truck or garage. For a roof repair, I'll pull up a 5-gal. bucket with the caulking gun, flashing, flat bar, roofing nails or whatever else I think the job requires. Undoubtedly I'll forget or need more of something, but at least I've saved a couple of trips down the ladder.

CHAIN

BLOCK

Levers will give you more lifting power

Lever posts out of the ground by wrapping a chain around the base of the post and slipping a long plank through the chain. Pry against a block resting on the ground to keep the lever from digging into the soil. Sometimes you'll have to excavate around the tops of stubborn concrete-embedded posts to remove some of the dirt trapping the top of the concrete.

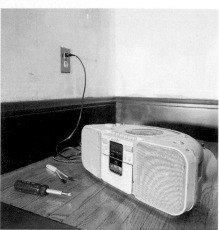

Listen to the music!

Find circuit breakers by plugging a loud radio into the outlet you're working on. You'll know you have the right circuit breaker when the music dies. But don't assume the electricity is off in all the other outlets or lights in the room. Before doing any wiring, plug the radio into other outlets you plan to work on. Some duplex outlets can have different circuits running to adjacent outlets. To be safe, test both the top and bottom with the radio. For lights, turn the light switch on and off to be sure.

Handle long, awkward pieces with clamps, blocks, screws and nails

The toughest solo jobs are holding up a full sheet of plywood, supporting the top row of drywall, and securing strips of siding or long boards in exactly the right position while you fasten them. Sometimes you can stick a clamp somewhere to support long boards, nail in a block directly below the work or even pound in a couple of nails to rest the two bottom corners of plywood sheathing while you fine-tune the placement and do the fastening.

Occasionally you'll need to place fasteners through finished surfaces, but don't sweat it. Nails leave relatively small, fixable holes and drywall screw holes are nearly invisible. These little insults are pretty tame compared with the mess you can have with a falling cabinet that you're trying to hold up while fastening!

Big, cumbersome cabinets are easy to hang alone if you first screw a level 1x4 through the wall into the studs at the right height. Then you can rest the cabinet while you fasten it to the wall. Holding 10-ft. gutter sections for fastening is a hassle. But support the far end with a clamp attached to the bottom of the fascia and it's painless.

NEW GUTTER

CLAMPS ON FASCIA BOARD

Use pivot points and balance to wrestle long ladders

I bet more broken windows and injuries happen from raising, lowering and moving ladders around than actually using them. The longer the ladder, the harder it is to control. Here's how to handle the longest ladders alone.

Anchor the feet of extension ladders against the base of the building and "walk" the ladder up to raise it. The solid wall keeps the feet from kicking out as the ladder's raised. To lower ladders, move the feet back against the building and reverse the process.

HEAVY WEIGHT ANCHORS LADDER FEET

2 Extend the ladder while holding it vertical

ANCHOR FEET AGAINST HOUSE

1 Anchor the base and walk the ladder up

3 Roll the top to walk the ladder sideways

HOLD HANDLE WITH RING FINGER; PLUCK STRING WITH THUMB AND INDEX FINGER

Snap chalk lines when you lack a third hand

Everyone knows how to pound in a nail to hold the end of a chalk line when they're alone, but what do you do on a basement floor? You use a brick to anchor it down, that's what. That's simple, but here's another trick that's a little tougher to master. When you have less-than-4-ft. snaps and you don't want to fool with or damage the surface with a nail, learn how to snap lines by holding the handle on the chalk box with the line extended past the mark. Hold the line tight and tip the box down so you can pluck the line with your thumb and index finger.

Use balance and grip to haul heavy plywood

Lift sheet goods by placing one hand under the sheet, slightly in front of center, and your other hand at the top, slightly behind the center. Hoist it so that the middle of the sheet rests on the ball of your shoulder. Your shoulder and back handle the bulk of the weight while your hands only need to balance it. Bonus: You'll be able to see where you're going, thread through doorways and even navigate up and down stairs.

1 Pull it out flat

2 Grip it top and bottom and lift with your legs

3 Balance it and carry it away

Wear a well-stocked tool apron to double your work speed

Since I gave up my career as a carpenter to become an editor, I've gotten lazy about strapping on the tool belt. It's usually on the ground with tools, squares and pencils strewn all over the place. So I spend half my time looking for lost tools. Invariably I'll get a board just where I want it and find my hammer out of reach.

Tuck all your basic, most-used tools in just the right pouch, and always return them to the same resting place. Pretty soon, you won't even have to look before grabbing the tool you need.

Using sturdy sawhorses and 2x12s is safer and more productive than reaching from ladders

Working alone on ladders can be inefficient and dangerous, especially because you'll be tempted to over-extend your reach and carry too many tools, paint cans, shingles or lumber when no one is on hand to pass you things. Nothing speeds up high, solo work like the spacious elevated work platform scaffolding provides. You'll be able to keep materials and tools at arm's length and safely reach a wide area without constantly moving ladders.

The scaffolding doesn't have to be anything fancy. When you have a job less than 10 ft. from the ground, set a couple of solid, crack-free, 2x12 boards (avoid large knots) over a pair of sturdy sawhorses for a platform you can move around on. Just make sure your setup is on even ground to keep the horses from collapsing, and avoid "walking the plank" by remembering that there are no safety rails. Keep plank ends close to sawhorses or they'll flip up when you step on the ends, like they do in slapstick movies (only it won't be nearly as funny in real life).

For higher jobs, like painting second-floor eaves or replacing windows or siding, go to the rental store and examine your scaffolding options. You can rent long, lightweight aluminum planks with various styles of jacks to support them and the same platform "section style" scaffolding you see the pros use on big construction sites. Tell the scaffolding supplier about the job you're planning to do and how high you'll be working to get help choosing the best scaffold. Most scaffolding can be carried in a pickup, but rental stores will deliver too. You'll forgive the cost when you see how your productivity increases.

2x12s

BLOCKS TO KEEP LEGS FROM SINKING

HEAVY-DUTY SAWHORSES

PLYWOOD SCREWED TO 2x4s

2x4s SCREWED TO SAWHORSE

SAW TABLE RESTS ON 2x4s

Extend your saw table with 2x4s and plywood

It's not always easy to find a willing helper to hold up long boards when you're ripping on the table saw. Here's a setup that you can rig up in just a few minutes.

Lay 2x4s perpendicular to sawhorses to support the lips of the saw table. Screw the 2x4s to the tops of the sawhorses. Lay a sheet of plywood directly behind the saw and lock it in place with 1-5/8 in. drywall screws.

CHAPTER 7

Pets

Bissell

Cat-proof potted plants

If you see a light bulb over your cat's head, they might be thinking, "Why go all the way downstairs to the litter box when all these potted plants are so much closer?" The solution is simple. Cover the soil around each plant with decorative rock. Thwarted by the rocks, your cat will rediscover the litter box. You can buy small bags of decorative rock at a craft or discount store.

Automatic accident cleanup

Our granddog, Max, came to stay with us for a couple of weeks, and he arrived with the Bissell SpotBot cleaning machine. It seems that Max had some G.I. issues, and we'd be bound to have some carpet cleaning chores during his stay. Max did not disappoint, and the SpotBot got quite a workout. After you scoop up the big stuff, you just plug in the SpotBot, put it over the spot, push the button and walk away. After it shuts off, you just empty it and rinse the reservoir. You can buy SpotBot for $150 at home centers and online.

— Travis Larson

Skunk vs. dog

If your dog gets ambushed by a skunk, do not bring them into the house for the cleanup. The stench will stay in your house for days. First, clean away as much spray as you can using lots of wet wipes. Then put your pup into the tub and use deodorizing pet shampoo to deal with the rest.

Repair scratches

To see how to repair pet scratches on your door, go to tfhmag.com/clawmarks

VINYL CARPET RUNNER

Clean up stinky messes

If cleaning up pet messes makes you gag, strap on a respirator with organic vapor cartridges. The charcoal filters will make the job completely odor-free.

Keep pets off the furniture

If you want a quick, inexpensive way to keep your dog or cat off your upholstered furniture, pick up a roll of clear vinyl carpet runner—the kind with the little spikes on the underside to hold it in place. Then cut pieces to fit your furniture, and when you leave the house, roll them out, spiky side up. Since most pets wouldn't willingly stretch out on a bed of nails, your furniture will be safe until you return. A 2 x 12-ft. roll costs $25 at home centers.

Pet-proof screen

If your dog or cat destroys window screen, replace regular screen with pet screen. It's available at home centers and at most places that do screen replacements. You can buy the pet screen and install it yourself, or take the screen and frame in and have it done for you. Pet screen is much stronger than regular window screen, so it resists tearing and other damage. Pet screen costs about 75¢ per sq. ft.

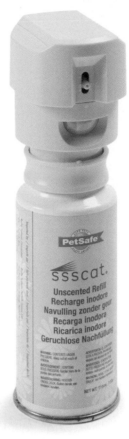

Keep your cat off the countertop

Do you have trouble keeping your cat off of your kitchen counters? If so, here's one solution: the PetSafe Ssscat Cat Spray Control System ($35 online).

It's basically an electronic head that sits on top of an aerosol can. The head—which requires four "AAA" batteries—has a built-in motion sensor and sprays a short blast of an odorless gas anytime kitty walks in front of it. The spray won't hurt, but your cat will sure think twice about jumping on the counter again. Be sure to buy extra refill cans if your cat is particularly naughty.

Entryway towel

Hang a dog-dedicated towel near the door for when your pet comes in with wet or muddy paws. Wipe those paws right there in the entryway and your floors will stay much cleaner.

Avoid floor damage

If your dog loves water, they probably make a mess with their water bowl. To protect your floor, pick up an inexpensive plastic boot tray at a home center or hardware store and put it under the water bowl. Problem solved!

BOOT TRAY

Out of sight, out of mind

Does your dog love to jump on the windowsills to bark at dogs they see outside? Some dogs get so excited, they break the window! One solution is to put privacy film on the lower sash of all the windows facing the street. A 48 x 78-in. roll costs about $20 at home centers. The film still lets in sunlight, but your dog can't see those canine trespassers anymore.

Train your cat to scratch a post

If you're just getting a cat and don't already know this, you've got to give them a place to scratch. You need something the cat will like better than your furniture. Most cats like sisal better than other materials. You can build a scratching post by wrapping a 3-in. PVC pipe or 4x4 with sisal or manila rope and making a stand, or you can buy scratching posts at pet stores or online. You'll have to train your cat to use the scratching post, but once you do, they will likely prefer the post to your furniture.

CHICKEN WIRE

Stop the digging

Some dogs are crazy about digging. If you've got a digging dog, here's a solution: Rake back the mulch and lay chicken wire over the ground. Use U-shaped landscape fabric staples to hold the mesh in place. Then cover the mesh with the mulch. Your dog will not dig in that spot any more.

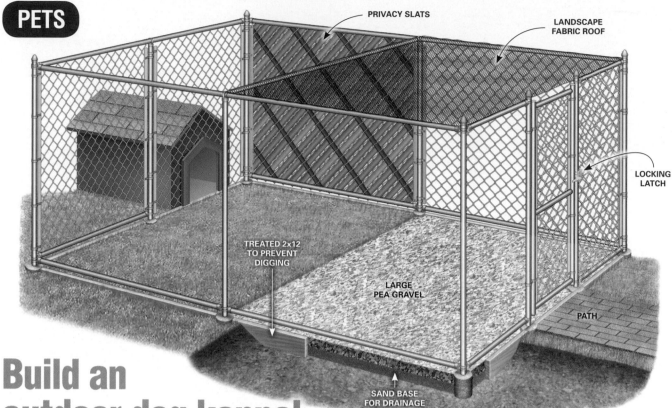

PRIVACY SLATS

LANDSCAPE FABRIC ROOF

LOCKING LATCH

TREATED 2x12 TO PREVENT DIGGING

LARGE PEA GRAVEL

PATH

SAND BASE FOR DRAINAGE

Build an outdoor dog kennel

Outfit your outdoor kennel with the proper flooring and drainage, a shady area and a windbreak. Pick up all the materials at your local home center. By Travis Larson

We contacted Lisa Peterson, director of communications for the American Kennel Club, for design advice and size guidelines for an outdoor kennel. We were hoping to get a sizing formula. But it turns out there's no such thing. Kennel sizing is based on how much time your dog will be spending in the kennel and how much room you have to spare. If your dog is going to be outside all day, he needs a larger kennel so he can run and exercise. If you make it too small, he'll take every opportunity to "get even" with you and your neighbors with nonstop barking and other bad behaviors. So larger is better.

For walls and doors, chain link fencing is your best bet (4 ft. tall minimum, and taller if you have a larger dog). It's affordable and easy to assemble, and you can buy premade wall and door sections at any home center. Buy a spring-loaded "snap clip" to secure the swing-down latch (some dogs can figure out how to open those latches and escape).

If your dog is a digger, you'll have to embed a "direct burial" treated 2x12 below the fence. Or bury the fence itself about 1 ft. into the soil. Those methods aren't foolproof, but they'll usually

prevent a "great escape." Screen off any sides that face streets or sidewalks by sliding privacy slats through the fencing. That'll cut down on barking and overall stress.

When it comes to flooring material, concrete may seem like the best choice because you can slope it for drainage and it's easy to clean. But it's actually a mistake. The hard floor will, over time, cause calluses, worn pads, splayed toes and painful joints. Instead, Lisa recommends either large pea gravel (some dogs eat smaller gravel) or large flat stones (flagstone). The irregular shapes actually help your dog develop stronger paws. But before you throw down gravel or set the stones, take the time to install a sand base for drainage at least 6 in. deep if you're building on clay. Then lay down landscaping fabric to prevent weed growth. You'll probably scoop out gravel along with the poop, so it'll need replenishing every year. If you have enough space, the ultimate dog oasis is a grassy area within the kennel.

Several companies offer composite flooring materials for dog kennels. It definitely looks better than gravel and is

easy to clean. But if your dog likes to chew things, it's not a good choice—unless, of course, your vet does free surgery. Plan on a surfaced path to the kennel. If you just have grass, you'll soon have a muddy path. All that mud will get tracked into the house.

Finally, dogs need protection from the elements. A doghouse isn't mandatory, but if you don't provide one, you should at least install a small roof and a windbreak. Dogs can withstand cold, but not cold and wind or rain. An elevated cot will get them off a freezing cold or searing hot floor. Even if you include a doghouse, provide other shaded areas in the kennel (landscape fabric stretched across the top works well).

When placing a doghouse, avoid the common DIY mistake of setting it in a corner (the roof is a perfect launching pad for a jump-over). Instead, locate it outside the kennel with an entrance hole cut through the fence. Or place it in the center of the kennel. If you're stuck with a corner location, make the fence higher in that area to prevent jump-outs.

Slow feeder for puppies

Some puppies eat their food so fast that they vomit it right back up. Instead of buying a slowfeed bowl, drill holes into a 12-in. length of 2-in. PVC pipe and cap the ends. Fill the tube with puppy food, and your dog will have to roll it around to get the food to fall out of the holes. Be sure the holes are large enough for the food to come out!

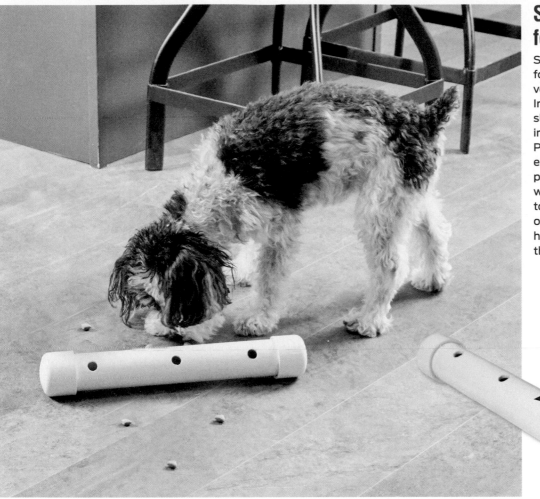

PVC PIPE

The big-dog diner

Do you hate seeing your big dog straining their neck every time they eat from their bowl? You can buy a pair of elevated dog bowls for $20 to $40 at pet stores, but you can also make your own out of a couple of cheap 2-gallon plastic buckets from a discount store. Just flip them upside down, cut holes in the bottoms with a jigsaw and set a couple of 2-qt. stainless steel bowls into the openings.

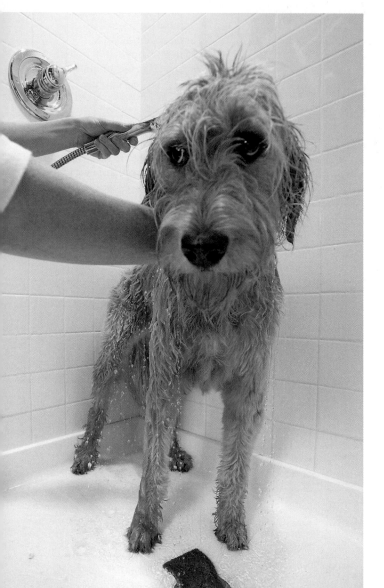

Dog food scoop

It's true that the tops of plastic jugs make good funnels. But if you keep the cap on and angle the cut, they also make handy scoops for everything from potting soil to pet food. We used a half-gallon jug to make this scoop.

SCRUBBING PAD →

Fur filter for dog bathing

I used to pay to have my dog bathed because if I washed my dog in the bathtub or shower, I'd end up with a clogged drain. Not anymore. To keep fur out of the drain, use a mesh-type scrubbing pad. In a shower, clip the pad to the drain plate with a bobby pin. In a bathtub, wedge two pads under the stopper from two sides. The pads catch fur but let water flow through.

— Travis Larson

Souped-up litter box

To make litter box cleanup just a bit more pleasant, keep the cleaning supplies in a handy spot—on the litter box shroud. Buy some adhesive-backed hooks and stick them to the side of the shroud. Buy a whisk and dustpan at a sporting goods or hardware store (they're made for cleaning small tents).

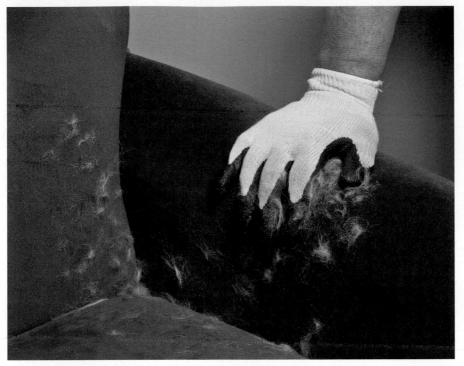

Pet hair remover

When we were moving my daughter from her apartment, I wore my nonslip rubber-dipped gloves that I had gotten at a hardware store. While lifting her upholstered chair, I brushed some dog hair off with my gloves and noticed the hair rolling up into a bunch, leaving the upholstery virtually lint-free.

Seeing it work so well, I kept at it, and in just a few minutes the whole chair looked great. I left the gloves as a housewarming gift for my daughter's new apartment!

— Spike Carlsen

Bunny rabbit A/C

Hot summer days are tough on bunnies. Here's a great way to recycle plastic water bottles and keep your bunnies cool at the same time. Fill the bottles with water, freeze them solid and then set them out in the rabbit hutches. The bunnies love to laze against the bottles as the ice thaws. This works great with puppies, too.

Bell training for dogs

Here's an easy way your dog can let you know she needs to go outside without any barking or scratching at the door. Hang some bells from the doorknob and your dog will quickly learn to associate the sound of the bells with the door opening. Soon she'll nudge them herself. You can speed things along by jiggling the bells and saying "Outside? Wanna go outside?" for a few days every time your dog goes out. Your dog will be able to "talk" to you about going outside even when you're somewhere else in the house.

Don't brush the dog—use a vacuum instead!

My dog has a heavy coat that requires a lot of brushing. I was constantly cleaning up the dog hair with the vacuum cleaner after I brushed her. It finally occurred to me that I could use my vacuum with an upholstery attachment to brush the dog. She was a little apprehensive at first, but now she loves it, and I do too. The vacuum sucks up all the loose hair so I don't spend any time cleaning.

— Travis Larson

Cat repellent

Tired of the cat jumping up onto the kitchen table while you're eating? Fill a clean spray bottle with water. Whenever the cat hops up there, give them a quick squirt. Eventually, the mere sight of the bottle in your hand will send your cat running.

Bird retrieval

A pet bird that gets loose can be difficult to recapture. Try closing the curtains and turning off all the lights. Birds don't usually fly in the dark, so it'll land and be easy to spot with a flashlight.

See-through door protector

Protect your doors from your dog's claws with a sheet of plastic. Buy 1/8-in. or thinner Plexiglas or plastic at any home center. Cut the Plexiglas so it fits just inside the door jambs and is 1 ft. higher than the reach of your dog. Most home centers will cut the Plexiglas for you, but you can also cut it with a utility knife and a straightedge. (If you have a large dog and need plastic above the doorknob, use a 3-in. hole saw to make a cutout for the knob.) Mount the Plexiglas to the door with 3/4-in. roundhead wood screws.

PLASTIC SHEET

Tinfoil couch-saver

Keep your cats off the couch with tinfoil. Tear off a piece of tinfoil long enough to cover the top of your couch, and set it on the cushions. The feel and sound of tinfoil drives cats nuts and they'll immediately jump off.

HOOK-AND-LOOP FASTENER

Private dining

To stop a dog from eating the cat's food, move the cat's dish into another room. Then attach adhesive-backed Velcro to the back of the door and to the front of the door trim. After filling the dish, hook up the Velcro so the door only opens 5 in. Now the cat can come and go and eat their meal in peace.

Pet-food dispenser

Build this bin and you can fill the dog dish with the flick of a finger and do away with that crumpled bag of dog food lying on the garage floor. It easily holds two 20-lb. bags of food and allows you to dispense it right into the dish. This bin even holds two types of food so the cat won't get jealous. You can put it together in a half day with basic power and hand tools.

Most of the materials for this dispenser can be bought from a home center or lumberyard. We used 3/4-in. clear aspen, because it's straight, soft and easy to work with. You can save some money by building it out of No. 2 pine boards. If possible, buy the 18 x 24 In. acrylic sheet already cut to size. To cut it without chipping it, you'll need a fine-tooth blade and a table saw.

"Blast gates" make handy food dispensers. Woodworkers use them for dust collection systems, so they're readily available at woodworking shops or by mail order ($9). Get the metal ones—the plastic ones don't slide as well. (One source is Rockler, rockler.com, part No. 20864.)

These gates do have limitations. Medium- to large-sized food works best; they can jam with small stuff like birdseed. If the gate jams, quickly open and close it firmly.

Follow the photo series for step-by-step assembly instructions. The acrylic requires special handling. Leave extra room around it so it can expand and contract freely. Carefully nail the perimeter molding so the nails don't nick the acrylic and crack it **(Photo 7)**.

Most types of hinges will work to secure the lid. We selected a short piano hinge. Cut it to fit with a hacksaw. The cabinet hangs on the wall on a cleat cut to 45 degrees **(Photo 8)**.

Figure A
Dispenser details

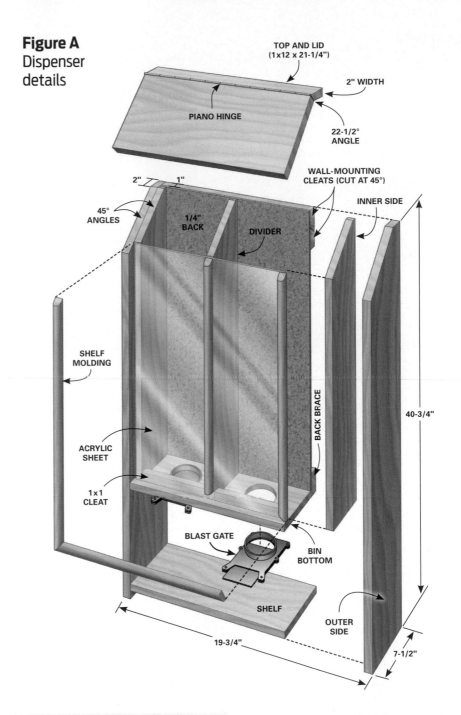

TOP AND LID (1x12 x 21-1/4")
2" WIDTH
PIANO HINGE
22-1/2° ANGLE
WALL-MOUNTING CLEATS (CUT AT 45°)
INNER SIDE
2"   1"
45° ANGLES
1/4" BACK
DIVIDER
SHELF MOLDING
BACK BRACE
40-3/4"
ACRYLIC SHEET
1x1 CLEAT
BLAST GATE
BIN BOTTOM
SHELF
OUTER SIDE
19-3/4"
7-1/2"

Materials

One 10' length of 1x8 aspen
One 9' length of 1x6 aspen
One 2' length of 1x12 aspen
One 2' length of 1x2 aspen
One 2' length of 1x1 aspen
1-3/4" x 8' quarter round or shelf molding
1-1/4" x 2' x 4' tempered hardboard
One 18" x 24" x .093" acrylic sheet
One 24" piano hinge
Two 4" dia. blast gates
1 lb. of 2-1/4" trim head screws
1 lb. of 1-1/4" screws
Eight 1" No. 6 flat head wood screws
Four 2-1/2" screws
Sixteen 3d finish nails

Cutting list

Two 1x8 x 18-1/4"—bin bottom and shelf
Two 1x8 x 40-3/4"—outer sides
  Note: Cut a 45-degree angle on one end set in 2" from the edge
Three 1x6 x 29"—inner sides and divider
  Note: Cut a 45-degree angle on one end set in 1" from the edge
One 1x12 x 21-1/4"—lid and top
  Note: Rip it to 22-1/2 degrees set 2" in from the edge. 2" is the narrow side.
One 1/4" x 29" x 18-1/4"—hardboard back
One 1x6 x 18-1/4"—mounting cleat
  Note: Rip in half at 45 degrees
One 1x2 x 18-1/4"—back brace
Two 1x1 x 8"—front cleats

SPEED
SQUARE

STRAIGHT
EDGE

LID

22-1/2-DEGREE BEVEL

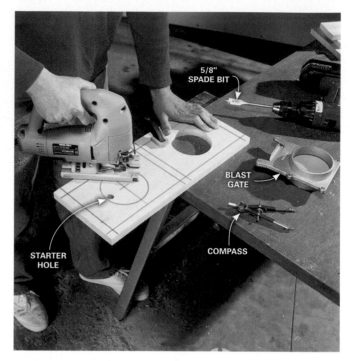

5/8"
SPADE BIT

BLAST
GATE

STARTER
HOLE

COMPASS

1 **Set** your saw to an angle and rip the lid (22-1/2 degrees) and mounting cleat (45 degrees). Clamp or screw the boards to your workbench and use a straight guide for these cuts. Cut the other parts to length **(see Cutting List, p. 271, and Fig. A)** using a speed square as a guide to keep the cuts square.

2 **Lay out** the bays on the bin bottom using **Fig. A** as a guide. Find the center of each bay and draw the circular cutout for the blast gates with a compass. Drill a 5/8-in. starter hole and cut out the openings with a jigsaw.

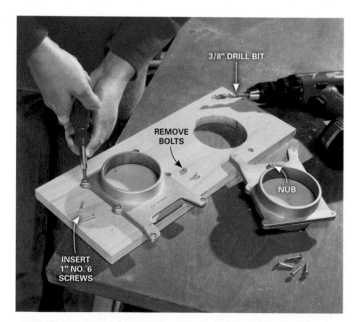

3/8" DRILL BIT

REMOVE
BOLTS

NUB

INSERT
1" NO. 6
SCREWS

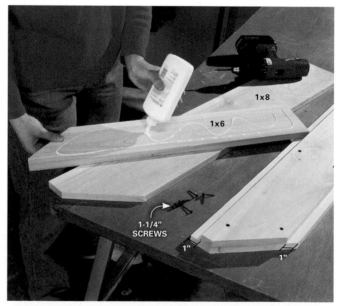

1x8

1x6

1-1/4"
SCREWS

1"

1"

3 **Mount** the blast gates in the openings. Replace the bolts that hold the two sides of the blast gate together with four 1-in. No. 6 wood screws. Don't overtighten or you'll pinch the gate closed. (Note: We also drilled a 3/8-in. hole to recess a little nub and bolt in the top of our blast gate.)

4 **Glue and screw** the two-piece sides together **(Fig. A)**. Use 1-1/4 in. screws and predrill with a 1/8-in. bit to avoid splitting the wood.

CENTER DIVIDER

BIN BOTTOM

MOUNTING CLEAT

5 **Predrill and screw** the center divider to the bin bottom with 2-1/4 in. trim head screws. Then add the sides, bottom, and top. Next attach the back and the top half of the cleat with 1-1/4 in. screws.

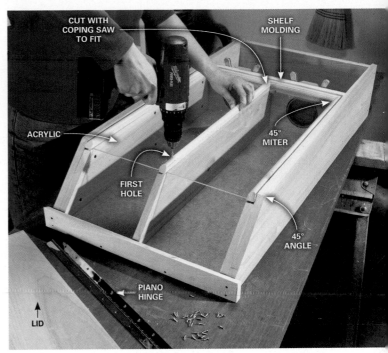

CUT WITH COPING SAW TO FIT

SHELF MOLDING

ACRYLIC

FIRST HOLE

45° MITER

45° ANGLE

PIANO HINGE

LID

6 **Set** acrylic in place, leaving 1/8-in. gap on all sides for expansion. Cut and fit the moldings **(Fig. A)**. Nail the sides and bottom moldings to the bin with 3d finish nails, sandwiching the acrylic in place. Set the center molding and predrill 1/16-in. nail holes through both the molding and acrylic.

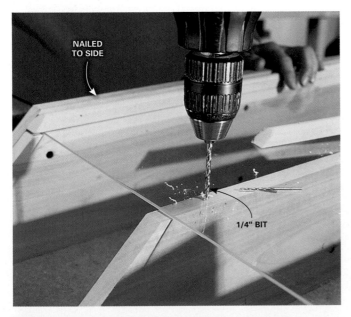

NAILED TO SIDE

1/4" BIT

7 **Remove** the center molding and enlarge the hole in the acrylic with a 1/4-in. bit to provide room for expansion. Press the drill gently so the bit doesn't grab and crack the acrylic. Replace the molding and nail it on. Cut the piano hinge to length and screw it to the top.

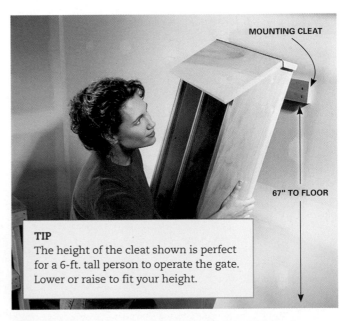

MOUNTING CLEAT

67" TO FLOOR

TIP
The height of the cleat shown is perfect for a 6-ft. tall person to operate the gate. Lower or raise to fit your height.

8 **Level and screw** the other half of the mounting cleat to the wall with four 2-1/2 in. screws driven into the wall studs. Hang the cabinet on the interlocking mounting cleats.

Dog Spots on Grass

Symptoms: Dog spots are round patches about 4 to 8 in. in diameter with dead grass in the middle, encircled by dark green grass. They're most apparent in the early spring when dormant grass first begins to turn green again.

Cause: Dog urine contains high concentrations of acids, salts and nitrogen, which burn (dry out) the grass roots and kill them. As rain washes the area, the urine is diluted and the nitrogen spreads, causing the grass surrounding the spot to grow faster and turn greener.

Remedy: You have to replant your grass; it won't come back on its own. But first you have to dilute or remove the caustic urine from the soil **(Photo 1)**. Thoroughly soak the area with lots of water. Let the hose run for at least three minutes. Then you can start the replanting process **(Photo 2)**. Add a half inch of new soil to help absorb any remaining urine **(Photo 3)**. Then you can spread new seed, as we show, or use a commercial yard patch mixture (available at most nurseries or home centers) or even sod. In any case, the secret of good germination is keeping the seed moist. And keep the area moist until the new grass is about 3 in. high.

Recovery time: Four to six weeks

An ounce of prevention

1 Soak your pet's favorite areas in your lawn to get the salts out of the root zone before they kill the grass.

2 Fertilize your lawn in the spring to boost the overall color and mask the darker green dog spots.

3 Train your pet to urinate in a designated area. Replace or repair the grass in this area annually or cover it with mulch.

4 Keep your pet well hydrated to make its urine less concentrated.

5 Become a cat person.

DOG SPOT

1 Soak the patch until the grass is sopping wet to dilute the urine acids and salts and wash them deeper into the soil, beyond the grass roots.

2 Scrape up the dead grass with a hand rake and remove it. Rough up the area to loosen the soil 1/2 in. deep. Seeds germinate better in soft soil.

3 Sprinkle on a 1/2-in.-thick layer of topsoil, then pepper it with grass seed. Cover with a pinch of new soil and press it to firm it up. Keep the area moist until the new grass is about 3 in. high.

Rainy-day doghouse

You may have seen the cute little doghouse that will stand up in the rain, but the price tag may have scared you away. Instead, make your own for a fraction of the price using a plastic storage bin. Cut an opening in it, flip it over on its lid and put a dog bed inside. Your dog can sit on the porch, watch the rain and stay perfectly dry.

UPSIDE
DOWN BIN

Low-fat dog treats

If your vet suggest you replace your overweight dog's high-calorie treats with plain rice cakes, take their advice. You may think they're tasteless, but your dog will likely go nuts over them! They're super low fat and they're a lot cheaper than most regular treats too.

Paws off countertops

Here's a great way to teach cats that countertops are off limits: Lay contact paper along the edge of the top, sticky side up. Cats hate the stuff and will avoid your countertops after a few sticky experiences.

Childproof = pet-proof

Like kids, pets get into places they shouldn't. To stop them I turn to inexpensive childproofing products: latches for cabinets, locks for doors, and gates for doorways. Discount stores carry some of these products. For a wider selection, shop online.

No-barking zone

Does your dog's barking in the car drive you nuts? Try this trick: Every time your dog barks, close the windows (watch her head). She'll quickly learn that barking means no fresh air and no slobbery tongue flapping in the breeze. After a few car rides, you'll both be driving around in blissful silence.

PETSAFE

High-tech pet doors

After the neighborhood raccoon discovered my doggy door, I installed a locking door that unlocks when it detects the transmitter on my dog's collar. Unlocking sometimes takes a few seconds and the door has jammed a few times, but it keeps out the wildlife and stops winter drafts much better than the old low-tech door. There are also motorized models that open the door automatically. To browse a wide variety of doors, check out petdoors.com. (800-826-2871).

Portable water dish

If you and your dog take long walks together, you both probably get pretty thirsty on hot days. Before leaving the house, stuff a plastic shower cap in your pocket. That way, you can give your dog a drink from any handy tap, drinking fountain or your water bottle whenever they need a slurp.

SHOWER
CAP

PAN OF
WATER

Paint tray birdbath

Molly, our cockatiel, loves to take
baths—and her favorite bathtub is a
plastic paint tray. The ribs on the
bottom of the tray give her traction,
and the tray's slope lets her wade in
the shallow water until she's ready to
move into the deep end. Paint trays
are cheap and easy to clean, and
they also make great turtle pools.
— Gary Wentz

Ant-proof pet food dishes

Every summer, ants invade our kitchen, and one of their favorite
destinations is our dog's food bowl. We came up with this simple way
to keep them out of her bowl—we set her dish in a pan of water. Not
only does it keep the ants out of the dog food, but Sage can take a
gulp of water from the pan whenever she needs a drink.

Wind-proof dog dishes

How many times have you gone outside to fill your dog's
food or water dish only to find that it's blown halfway
across the yard? The really heavy pet dishes are
expensive, but here's a cheap dog dish that won't blow
away. Fill a plastic ice cream bucket with a couple of
inches of sand, and then put a second container the
same size inside it. Use the inside bucket as your dog's
dish and it'll stay right where you put it.

SAND

Modern Console

Mimic a mid-century modern classic by turning a simple shelving unit on its side, wrapping it with plywood inside and out, and attaching legs. Our materials cost was about $250.

Build it

Notice that the end panels of the original assembled Kallax shelving unit protrude beyond the sides. Remove both panels **(Step 1)** and trim off the protruding edges **(Step 2)**. Then reattach both panels flush with the sides **(Step 3)**. Cut hardwood plywood panels to wrap around the unit **(Step 4)**. Make the top and bottom panels long enough to cover the side panels, and cut the side panels to fit tightly between the top and bottom pieces. Cut all the panels wide enough to create a 3/16-in. lip around the front of the shelving unit. Adhere iron-on edge banding to these pieces.

Fasten the panels with flat-head sheet metal screws after drilling countersink pilot holes through the unit. The unit's frames are hollow, so be careful not to punch through their thin faces when drilling the countersinks. Make sure the screw heads seat flush.

Cut plywood to cover the bottom and sides inside the unit **(Step 5)**. Don't fasten these pieces with screws; instead, go for a friction fit. Apply iron-on edge banding to the exposed edges.

Remove all the plywood parts to apply finish. Finish the legs too. Reinstall the panels and inserts—tack the inserts with small nails or brads. Then attach the legs **(Step 6)**.

Basic unit

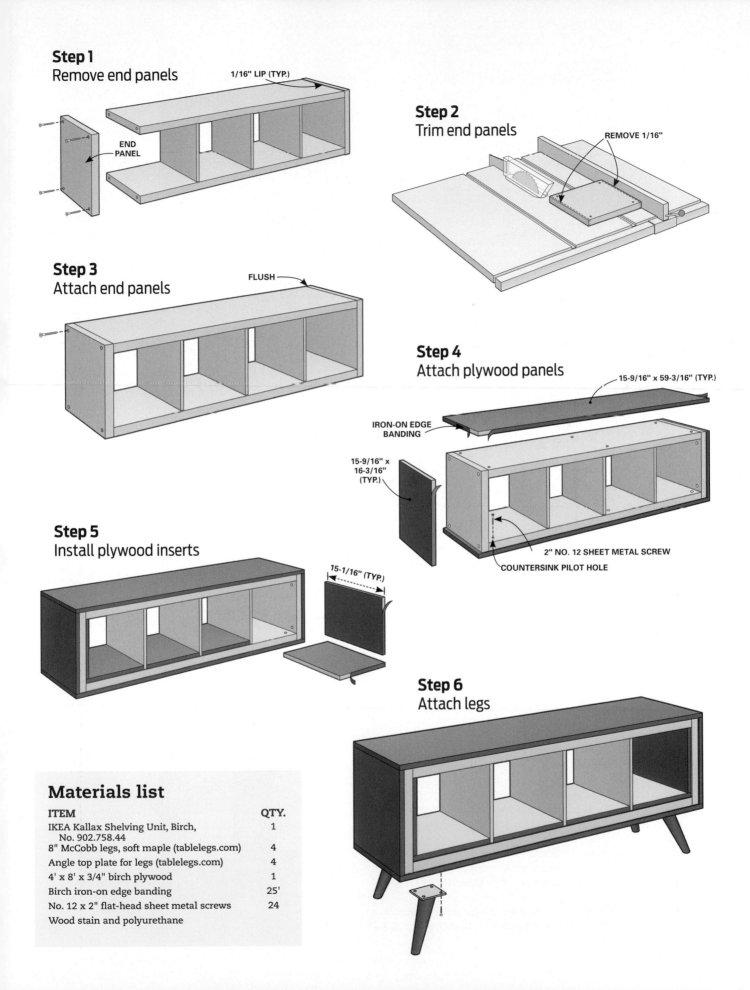

Step 1
Remove end panels

1/16" LIP (TYP.)

END PANEL

Step 2
Trim end panels

REMOVE 1/16"

Step 3
Attach end panels

FLUSH

Step 4
Attach plywood panels

15-9/16" x 59-3/16" (TYP.)

IRON-ON EDGE BANDING

15-9/16" x 16-3/16" (TYP.)

2" NO. 12 SHEET METAL SCREW

COUNTERSINK PILOT HOLE

Step 5
Install plywood inserts

15-1/16" (TYP.)

Step 6
Attach legs

Materials list

ITEM	QTY.
IKEA Kallax Shelving Unit, Birch, No. 902.758.44	1
8" McCobb legs, soft maple (tablelegs.com)	4
Angle top plate for legs (tablelegs.com)	4
4' x 8' x 3/4" birch plywood	1
Birch iron-on edge banding	25'
No. 12 x 2" flat-head sheet metal screws	24
Wood stain and polyurethane	

Craft Center

Build a worktable with a huge surface, convenient storage and easy mobility by sandwiching three small storage units between a base with casters and a plywood top with hardwood edging. We spent about $330 on materials for the table shown here.

Build it

Cut hardwood plywood for the top and base and install hardwood edging and iron-on edge banding as shown in **Step 1**. Position two Kallax shelving units back to back and fasten them to the base with flat-head sheet metal screws after drilling countersink pilot holes through the Kallax frames **(Step 2)**. The frames are hollow panels, so be careful not to punch through their thin faces when drilling the countersinks. Make sure the screw heads seat flush.

Install the third Kallax unit across the front of the base, using the same method. Then tip the assembly over onto the top and fasten it as before **(Step 3)**. Install locking swivel casters **(Step 4)**. Then tip the assembly right-side up and round over all the top's sharp edges with a router and a round-over bit. Complete the job by installing Kallax drawer inserts and applying your favorite finish to the top **(Step 5)**.

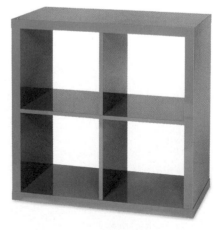

Basic unit

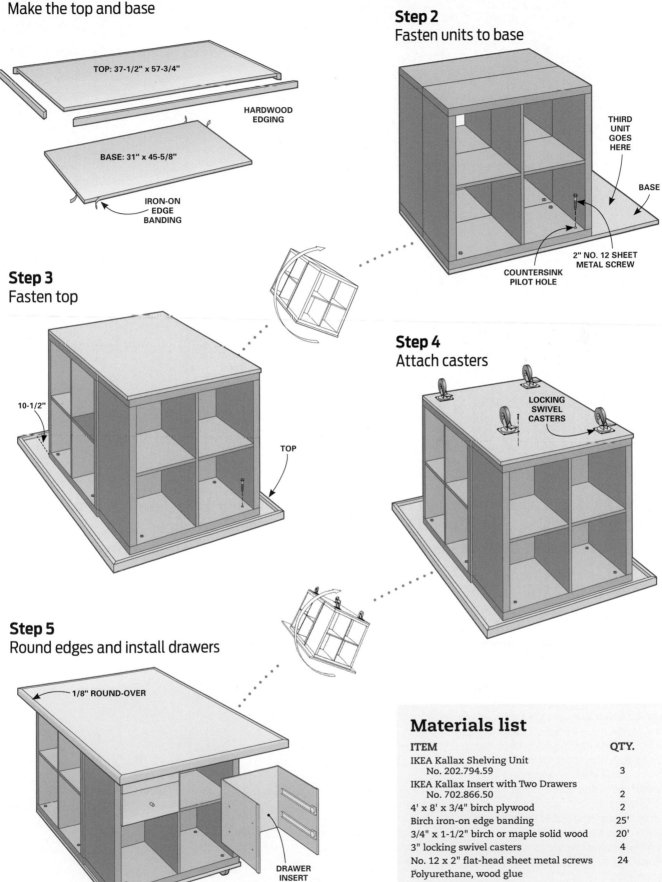

Step 1
Make the top and base

TOP: 37-1/2" x 57-3/4"

HARDWOOD EDGING

BASE: 31" x 45-5/8"

IRON-ON EDGE BANDING

Step 2
Fasten units to base

THIRD UNIT GOES HERE

BASE

2" NO. 12 SHEET METAL SCREW

COUNTERSINK PILOT HOLE

Step 3
Fasten top

10-1/2"

TOP

Step 4
Attach casters

LOCKING SWIVEL CASTERS

Step 5
Round edges and install drawers

1/8" ROUND-OVER

DRAWER INSERT

Materials list

ITEM	QTY.
IKEA Kallax Shelving Unit No. 202.794.59	3
IKEA Kallax Insert with Two Drawers No. 702.866.50	2
4' x 8' x 3/4" birch plywood	2
Birch iron-on edge banding	25'
3/4" x 1-1/2" birch or maple solid wood	20'
3" locking swivel casters	4
No. 12 x 2" flat-head sheet metal screws	24
Polyurethane, wood glue	

Built-in Bench

Create a classic mudroom bench by fastening base molding and a new top to a cabinet designed to display a flat-screen TV. Our bench materials cost about $250, plus $50 for base molding. Your base molding cost will depend on the type and quantity you choose.

Build it

Assemble the Hemnes TV unit through Step 27 of the manufacturer's instructions. Move it into position and shim the legs as necessary to level it. Then install a support block under the rails beneath the center divider **(Step 1)**. This allows the unit to be used as a bench. Fasten the unit to the wall through its upper back rail **(Step 2)**.

Build a new top by gluing hardwood edging to 3/4-in.-thick hardwood plywood and then rounding over all the sharp edges **(Step 3)**. Sand the top, stain it and apply your favorite finish. Use corner brackets to fasten the top to the bench **(Step 4)**. Then fasten base molding around the bench to build it in **(Step 5)**. Install the drawers to complete the project.

Basic unit

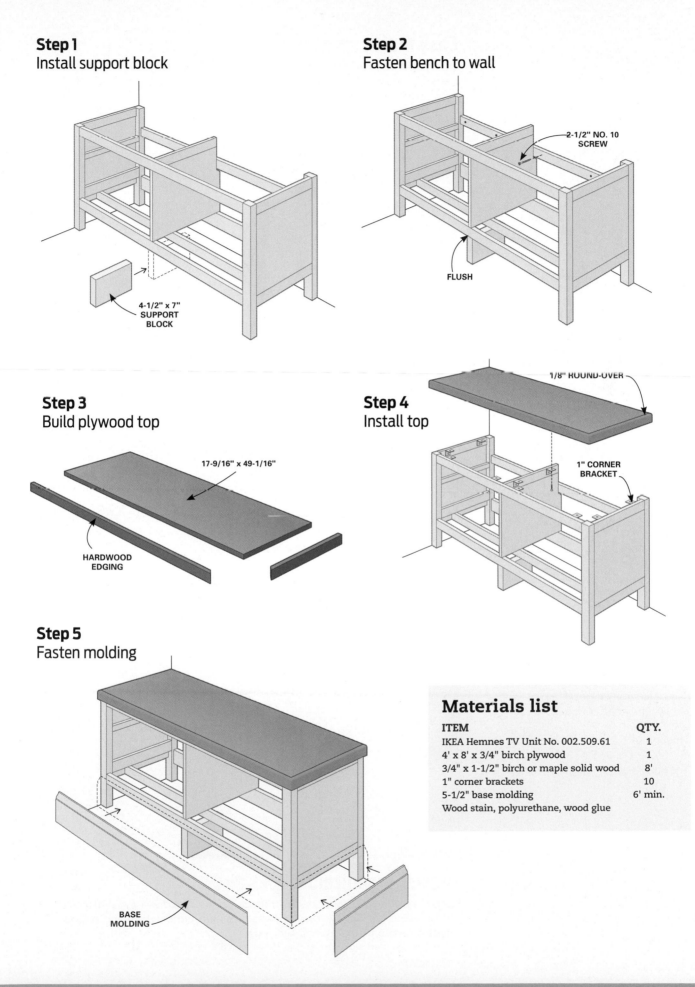

Step 1
Install support block

4-1/2" x 7"
SUPPORT
BLOCK

Step 2
Fasten bench to wall

2-1/2" NO. 10
SCREW

FLUSH

Step 3
Build plywood top

17-9/16" x 49-1/16"

HARDWOOD
EDGING

Step 4
Install top

1/8" ROUND-OVER

1" CORNER
BRACKET

Step 5
Fasten molding

BASE
MOLDING

Materials list

ITEM	QTY.
IKEA Hemnes TV Unit No. 002.509.61	1
4' x 8' x 3/4" birch plywood	1
3/4" x 1-1/2" birch or maple solid wood	8'
1" corner brackets	10
5-1/2" base molding	6' min.
Wood stain, polyurethane, wood glue	

Keep those hacks coming!

You know that feeling when you see something and wonder, why didn't I think of that?

As editors, we get that feeling all the time when we read the ideas that our clever readers and followers send to us. When you've come up with an innovative solution to a common (or not-so-common) problem around your home or yard, why not share it, right?

Here are four pages of our most recently published hacks that we're happy to share with you. Whether you call it a tip, a hint or a hack, if you've got an ingenious idea that you'd like to share, please send it to submissions@ familyhandyman.com.

Thank you!

The editors at Family Handyman

Easy mulch spreading

Mulching around flowers and bushes in tight quarters is easier if the mulch is in a small container. So, place buckets and pails in your wheelbarrow and fill them with mulch. It doesn't matter if the mulch misses the bucket and lands in the wheelbarrow. Once you've emptied the buckets, dump the contents of the wheelbarrow in an open area and spread it out.

— Eric Swartz

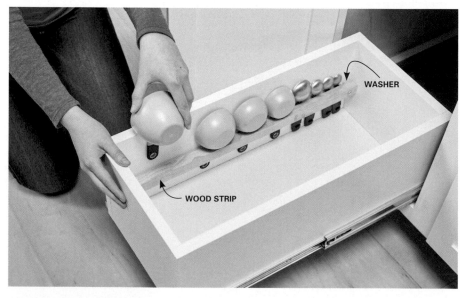

Drawer organizer

Keep measuring cups and spoons from cluttering up a drawer. Just attach a strip of wood to the drawer's side. Install washers behind the wood strip to create a gap for the handles to slide into.

— Chris Grimal

MARBLES

Make your own lazy susan

I was shopping for a lazy Susan for my spices, but the ones I found were expensive and wouldn't fit in my cabinet anyway. I made my own with two matching pie tins and marbles. You just spread a single layer of marbles in the bottom tin and set the other tin on top. Spins just like the store-bought variety!

— Carol Schultz

No-smell gym bag

A gym bag can get stinky after a while, but here's an easy way to prevent that. Put silica gel cat litter in a small square of fabric and close it with a zip tie. The crystals absorb odor-creating moisture, keeping your bag fresh. Replace the crystals once a month or as needed.

— John Burfeind

SILICA GEL
CRYSTALS
IN A BAG

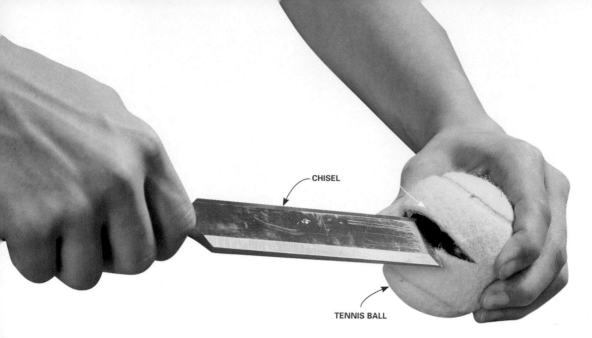

CHISEL

TENNIS BALL

Protection for big blades

If you have wide chisels sliding around in your toolbox, here's a good way to protect their cutting edges (and your fingers). Cut a slot in a tennis ball using a utility knife. Stick your chisel in the slot and you'll have no more worries.

— Noel Hansen

Handy camping kit

My family does a lot of camping, and I always had trouble rounding up all the little items we needed and keeping them organized. First aid supplies, bungee cords, clothesline, bug spray . . . . Then I loaded it all into a fishing tackle box, and now we're always ready to go.

— Lynn Magers

OVEN CLEANER

DRILL BIT

Get the gunk off drill bits

The heat produced during drilling causes resin to build up on drill bits. Resin-coated bits cut poorly and heat up and get dull faster. To remove the resin, spray the bit with oven cleaner and let it soak for a couple minutes. Then scrub it with a toothbrush and rinse with water.

— Virgil Petersen

A stop block for long cuts

Setting up a stop to make repeat cuts is definitely a time-saver. Here's my solution for cuts that extend beyond my saw's fence. I attach a long 1x4 to my saw fence and use a stop block I made from a short piece of 1x4 and a 1/4-in. plywood lip. I just slide the stop block to where I need it and clamp it into place.

— Ted Kanon

STOP BLOCK

1x4

PHONE CHARGER CORD

BINDER CLIP

Cord control

Here's an easy way to keep cords and cables from slipping off a desk. Clamp a binder clip onto the edge of your desk and run the cable through it. For cords with large ends, squeeze the clip's handles to remove them, slip in the cord and reinstall the handles.

— Carter Janacek

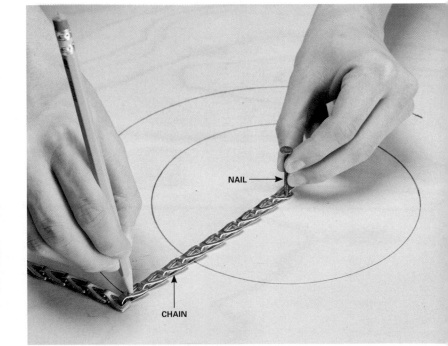

NAIL

CHAIN

Draw a circle with a chain

To quickly draw a circle or mark a radius, put a nail through one end of a chain and into the workpiece and use the nail as a pivot point. Insert the point of a pencil into a chain link at the desired radius and draw the arc or circle while keeping the chain taut.

— Mike Murphy